Harald's Garland

A Collection of Short Stories and Essays

Harald Lutz Bruckner

Harald's Garland: A Collection of Short Stories and Essays

Published by Hideaway Park Press
Green Valley, AZ

ISBN: 978-1-0878-5350-5 (paperback)
ISBN: 978-1-0878-6080-0 (ebook)
LCCN: 2020900712

Books by Harald Lutz Bruckner

The Blue Sapphire Amulet

The Birken Saga
A Trilogy

Book 1 *Escape on the Astral Express*
Book 2 *A Wanderer on the Earth*
Book 3 *The Born-Again Phoenix*

Harald's Garland

Lighthouse Mystery

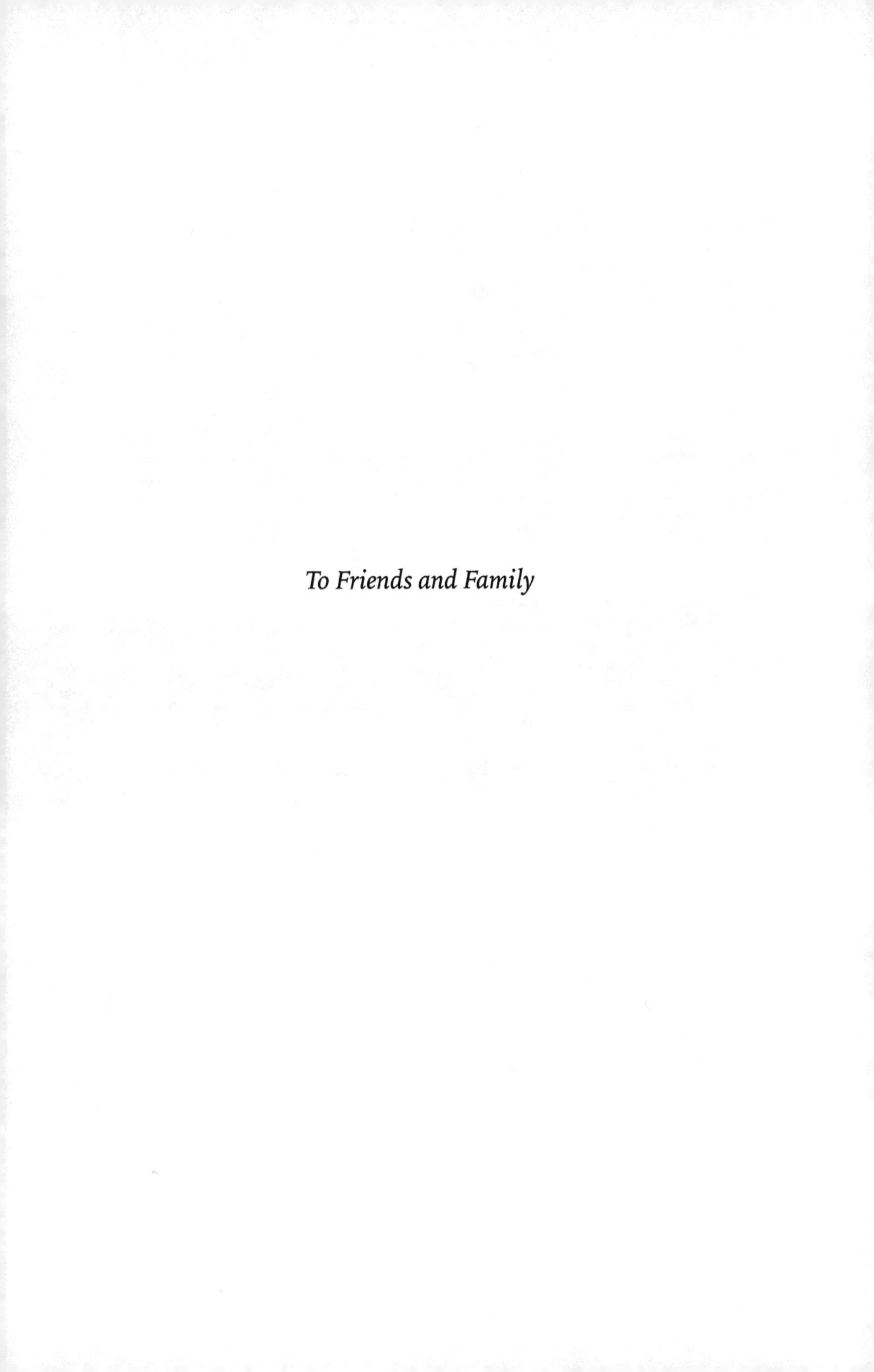

To Friends and Family

Contents

Rise and Fall of the Hahnenkamms

"DID you hear that?"

"How could I not? It sounded sort of muffled. You see that pale-blue Mercedes ahead? It looks like it's smashed against the side of the house on the corner. Let's approach with caution. I have a strange feeling about this one, Franz."

Adolf jumped out of the car, his hand reaching for the gun in his holster. "Come close, Franz, and give me a good flash into Pale Blue." The light bounced off the smooth leather covering of the dashboard. Adolf gasped. "Franz, we heard right a few seconds ago. Look at the guy in the driver's seat. What's left of him. Half his face is gone. Get on the horn and call for backup. This one's too big to handle just for the two of us. Don't touch a friggin' thing before you put on some gloves!"

Sirens were blaring as they approached the corner of Rosalindenstrasse. People were pouring out of neighboring houses or leaning from windows as three blue-flashing cruisers reached the area near the accident. *An accident*—at least that's what the curious onlookers suspected. All they saw was the pale-blue Mercedes smashed against the corner of Rosalindenstrasse 36. Officers Friedrichs and Meister made sure no one got close enough to glance at the dead man inside the car.

Sergeant Apfelbaum was the first to exit from one of the police cars summoned for backup. "What happened here? Why the call for assistance? Looks like a fender bender to me! Are we dealing with a drunken bum who got a bit too close to his own house? What's your name?" He faced Officer Friedrichs. "Are you two new on the force?"

"Adolf Friedrichs, Precinct Thirty-Seven." He clicked his heels. "My partner is Franz Meister. We've been on the force since 1986. Just patrolling the neighborhood. We were about a block from the scene when both of us heard a muffled, popping sound. We thought it sounded like a gunshot. That's what prompted us to investigate. Spotting the dead man behind the wheel, I instructed Meister to call for backup. We haven't touched a thing. All is exactly the way we found it. Shall we get rid of the onlookers? No doubt we are looking at a crime scene."

"You're damn right; it wasn't just a fender bender," added Meister.

Apfelbaum aimed his bullhorn, blasting his message to the bystanders. "Folks, you better head back to bed. This ain't a movie set. We have no need for extras. Unless you saw or heard anything we should know, don't bother to stick around. So clear out—*schnell, schnell* [quickly]. We've got our work cut out for us."

As his vision swept over the crowd, he saw a guy approaching the vehicle, his camera pointed at the dead driver. "Did you not understand me? Hand me that camera, you damn fool! You are interfering with a police investigation."

Totally caught off guard, the man turned over his camera to Apfelbaum. With a single deft motion, Apfelbaum flipped open the back of the camera and ripped the film off its spool. He tossed the cellulite snake into the guy's face. "I hope this teaches you a lesson. You are lucky; I'm a Leica buff myself. Had it been any other brand, I would have kicked the shit out of it." He practically shoved the camera into the offender's gut. "Now beat it!"

Apfelbaum and his crew peered into the vehicle; the driver's suit coat was oozing with congealing blood. One of the men opened the door of the Mercedes on the driver's side. Apfelbaum got the full picture. "Holy shit! He's wearing pigskin gloves and is gripping a Glock 17 with his left hand. Don't touch that gun until we check for prints, Sattler. He must have fired that thing with his left paw. Put your safety gloves on before searching the body and car. Check the glove compartment for registration and insurance documents. We might learn who this guy is—or should I say, *was*?"

Moritz Sattler, Apfelbaum's partner, started the search of the car. He stared at the papers facing him. "The vehicle is registered to a Ferdinand Hahnenkamm." Glancing briefly at the right side of the man's face, he volunteered, "He's a mess, but this guy doesn't look like he's eighty-five years old. Maybe we are looking at stolen wheels?"

Apfelbaum yelled, "Keep searching."

Two of Apfelbaum's young sidekicks dragged the bloody remains out of the Mercedes and placed the corpse into a body bag. Apfelbaum's voice carried over the sirens from the approaching paddy wagon that would carry the dead man away: "Don't leave any stones unturned when you strip him at the morgue. Under the circumstances, a thorough search of anything he wears must be conducted if we are to learn who he is. Sattler, you ride in the paddy. I'll see you at the mortuary."

No sooner did the sirens of the departing vehicle fade in the distance when a tow truck appeared around the corner and hauled Pale Blue away. Windows darkened as gawking neighbors retired one by one. For the disappointed onlookers, the late-night show was over. For the men in blue, solving the mystery of the dead man found at Rosalindenstrasse 36 had just begun.

Sergeant Apfelbaum stormed into the morgue. "What'ya find in his pockets? Anything? And don't give me that 'Nothing' shit! He must have had something in all those damn pockets."

The coroner came to Sattler's defense as he stood next to the naked corpse covered with a clean white sheet. "He helped me strip this guy. He turned every pocket inside out. That's his wallet. There were 212 marks and fifty pfennigs in the wallet in the right back pocket of his pants. The only other things we found were a dirty handkerchief soaked in blood in the left breast pocket of his suit jacket and eight chips from the Siegburg Casino in his left front pant pocket. They were coated with his blood and only identifiable after we washed off the sticky mess. We checked the gun for fingerprints. There were none. Wiped clean. The guy carried neither a driver's license nor a mandatory personal ID. Sattler could not have been more thorough in his search."

"What'ya think happened, Doc? You got any ideas?" asked Apfelbaum.

"At this point I'm unwilling to call it suicide although one might assume that's the case from the way he gripped that revolver with his left hand. Sure was a direct hit to his artery on the left side of his face. Either he or whoever shot him knew what they were doing.

"You know your next step. Find out who Ferdinand Hahnenkamm, the apparent owner of the car, is. That's the best lead you have at the moment. Your buddy, Sattler, was right. It ain't the guy lying on that table. This man is somewhere in his late forties. At worst, in his early fifties. According to the documents in the glove compartment, Ferdinand Hahnenkamm would be eighty-five. *And that age this one is not!"*

"Let me take another peek at our friend." Apfelbaum pulled back the sheet, exposing most of the corpse. "Is that his natural hair color? Looking at the color of his skin and his body hair, he looks more like a redhead than that dark color on his scalp. I hadn't noticed that in the darkness of the car. The mess of all the blood sure didn't help. You cleaned him up good!"

Coroner Diebel faced the sergeant; he cringed at Apfelbaum's language. "Absolutely. Just look carefully at the center of his scalp. Without a doubt, this deep auburn is not the man's natural hair color. No question, it's a good dye job. Makes you wonder. He did have a pretty good crop of hair before the insult. The touches of gray on his right temple gave me a hint of his age," said Coroner Diebel.

"I'll check on Ferdinand Hahnenkamm first thing in the morning. That Mercedes has been around for a few years, although it looks in great shape on the outside. It's a 190-E

Benz. Good car. Of course, after the shooting, it will need major work on the inside and some restoration on the outside where he got too close to the building. For now, it's impounded until this case is solved. I need to get some sleep; I was supposed to be off duty three hours ago," stated Apfelbaum.

Diebel covered up the corpse before he shoved the gurney into the icebox and slammed the steel door with vigor. An autopsy would be done in the morning. "Night, gentlemen! You'll have the full report later tomorrow."

Ӿ

Apfelbaum was at his desk by nine o'clock in the morning. He was nursing his second cup of coffee when he reached for his phone. He dialed the Motor Vehicle Bureau.

"Motor Vehicle Registration, Fräulein Reif speaking. How may I direct your call?"

"Sergeant Apfelbaum, Precinct #41. We impounded a Mercedes 190-E after a shooting last night. The documents in the car suggest that the vehicle belonged to a Ferdinand Hahnenkamm. I need a little more info on the owner. Can you help me? Or tell me who can?"

"I believe I can check that for you. Was that Hahnenkamm with two Ms?"

"Yes'm!"

"Just a moment, please." Five minutes went by. Apfelbaum was tapping his desk with his pen, a nervous habit of his. He wasn't the most patient man on the force. He heard Fräulein Reif pick up the receiver.

"Ferdinand Hahnenkamm was born in 1910. He bought the car new in 1983. Our records indicate that he died in May

1990. His wife signed the title over to their son, Walter, in August 1990."

"You got any dope on the wife and son?" More tapping on the desk.

"All we have on her is her birth date and the year she died. She's from 1911 and died in 1995. Walter, their son, was born in 1947. He's been involved in several serious car accidents. Hahnenkamm Jr. has been in the clink twice for DUI—big time. His last residence of record is Rosalindenstrasse 36 in Essen. That's all I have for you without further digging!"

"Thanks, Fräulein Reif. That's a heck of a lot more than we had last night." He placed the receiver back onto the cradle—none too gently.

"I'll be damned! Doc Diebel was right on with the estimate of this guy's age. He was forty-nine in June. Sattler, you got it right too. You were wondering last night if he slammed that car into his house; and that is exactly what he did. Supposedly he lives at the corner house where we found him. Let's hightail it over there and find out what that's all about."

Apfelbaum and Sattler jumped into an unmarked cruiser and were on their way. They pulled up in front of Rosalindenstrasse 36 in no time flat. "Not too much damage to the house," noted Sattler. They walked up to the entrance and checked out the names next to each doorbell.

"There's a W. Hahnenkamm on the second floor." Apfelbaum pressed the doorbell repeatedly without getting any response. "You think he was a bachelor? Him lying in the morgue would be 'splaining why no one answers the door. Wanna try ringing the neighbor on the same floor? Who knows?" Sattler shrugged his shoulders and looked at the name. "It's a weird one. 'Dingdong'? I'd change that handle in a heartbeat if I were stuck with it." Sattler laid his thumb on the button and pressed firmly. A buzzer sounded and the door opened.

Clutching the highly polished wooden bannister, the two cops climbed the stairs to the second floor. "Nice to see an old house so well taken care of. I noticed on the cornerstone it was built in 1906. Obviously, it must have survived World War II," commented Sattler.

Catching their breath, they were greeted by Lady Dingdong, clearly advanced in age. She was puzzled to see the two uniformed men standing in front of her. They flashed their police badges and introduced themselves properly. Apfelbaum spoke first.

"Sergeant Apfelbaum!" He stuck out his right hand to greet the woman. "This is my colleague, Sergeant Sattler. We are here to investigate an incident that occurred in front of this house after 23:00 last night."

"It's a pleasure to meet you, officers. I'm Amalia Dingdong. How may I be of service to you? Please step into my parlor. I would like to sit before we proceed. I am eighty-five years old. Although I'm pretty spry for my age, I just don't want to stand here in the hallway and look up at you tall, handsome men during a lengthy conversation. It simply is too hard on my aging neck. Forgive me, what did you say this is about?" The lady extended her hand, inviting Apfelbaum and Sattler into her living room. They glanced around, noticing that it was elegantly furnished. The lady obviously had money and good taste.

"Didn't you hear all the sirens last night? The whole neighborhood seemed to be looking on when we arrived on the scene," said Apfelbaum.

"No. My bedroom is in the back of the house, and when I shed my hearing aids before I retire, I'm pretty much dead to the world. I went to bed shortly after 22:00. I'm the oldest resident in the building. Most of my neighbors work and are gone during the day. I believe the young Mrs. Hahnenkamm, across from my apartment, is on vacation. She and her twelve-year-old son have been gone for a few weeks. I heard her tell another neighbor that they planned to visit her relatives outside Stuttgart. She and her husband, Walter, own this house. I rarely see him; he seems to enjoy being absent from the scene."

As Lady Dingdong spoke, Apfelbaum and Sattler watched her closely. They winked at each other, both registering that apparently she didn't have a particular fondness for her neighbors, the Hahnenkamms.

"Would you care for tea or coffee? I have both. If it was later in the day, I might have offered you a cognac. Of course, I realize this is not a social call and you are not to imbibe while you are on duty."

"Right, ma'am. No cognac for sure, but I wouldn't mind a cup of coffee. What about you, Sattler?"

"Sounds great. It's been a short night. I'll take mine with a healthy dash of cream. No sugar, please."

"No "cow" for me, but three lumps of sugar would do the trick."

It took no time at all for Frau Dingdong to reappear. "Here we are, gentlemen." She set the pretty collectors' cups in front of them.

"Do you by any chance know of a way we could get a hold of Frau Hahnenkamm? It's pretty important we do. We found her husband shot to death in front of this house last night. He was seated in a pale-blue Mercedes; he apparently rammed into the side of this building before he died. He's in the precinct morgue; an autopsy is being performed as we speak," said Sergeant Apfelbaum.

"Oh, my God!" was all she said, loudly. She turned her face away from the police officers. In an almost inaudible aside she muttered, "Good riddance to the bastard!"

"What were you saying, ma'am?" said Apfelbaum.

"Oh, I was just sending a quiet, short message to the man upstairs. That's too bad. I'm glad his mother didn't live to experience this. She's been gone for a little over a year. She was my closest friend from the time we were little girls. We were born the same year, attended the same schools, and treasured the good and the bad years we were destined to share. I miss Elsa terribly. Such a kind lady. She outlived Ferdinand by five years.

"I'm sorry to say, I have no clue where the young woman's family lives. I know it's in the vicinity of Stuttgart. I never had an amicable relationship with the young folks, although I've known Walter since the day he was born. How well I remember."

"Pray tell. Would you mind telling us a bit about young Hahnenkamm now lying dead in our morgue?"

"Not at all. He was an unexpected godsend to my dear friend!"

"Where do I begin? I suppose at the beginning. Elsa and I were born a week apart not too far from this house; that is, I was born a couple of streets over from Rosalindenstrasse. Elsa was actually born in this very place. At the time, the building was merely five years old. It was her father's pride and joy. Elsa's mother often told the story of the *Richtfest* [the day when a young tree was mounted on the almost completed roof, symbolizing the establishment of the house's roots with the promise of a long and prosperous life]. Elsa and I met the day we started in kindergarten. My God, that was eighty years ago. Where have the years gone? We were four years old when our fathers marched off to fight for Germany in the 'Great War.'"

"That's a long time ago. Are you sure you are up to sharing the whole story of the Hahnenkamms' lives with us?" said Apfelbaum.

"I won't go into all aspects of the Hahnenkamms' lives; they only came into play in 1932 when Elsa married Ferdinand. She was such a beautiful bride. My story begins with the life of my dear friend, Elsa Krämer.

"She had an older sister and brother at the time. Her younger sister was born when Elsa was eight years old. Georgine was our living doll until we outgrew playing with dolls. By the time we were in our teens, Georgine was a handful. Her father spoiled the heck out of her. Georgine never could do any wrong."

"Well, are we ever getting to the present, dear lady? How much time do you think we have?" interrupted Sergeant Apfelbaum.

"My good man, if you want me to take you into the present, you'll have to suffer with me through the past. That's all there is to that. Would you two care for another cup of coffee? At the rate we are going, we may sample my Remy Martin or Louis XIII after all."

"Nothing but the best, lady! For now, let's stick with the coffee. May I use your phone? I better let my superior know we are onto something and may be gone for a while."

He dialed the number at Precinct #41. "Apfelbaum here; put me through to Kirsch."

"Commander Kirsch speaking."

"Hi. It's Apfelbaum. We made some interesting discoveries at the Hahnenkamm house. The guy's wife is out of town, and no one knows where she and their kid are visiting. Closest I got, they are somewhere near Stuttgart. That covers a lot of territory. Their next-door neighbor, a delightful eighty-five-year-old lady, is filling us in on some interesting background." He winked at Amalia Dingdong.

"The lady isn't too friendly toward the young Mrs. Hahnenkamm, the guy in the morgue, and their twelve-year-old son. On the other hand, she is a gold mine of info re the older Hahnenkamms. We may be a while. Some of what she has to say might shed light on the case. Hope you don't mind. Sattler and I are sitting at the edge of our seats. See you sometime. Not sure when."

"You do as you see fit. Sounds like we are going to have a lengthy visitor in our mortuary." Kirsch hung up the phone. Apfelbaum gave Amalia another wink, encouraging her to continue her story. "Thanks for the refill on the coffee." Sattler nodded his head in agreement.

"Elsa Hahnenkamm and I had a wonderful life for most of our years. As we became elderly, so to speak, not all that was gold glittered, especially when it concerned Elsa. She should have been queen for a day to her last breath. That's why I'm so bitter. But let me take you back to happier days.

"Elsa was always a beautiful girl. She was elegant, well

groomed, and stylish in the latest of fashion. I had a hard time keeping up with her. By the time we were sixteen, we were accomplished dancers. The rake who taught us the latest dances in vogue was Elsa's brother, Arthur. His idol was Fred Astaire.

"We'd walk into the Kasanova on Arthur's arms all decked out in the latest flapper dresses and he always in a black tie and tux. It never failed: when our threesome showed up, we'd stop the show. The band would switch to a quickstep or the latest tango or foxtrot, and Arthur would present one of us on the *parquet* to the full applause of those in the house. When Arthur and we walked in, other dancers cleared the floor. At first they called Arthur and Elsa 'Fred and Adele'; later it was 'Fred & Ginger.' Everyone adored them.

"I don't remember how often Elsa was the Queen of the Rose Monday parade during Carnival. Twice, I was her first attendant. We truly enjoyed our lives. Arthur had taught Elsa to drive; by 1929 she had her own car. Tooting around Essen in Elsa's sporty little number, the two of us were viewed as notorious by other jealous females.

"Neither Elsa nor I were particularly interested in pursuing academics. She got into the habit of working a few hours in the parental business, and I enjoyed finishing school being groomed for that 'MRS' degree. Our free time was dedicated to Arthur's motto *'live, live, live!'* His father wanted him to be a lawyer or physician. He chose to be a butcher in the daytime and a dancer and barfly at night. Arthur practiced what he preached. He *lived!*

"All that carousing came to a screeching halt when Elsa and I were married to a couple of great guys in 1932. As a matter of fact, we were married the same day in the same church. It was almost like a double wedding. Elsa was a stunning bride on the arm of her ailing father being led into the arms of Ferdinand Hahnenkamm, a well-to-do gent from Wanne-Eickel, of all places. I married Otto Dingdong.

"I almost insisted on keeping my maiden name, Amalia Dorothea von Eichendorff. I'm a great-great-great-great, etc., daughter of Joseph Freiherr von Eichendorff, a famous nineteenth-century Prussian poet, novelist, playwright, literary critic, translator, and anthologist. It took a mad love for my future husband not to object to becoming a Dingdong. I was always glad there were no little Dingdongs to worry about. Even after Otto was killed in Stalingrad, the thought never occurred to me to change back to my maiden name. I know it's the source of much amusement for most people—including you two gentlemen. I couldn't help reading the smirks on your faces when I first introduced myself to you. That's OK. I've gotten used to it over the past sixty-four years."

"Sorry we were so obvious! It's not your name that is important to us; it's your charm and the delightful telling and sharing of the Hahnenkamms' story you're willing to impart to us that captivates and keeps us listening to you," said Apfelbaum. Sattler smiled in agreement.

"At first, Elsa and I suffered from separation anxiety when she and Ferdinand settled in Wanne-Eickel, where his ancestral home and business were located. Of course, we realized quickly that we weren't worlds apart and could easily visit each other by hopping on a train and be there in less than an hour.

"Otto was a rising star in the banking world, and Ferdinand was successful in expanding the familial enterprise. Both Elsa and I enjoyed a certain degree of affluence, affording us the elegant homes in which we lived. Arthur married a couple years later and took over his father's business in Essen. Clearly, those fun-filled days of the roaring twenties were behind us.

"Somehow the turbulent changes on the political horizon didn't impact any of us as much as they did many others until all suitable young men were drawn into World War II in 1939. What Elsa and I regretted the most in the early years of our respective marriages was the fact that we were not destined to have children. Elsa was fortunate enough to have two nephews by her older sister, Helena. Being godmother to both boys filled a certain void in her life. Being an only child, I was denied that experience.

"After Ferdinand was inducted, Elsa closed their business in Wanne-Eickel and spent much time traveling and with her family in Essen. She and I were closer than ever, especially when I was widowed in 1942 and Arthur went MIA during the military debacle called Stalingrad.

"While my home in Rüttenscheid survived the war unscathed, Elsa's home in Wanne-Eickel was flattened during a bombing in 1944; the parental home on Rosalindenstrasse was severely damaged in 1945. Elsa had no idea what happened to Ferdinand during the waning months of the war. I was fortunate enough to have Elsa share my home during the twilight of the Third Reich and the collapse of the country. Both of us were stunned when Ferdinand appeared at our doorstep in August 1945 looking more like an escapee from a concentration camp than the healthy-looking young man both of us recalled."

Sattler coughed, getting Amalia's attention. "Ma'am, after all this coffee, I need to use a restroom. Could you point me in the right direction?"

"Oh, of course. Down that hall; it's the second door on

your left. Both of you, feel free to use it. I should have thought of that myself." When Sattler returned, Apfelbaum excused himself to do the same. Amalia went to her bedroom, needing a potty break herself.

"What do you think, Sattler? This is turning into quite the story. I can't wait for her to get to the juicy stuff. I know we are still officially on duty. Hope you don't mind, but the next time she offers me some of that fancy cognac of hers, I won't decline. I'm even considering accepting a bite to eat if she should ask."

"I thought you would never come up with that suggestion. I've been ready for a shot and some munchies for the last hour or so."

"Glad to know you're seeing it my way. Here she comes. Let's see if she reads our minds," said Apfelbaum.

"Thanks for letting me take a little break. I needed that. Now, how about a little refreshment? I have the fixings for some *Schnittchen* [finger sandwiches] in the house. What may I serve you to drink, gentlemen? Would you care for some cognac or something different?"

"We thought you'd never ask. No, just joking," said Apfelbaum. "I'll relieve you of some of that fancy Louis XIII. What about you, Sattler? I know cognac is not exactly your speed."

"If you have it, I'll have a Dortmunder and a shot of schnapps—anything but cognac. Thanks."

"No problem. It's all on hand; I like a good glass of beer now and then myself. I'm delighted with your company. At my age, most of my friends are gone. Not having family or friends, it becomes a lonely existence. It's not often that I get to talk to, never mind entertain, two handsome young officers. It seems I have you enthralled listening to the telling of my story." She got up and reached for a crystal snifter, pouring a healthy drink for Apfelbaum. "I'll be right back with your beer and a shot." After both men had their drinks, she excused herself for a few moments, wanting to fix the finger sandwiches in her very modern kitchen.

"May we help you with that, Ma'am?" inquired Sattler. "No need for that. You men enjoy your drinks, relax, and rest your ears. I won't be long. Haven't done this in a long while. Always loved to entertain. It's my distinct pleasure to have you in my home."

Fifteen minutes later she walked in with a large platter of enticingly arranged finger sandwiches. They might have been prepared by a top-notch deli in the neighborhood. She placed napkins and China plates on the cocktail table and encouraged them to help themselves. "How about it if I refresh your drinks before I join you for a bite?"

"Thanks, that would be nice. What are you drinking?" said Apfelbaum.

"Nothing alcoholic. I'll have some Perrier. Right now I need to keep my wits about me if you want me to finish my tale of the Hahnenkamms.

"As I said, before we decided to take a break, Elsa and I were both stunned by Ferdinand's reappearance. At the time, I was the first to find my voice: 'Where have you been? How did you find Elsa and me?'

'When I found myself on the doorstep of Helena's house, I scared the hell out of all of them. They thought they were seeing a ghost. It was from Helena that I learned of your existence. And that's how I got here and found you.'"

"'East of Vienna, I became separated from my company during the last skirmishes and engagements with Russian troops. When the artillery fire ceased, I crawled out of the woods and hid in a farmer's barn for two days. I took off my uniform and put it under some hay in the barn. All I had on was my dirty underwear and socks and boots. I must have been quite a sight when I finally emerged from my hiding place and faced the old farmer and his wife. They were scared shitless, believing at first I was a Russian deserter. When I addressed them in German, they were relieved and offered me shelter for a couple of days. I was thankful to them for feeding and clothing me.

'The old man was kind enough to part with the best of his old prewar bicycles. I started on the first leg of my long journey home to Wanne-Eickel as dusk set in. For the first two hundred miles, I moved from town to town and from barn to barn mostly at dusk and in early evening. Some farmers never even realized that I had slept in their barn for a few hours. Here and there, I became daring enough to face an owner and beg for a piece of bread or whatever. Most nights I devoured half-ripened apples I had ripped off trees as I was riding by on my bike. When the bike gave out, I hoofed it. It took me more than three months to conquer the one thousand kilometers plus to reach home.'"

"Man, that was some hike when you stop and think about it," interrupted Apfelbaum. "You ain't kidding," agreed Sattler.

Amalia smiled as she continued her tale. "Ferdinand made a remarkable recovery; within a few weeks, he returned to Wanne-Eickel and began to build a humble structure on the site of their former business and home. None of their personal belongings were destroyed, due to Elsa's foresight to transport anything of value to safe storage with relatives living in Swabia in 1943.

"When Arthur did not return by late 1946, Elsa's parents encouraged Ferdinand to assume responsibility for their business in Rüttenscheid. Elsa and I were elated that she would remain close to me in Essen.

"Within weeks, a joyous Elsa hugged me on my doorstep. 'You'll never believe this. I'm with child and will be a mother by next June. Can you imagine this after being married to Ferdinand for more than fourteen years? He is positively euphoric.'

"So was I. Getting over my first shock after learning of Elsa's good fortune, I was jealous and envious of her. How I would have loved to have a child by my dear Otto—Dingdong or not. It wasn't meant to be. I consoled myself and looked forward to the birth of Elsa's child."

ꭗ

"Walter Hahnenkamm was born as anticipated in late June 1947. Elsa didn't really suffer a difficult birth. When the baby slipped from her womb and announced its arrival with a healthy outburst of energy, Elsa was overjoyed to learn that she had delivered a boy who would carry on the family name. The baby was rushed from the birthing room; he was washed and dressed before being presented to his parents.

"By the time the nurse brought little Walter to Elsa's room for a first viewing, Ferdinand was standing next to her bed anxious to behold their creation. They placed the baby into her arms and she counted his cute little fingers; the toes had to wait until later. Gently, she removed the tiny knit hat from his scalp. Elsa couldn't believe her eyes. She screamed, *'Oh my God, he has a head full of carrot-red hair!'*

"She sobbed uncontrollably as she looked up at Ferdinand. 'You have dark hair, and I'm a blonde; how did we wind up with a red-haired kid?'

"One would have thought she had given birth to a monster. Ferdinand finally said, 'Remember, both my father and my older brother, Junker, have red hair. It's in the family for sure. The milkman had nothing to do with it!'

"Once she recovered from the initial shock, she voiced her solution to the 'problem' as she saw it. 'Hydrogen peroxide does wonders for my hair; why not for him?'

"Within days of being discharged from the hospital and much to the shock of everyone in the family, little Walter was transformed into a bleached blonde. He remained a blonde until six months before he started kindergarten. Elsa reluctantly appeased Ferdinand and let Walter be a natural redhead. By this time, the carrot red had darkened to a somewhat more acceptable shade as far as Elsa saw it. There was no question about it; Walter was terribly indulged by both of his parents but also very much loved. They had never expected to celebrate parenthood.

"Walter was given every opportunity to succeed in whatever whimsy he elected to pursue, be it his attempts at being a musician, an ice skater, a race car driver, or whatever. He even tried his hand at becoming a butcher. He never truly became accomplished at anything; the closest he came was being somewhat gifted at hockey. And, of course, he became extremely skilled at spending his parents' money.

"By the time he was eighteen, he had smashed three new

Mercedes, including the one he had received as a present from his father. In his mid-twenties, he had actually become rather handsome. His hair was always professionally styled and dyed a dark auburn.

"To his parents' chagrin, he announced that he was marrying a girl of whom they knew little. The girl's parents were poor, and Walter expected Elsa and Ferdinand to pay for an elaborate wedding. The girl was pregnant with his child.

"I was invited to the wedding celebration. After dinner, Elsa and I needed to use the ladies' room. While using the facility, the bride and her attendants walked in and proceeded to discuss vociferously how successful they had been in duping the groom and his family into believing that the bride was knocked up. Their plan was to milk the Hahnenkamms for all they were worth.

"Needless to say, they were flabbergasted when Elsa and I emerged from our respective stalls. The bride had not envisioned meeting the wrath of God in the ladies' room when Elsa turned on her: 'You cheap piece of trash. You and your entire tribe better be out of the establishment within fifteen minutes. Take a good look at our son as you pass him by. It's the last time you will see him other than in court when your marriage is annulled. You'll never see another mark from this family!'

"Elsa then walked up to Ferdinand and told him what she had discovered. 'Tell our son, the party is over!'

"She picked up her purse and settled the bill with the restaurateur in cash. Walter had never seen his mother so angry and in such a state. Once again though, his parents shielded him from assuming his responsibilities. Of course, in this case they protected him as well as themselves."

"Mrs. Dingdong, this is beginning to sound more revealing

by the minute. Our man in the morgue is indeed a person of interest. Sattler and I can't wait to hear the end of this story."

"Walter married a second time when he was thirty-six and presented his parents with a grandson the following year. Horst was seen as the joy in Elsa and Ferdinand's autumn years. They had moved into an elegant modern apartment in a neighborhood that particularly suited Elsa. The responsibilities of managing the large house and business were turned over to their son. Grandson Horst was only six years old when Ferdinand suffered a massive heart attack. Ferdinand knew he hadn't long to live when he said to Elsa, 'Watch out for our son. He's a bad seed. Never divest yourself of anything, and never sign anything without benefit of legal counsel. I've done everything in my power to protect you. There are things you do not know about our son, matters which I've settled not wanting to upset you. Elsa, mark my words, and never forget what I'm trying to tell you. I hope he doesn't end like my brother, Junker, who gambled away his fortune. They found him in an alley in Witten; he had shot himself in a drunken stupor.'

"Ferdinand fell back into Elsa's arms. He was dead.

"Less than two years passed when Walter made his first move. 'Mother, if you want us to continue living in the old house, you must spend beaucoup money and update that mausoleum. I need at least one hundred thousand marks to make that place livable for us. We deserve to live in the style to which we've become accustomed. Don't give me any crap; I'm well aware of how much money you have in your bank accounts. I could ask you for my share of the inheritance, which is fifty percent of what Father left you. But I won't; I'm not that stupid. I want it all by the time I'm done with you. And you better meet my demands if you want to see Horst again.' He slammed her purse on the table. 'Write the fucking check before I beat the shit out of you!'

"Elsa wrote the check for one hundred thousand marks and handed it to her son. As soon as he left the apartment, she called me and told me what happened. When I arrived at her place, she was sobbing and practically fainted in my arms. I always had some inkling of what might happen after Ferdinand's death. But never had I dreamt of witnessing such depravity. This was just the opening salvo.

"By the time Horst was eight years old, he was told by his father to kick the old lady in the shins if she didn't fork over what he demanded. Walter insisted that he be the sole agent to collect all rents from properties owned by Elsa. When she refused to sign the documents, he had her declared mentally incompetent by a physician, only too willing to accept the 'thirty pieces of silver' for the ugly deed. After Elsa's eighty-first birthday, he moved his mother out of her elegant apartment with most of her furnishings into the oldest and smallest apartment in this old house. It was the only part of the building never updated since 1906. With furniture piled to the ceiling, the tiny hovel resembled an ugly warehouse. Anything suitable for a quick sale was turned into cash.

"Walter and his wife Elke lived in the thoroughly modern quarters above her and provided Elsa with minimal and substandard nourishment, had her telephone service cut, and controlled who she saw. And that included me; her captors didn't want me to look after her. I had to sneak downstairs in the dark when I wanted to see Elsa.

"The name of the previous tenants of the tiny apartment was Nix. Elke insisted on not changing the name tag at the house directory. In her opinion, the name suited her mother-in-law. [*Nix,* in German slang, means 'nothing.'] Elsa's heirs thought of her and treated her indeed as if she was *nothing*. They had every intention of starving her to death. After she had a mild stroke, she was hospitalized in quarters meeting the needs of the poorest of the poor. Upon being discharged, Walter and Elke transferred Elsa to a home for the indigent. It was there that she died in 1995. She was buried next to Ferdinand in the family plot without adding her name on the grave marker. Walter made sure his mother remained *'Nix'* even in death. At last, he had made good on his word; Walter had taken his mother for all she had—her dignity, her wealth, and, ultimately, her life."

"That brings us to the present," said Officer Apfelbaum. "I suppose we could get a warrant and search their apartment in his wife's absence. I would like to have a photo of Walter before we take a ride out to the Casino in Siegburg. That should be our next step. You don't by any chance have a fairly recent photo of the gentleman, do you?"

"Don't call him a gentleman in my presence. He was a monster. Now I can share with you my softly spoken aside when we first met this morning. I said, 'Good riddance to the bastard'— and I meant it. To answer your question, I have a photo of him and Ferdinand that was taken about six years ago shortly before his father died. He hasn't changed all that much, especially with that professionally styled hair and dye job. Anyone who knew him well enough would recognize him. Let me get it for you; it's in one of the drawers in the desk in my bedroom. I couldn't keep it on display after what that scumbag did to my friend." Amalia left Apfelbaum and Sattler alone for a moment.

⋇

"Let's stop at the office and pick up those chips before heading for Siegburg. We'll briefly fill in Kirsch if he's still on duty. I want the goods on this guy," said Apfelbaum. Sattler had had other plans for the evening but concurred with his colleague that a night visit might be a better time to get info re the habits of a certain Walter Hahnenkamm.

When Amalia returned with the photo in question, Apfelbaum clued her in on their intent to pay a visit to the Siegburg Casino that very night.

"Here are our business cards. Please get in touch with us as soon as Frau Hahnenkamm should appear. We've decided not to make any effort to search for her and will keep this out of the papers for as long as possible. Only when we know more about this character shall we proceed. In the meantime, stay in touch with us as soon as you see the whites of Elke Hahnenkamm's eyes—and let's not forget 'darling' little Horst. It's been a pleasure being with you, Amalia Dorothea von Eichendorff Dingdong."

"The pleasure has been all mine, officers." She shook their hands and smiled broadly as Apfelbaum and Sattler departed.

⋇

"Hit the gas, Sattler! I was glad they hadn't locked up Hahnenkamm's stuff in the evidence locker. It was sort of surprising but fortunate for us. I bet you Kirsch wasn't aware of the slip. Diebel must have been bushed after that late-night arrival. Had Kirsch seen that, the shit would've hit the fan!"

ℵ

The officers walked into the Siegburg Casino an hour later and headed straight for one of the busiest roulette tables. Apfelbaum sidled up to the croupier and paid close attention to what the man was doing. Looking at the chips on the table, he knew that the ones recovered from Hahnenkamm's pant pockets had indeed originated at the Siegburg Casino.

A number of players lost considerable amounts of money and walked away from the table. There was a momentary lull in activities when Apfelbaum seized the opportunity. He held up Walter's photograph to the croupier. He could tell immediately that Walter was no stranger to the man.

"Do you know this gentleman?" With that, both he and Sattler flashed their credentials. "May we go someplace where we can talk? It's urgent business. What's your name?"

"Herrmann Meier. Let me get my boss's attention." He raised his arm, waving it repeatedly.

Finally, a well-dressed gent approached. "What's this about? Is there a problem? I'm Fritz Deerendorf, the casino manager."

Apfelbaum responded, "Nice meeting you. There's no problem; we just have a question or two about an apparent frequent patron of your casino. Do you recognize this man? Obviously, Meier did when he glanced at the photo a moment ago."

"Let me see it. *Oh, yes*! We know Herr Hahnenkamm very well. He spends many hours indeed at our gaming tables. Lately, he hasn't been too lucky. As a matter of fact, yesterday he lost his shirt at that table over there!"

"May we talk in your offices for a moment? We'd rather not entertain your patrons and stop Meier, here, from making more money for the house."

"OK, you are catching us on a slow night. Step right in, gentlemen, and have a seat. Now, what can I do for you?"

"When you said Hahnenkamm lost his shirt, how elegant a shirt was it?"

"He lost 85,000 marks just last night. That was about the worst day he had this week. Actually, he wrote us an IOU for 20,000 marks. Is there a problem?"

"Did you see him leave? Was he sober, or did he have too much to drink?"

"Please don't tell me he was in an accident! Actually, I thought he was pretty sober when he got into that old Pale Blue that used to be his dad's."

"Did he have any words with anyone here before he gave you the IOU and left?"

"No. He certainly had no words with me. I knew he'd be good for his debts; he's never stiffed us out of anything."

"I must tell you, Herr Deerendorf," Apfelbaum cleared his throat, stalling to get the man's full attention. "Walter Hahnenkamm is dead. He drove Pale Blue home and got a bit too close to the side of his own house. When he was found by a couple of our men on routine night patrol, he was seated inside the car. The left side of his face was blown away by a point-blank shot to his head. He was dead when they found him. Can you think of anyone who might have done him in? Also, do you recall if he was a lefty?"

"I'm blown away. How is that possible? Yes, he was quite the gambler, but he was very much liked by all patrons and our staff. He was Mr. Debonair. He always came alone to the casino. Once he ran into one of our regulars, a lady—Madame Georgine. They didn't speak to one another. He told me later she was his mother's younger sister and that they were arch enemies. He never drank much. Perhaps a cocktail, a beer, or a glass of wine. I've never seen him drunk and never act as anything but a gentleman."

Apfelbaum swallowed hard as he mouthed to Sattler, "Must be a case of dual personality."

"Heh, I almost forgot. He was a lefty. Saw him write, eat, smoke, etc.—always with his left hand," said Deerendorf.

"Thanks for your cooperation and the info on Hahnenkamm. We have a much better picture, Herr Deerendorf. We'll see ourselves out. Thanks again."

They put on their caps and walked out to the car. Meier looked busy when they walked by his roulette table.

"What's your verdict, Sattler? Was it murder or suicide? Any hunch about it?"

"Knowing what we know now, that Hahnenkamm was apparently very skilled in using his left hand, I'm inclined to believe he did it himself. We need to do a little checking into his finances. That will be another important clue."

"I concur. Exactly my feeling. We'll do some checking tomorrow. Let's call it a day after dropping off Hahnenkamm's stuff at the lock box. We'll fill in Kirsch and write the report tomorrow morning. I'm bushed. It's been one hell of a day and night!"

Sattler jokingly clicked his heels. "My sentiments, exactly!" said he as he walked toward his motorbike.

Apfelbaum spotted the night secretary. "Are you by any chance super busy? If not, would you be so good and transcribe my tape for the chief? Just put it on his desk when you are done. Very interesting! Very interesting, indeed! Thanks!"

"No problem! Anything for you, Officer Apfelbaum, anytime."

Ж

Apfelbaum and Sattler sat across from each other at their double desks. Fräulein Reif had done some digging for them. Both guys picked up their phones on the first ring. Apfelbaum covered his mouthpiece for a split second. "This ought to be good!"

"Yes, Fräulein Reif, what'ya find out?"

"Sorry, Apfelbaum; it's Commander Kirsch. Enlightening report you left on my desk. When on earth did you have the time to write in that much detail? This guy's more colorful than I expected. Guess you can't judge a book by its cover, to use a cliché."

"Actually, we used our noodle for a change. I had my recorder running all the time Amalia Dingdong was talking. We had the night secretary type it up; luckily, it was a slow night."

"Smart move. I see a call coming in. This might be Reif for you. Let me know what she found out."

"Yes, Fräulein Reif. Apfelbaum speaking. Got some juicy details for me?"

"I'm not sure about juicy. I had to reach out to the City Clerk for some of the info. Obviously, I have no access to his bank accounts. By the way, they are all exclusively in his name. Both properties in Wanne-Eickel and in Essen are mortgaged to the max. When he inherited them a year ago, they were debt free. That should tell you something. We might and we might not get access to bank records when Frau Hahnenkamm returns from wherever. It might take a court order should it be deemed necessary to have a look at them."

"Thanks! Very helpful info," said Apfelbaum setting the phone back into its cradle. "Let's have a chat with Kirsch and Diebel. I want to hear what they speculate."

Kirsch closed his office door. "Well, gentlemen, what do you say?" Diebel spoke first. "From what I read and have seen and heard, he had good reason to kill himself. What still puzzles me are the use of the gloves and the gun wiped clean of any fingerprints. Why would someone in that state of mind be concerned about leaving fingerprints? I have no problem with him being a lefty. Those who function in that mode become very adept at doing anything effectively."

"Sattler and I wondered the same after initial discussions and findings. "After listening for hours to Amalia Dingdong, we figured that bastard was mean enough to make it look like someone murdered him. We share Dr. Diebel's assessment that he committed suicide after that last horrendous loss at the Siegburg Casino. For now, let's keep him on ice until Madame Hahnenkamm returns. That ought to be a shocker for her and that miserable kid of theirs. Amalia Dingdong will call us the moment she hears any signs of life across the hallway. She will not speak to the young woman. It will be up to us to break the news."

Ten days went by before Amalia heard activities across the

way. Actually it was Horst maneuvering the stairs on roller skates that alerted her to their presence. She confirmed what she suspected by viewing the annoying activity through her "spy." Horst wasn't aware that he was being observed. It was ten in the morning when she dialed Apfelbaum's extension.

"Hallo, Officer Apfelbaum." He recognized her distinct voice immediately. "*Guten Morgen*, Frau Dingdong. Any news from across the hallway?"

"Yes! They must have returned late last night. I wonder how she reacted to the empty apartment? I'm sure the bed was untouched, and I doubt he left any kind of note. He never struck me as that considerate. Of course, if he planned his demise before he left that day for another round at the casino, perhaps there was a note. Although, seeing the boy on roller skates in the stairway would indicate to me that Frau Hahnenkamm doesn't have a clue—and I intend to keep it that way. It's all in your hands."

"Thank you, Frau Dingdong. Sattler and I are on our way. We'll be knocking on Frau Hahnenkamm's door shortly. Thanks again for your discretion."

Apfelbaum and Sattler rang the doorbell ten minutes later. They looked at each other walking up to the second floor. There was no doubt in their minds that Frau Dingdong's spy was in use. Elke opened the door and gasped when she saw both men in their blues, greeting them with, "Are you sure you pushed the correct button?"

"Are you Frau Walter Hahnenkamm? If so, you are the person we wish to speak to. Please put on a coat or jacket and come with us."

"Why? And where to? What about my son? He's playing on the street."

"Bring him along. It concerns his father, your husband. We need you at the police station."

Elke's eyes were wide open; she stared at the two officers. She didn't ask another question. On the street, she called Horst over. "Take those skates off and get in this car. We have to go with these men. It's something about your father. Just keep your foul mouth shut." For once, he minded his mother.

Ж

Commander Kirsch and the coroner, Dr. Diebel, had staged the morgue scene. The gurney bearing Walter Hahnenkamm had been removed from storage and turned in such a way that any onlookers were first exposed to his relatively unblemished right side. His body was still completely covered with a stark-white sheet.

Apfelbaum and his entourage entered the morgue. Elke wasn't quite certain where this was headed. Somehow she recalled having observed a similar scene in a movie. She was looking back and forth from the men behind the gurney to Apfelbaum and Sattler.

Dr. Diebel couldn't stand the suspense any longer; he wanted to see the reaction on the face of the presumed wife of the dead man in his custody. With a swift motion of his left arm, he pulled back the sheet exposing the right side of Walter's face. Elke screamed as she reached out to her dead husband.

Diebel said, "We are sorry, but we needed you to confirm that this is indeed your husband. He was found dead in his car twelve days ago. We believe he died as the result of a self-inflicted gunshot wound. No one knew where you were; it's for that reason the police couldn't reach you."

"What makes you think he killed himself? Wouldn't he have left me some kind of note? How did you even know who he was and where he lived?"

"All that was done by linking the car registration and insurance papers for the Mercedes to your husband. The casino chips in his pant pockets led us to Siegburg where your husband lost 85,000 marks early in the evening before he shot himself. There is an IOU for another 20,000 marks held by the casino. Your house in Wanne-Eickel as well as your house on Rosalindenstrasse no longer belong to you. They are mortgaged to the hilt. We have no idea if there is any money left in your bank accounts. Does this answer your questions?"

"I'm shocked! Please drive us home." She didn't shed a tear; Elke grabbed Horst by the hand as she turned away from her dead husband. Had she seen him from his left side, she would have fainted—all present were certain of that.

"Your husband's car will be released to you later today. Please let us know where you wish it to be towed. The vehicle is in need of some repair and a major detailing job on the inside. The seats in front may need to be replaced. His body will be transferred to the Parkfriedhof by Heidenkamp Funeral Services. Under the circumstances, we believe you would not want an open casket. Correct?"

"Absolutely not!" was all she said.

"Heidenkamp will discuss all details with you. Again, please accept our deepest sympathies."

The funeral took place four days later. There was no obituary in the papers. A small paragraph on page three of the *Westdeutsche Allgemeine Zeitung* [WAZ paper] mentioned the accident and the death of forty-nine-year-old Walter Hahnenkamm whose services would be at the Parkfriedhof. Further details were available through Heidenkamp Funeral Services; their telephone number was listed.

Amalia Dingdong read the blip in the WAZ and decided to attend the funeral. She would be disguised by a veil of darkness and remain in the background. While she detested the dead man, he was the son of her closest friend, and she knew him since the day he was born. She suspected a relatively small group of mourners would be in attendance. For that reason alone, Amalia was pleased with herself that she had resolved to take a cab to the Parkfriedhof and pay her respects. Riding in the cab, she thought about Otto, Elsa, and Ferdinand. They were all resting now in close proximity at the cemetery. Otto probably would have chided her for attending "that monster's" funeral and would have called her a hypocrite. *So what?* she thought.

When she got to the gravesite, she stood back but still had a good view of the happenings. The service was brief, with no long-winded speeches by the young minister. What happened next, she couldn't believe. She knew she needed to share her observations with Officers Apfelbaum and Sattler.

Unobserved, she walked away from the gravesite. She engaged a cabbie and asked to be taken to Precinct #41. When she entered the station, no one was more pleased to see her than her two handsome men in blue. She might have been eighty-five, dressed in stark black, and heavily veiled, but she had a regal bearing and an aura of unmistakable elegance. Amalia Dorothea von Eichendorff Dingdong was a class act.

Apfelbaum and Sattler rose from their chairs immediately extending their right hands in greeting, gently shaking Amalia's gloved hand. "To what do we owe this honor? You are brightening our dreary day with your surprise visit."

"I've just attended Walter Hahnenkamm's funeral at the Parkfriedhof. His wife didn't even see me standing in the background. To help my case, I was well disguised—don't you agree?"

"Great veil!" said Sattler.

"There were few mourners beside the son, Horst, and his mother. I believe I counted fourteen other people. None I knew and none who knew me. The minister conducted the service with extreme efficiency. They had barely started tossing the first shovel of dirt on the coffin when a stunning black Mercedes limousine pulled up right in front of the gravesite. The chauffeur jumped from his seat, opening the left rear door. An elegantly attired blonde stepped out and carried a large bouquet of expensive red roses in her arms. You should have seen *her* black dress and hat. *And those legs*. You men would have gone gaga. She stepped right in front of Elke, the wife, and tossed the roses into the grave. As she did, she turned to face Elke Hahnenkamm. I couldn't help hearing what she said: 'I'm also Frau Walter Hahnenkamm. He built a beautiful home for me and our daughter in Mühlheim. You will hear from my attorney in short order.' She quickly rushed back to her car. The chauffeur held the back door open for her and hurriedly pulled away from the scene. All, including myself, were left speechless."

"I'll be damned! A bigamist to boot!" was all Apfelbaum could say as he struck his desk with his right fist. Sattler suffered momentary *Maulsperre* [lockjaw]. Recovering from the initial shock, he smiled at Amalia and got out of his chair. He then extended his right hand: "Thank you, Frau von Eichendorff Dingdong!" Apfelbaum followed suit with his gesture of gratitude. Holding her head high, her back straight as she was taught as a young girl, Amalia merely smiled as she walked out of the station, leaving her two charming gentlemen in blue behind—staring into infinity. Apfelbaum and Sattler wondered what thoughts the great lady carried away with her.

Lost & Found

TRAVELING by air has become such a "joy"! Domestic travel between major U.S. cities seems to take almost as much time as transatlantic flights did in the not-so-distant past. Hardly any airline gets you to your destination nonstop. Whoever invented the idea of routing passengers via so-called hubs did not have expediency and a traveler's convenience in mind.

Recently, my wife and I embarked on a domestic journey from Denver to Milwaukee. We were ready and waiting to be whisked away to Denver International Airport by the local shuttle service at 8:30 a.m. That turned out to be a positive beginning of our sojourn. A late-winter storm made road travel a rather slick experience. It was great to leave the driving to an experienced chauffeur.

We pulled up at a Starbucks coffee house for refreshments and potty stops. Our arrival at the airport at 11:15 a.m. got us there in plenty of time to manage all current security checks with ease. In this case, e-tickets worked well. Checking in was a cinch. "What time is our flight leaving?" asked Laura.

"Departure is scheduled for 12:55 p.m. I think we want to

grab a bite to eat before getting on the plane. Remember what Gardenia told us about her experiences just a few weeks ago. Although she was on a lunch flight, she was offered nothing but a drink and a few pretzels. How about some pizza?" said I.

That sounded OK to Laura. We didn't get much for our money, but it was adequate to tie us over until dinnertime. We made our way through the security check point and luckily did not set off any bells or alarms. Furthermore, for once we were not selected for a random check as we observed what was happening to fellow travelers. Their bags were scrutinized, their shoes x-rayed, and their bodies physically searched. *How lucky could we be?*

Having passed this hurdle, we made our way to the gate of departure. We were passing a few gift shops and several small stores selling books and newspapers. I purchased a *USA Today* since I wanted to see what the weather would be like in Milwaukee. My wife was bored. She was missing her handiwork. In the past, when traveling, she always had her stitching things with her. She loves working counted cross stitch to while away the time. Not on this trip, since the little scissors she needed were considered forbidden contraband.

She finally decided to write some notes, managing to kill time while I read the paper. About twenty minutes past noon she got up: "I am taking these letters to the mail box. I saw one just after we passed through the security check. Keep an eye on my coat." And she was off. At 12:30 p.m., they began boarding first-class passengers and those having memberships in platinum and gold clubs. I could tell that the flight was oversold; standbys were lining up by the check-in desk.

I got up from my seat, gathering our coats, etc. Looking in

the direction where the shops and the mail box were located, I could not see hide or hair of my wife. The clock kept ticking away and no sign of Laura. I began to panic when the last call for passengers with assigned seats was issued. I ran all the way back to the security check point and briefly looked into various shops that might have held her interest. Still no sign of my spouse.

I ran back to the gate, hoping to have missed her and to find her there waiting for me. No such luck. I stepped up to the desk, telling the friendly Delta employee my name and that apparently I had lost my wife somewhere along the concourse. He offered to page her. *What a great idea,* I thought.

"Laura Birken, report immediately to gate C22—you are about to lose your seat," boomed the man's voice over the intercom. That should do it for sure. They began boarding some of the standby passengers.

So much for getting to the airport on time, I thought. *Where the hell is she? What will happen if we don't get on this flight? Our connection in Cincinnati sure will be out of the question even if they get us on a later flight out of Denver. My God, maybe somebody accosted her. Maybe she is lying in some restroom. Maybe she got sick? There are too many maybes.* I charged up the concourse again. Still no sign of Laura. I turned around and raced back to the gate. And then I saw her standing by the desk, now looking for me.

"When I got back here, this gentleman told me you were looking for me. I am so sorry."

"Where the hell were you? Didn't you hear them page you? I can't believe this is happening. Let's get moving and get on this damn plane. You are lucky that they are still holding our seats." As we rushed down the gangplank I called her stupid and other endearing names. I was happy and angry at the same time.

When we were finally seated on the plane and buckled in, she proceeded to reiterate what had happened. "I mailed my letters, looked at a couple of books in one of the shops, and finally went to the restroom. I never heard them page me. Suddenly, I looked at my watch and realized what time it was. I was shocked; it was almost one o'clock! I must have fallen asleep. When I got to the gate, I was even more shocked not to see you there. I'm so sorry. I won't do that again. I can just imagine what you went through."

"No, you can't. I thought you were kidnapped or lost. But I'm glad you found me just in time." For the rest of the journey, she didn't dare leave my side.

Manna from Heaven

EVER since I was a child, I have had much respect for fire. I was about five years old when I observed the results of a careless person causing a major fire at a neighbor's apartment. It almost cost the lives of two young children. Several years later, playmates of mine decided to experiment with a book of matches under a loaded hay wagon stored in a barn that was filled to the rafters with fresh hay and straw. Once the hay strewn on the ground had caught fire, they fled and closed the barn door. It didn't take long before the roof literally blew off the structure. The gases from the fresh hay had caused a major explosion, resulting in one of the most spectacular fires the little town of Kőndringen had ever observed.

And then there were the unbelievable scenes of destruction by fire in my hometown during World War II. After the attack of September 23, 1944, it seemed the entire city of almost 800,000 had been torched. The block of older apartment houses directly across from my parents' building was standing in flames. It was so light at eleven o'clock at night that one could have read a paper without benefit of other illumination.

Charred bodies pulled from the burned-out homes were laid on the sidewalks, covered up with papers. I was ten years old; I never forgot.

As an adult in my own home, I have been known to conduct routine inspections of the house before retiring. Laura has often heard the question, "Have you unplugged your iron?"

It used to drive us crazy when we were traveling back and forth between two homes: "Did you make sure the coffee pot was put away? What about the toaster oven? etc." Eventually, we made checklists for both homes. Nothing was ever checked off unless the status had physically been observed. It gave us much peace of mind as we were sailing across the prairies of the West. Just today, Laura said, "I'm so glad we are in the habit of always disconnecting all our electrical appliances when we are done with them." I could not have agreed more with her.

My family, living in a Seattle-type climate in Germany, always craves the few sunny days given to them by the weather gods. The first question always used to be, "Is it snowing again?" When we would answer in the affirmative after we returned from our visit with them in May, they couldn't believe that we were thrilled at the few occasions when Mother Nature made a feeble and delayed attempt at correcting for its shortcomings during the regular snow season.

"We need the snow. It's our source of water for the dry summer to come." They listened to our rationales and made weak concessions of concurrence with our arguments for the need of snow and rain in our part of the world.

When the scenes of horror flashed across their television screens a world away acquainting them with Hayman, Missionary Ridge, and Glenwood Springs, the message finally rang loud and clear. They picked up their phones to check on our well-being: "How are you? How are the fires? How close to you are some of the places we hear about? It's on TV all day long. Have you had any rain lately? How dry is your forest?, etc."

Now they could understand our fear of fire, living in a tinder dry forest of lodgepole pines. They were crossing fingers and lighting candles at the church. "I have been blowing at the clouds, but no matter how hard I try, they don't seem to want to move west," my sister-in-law said. "It's like the war" was her response when I told her that I had made a list of things to consider taking in an emergency.

I not only made a list of things but also put down their locations. Things that are not constantly needed have been packed up and are conveniently stored in front of the cars in our garage—important papers relative to insurance, IRS, etc. Old family photos and albums, diaries, and stamp collections and boxes containing negatives have joined the emergency kit. Other things would have to be packed in a hurry should the need arise.

The advice given by the media to be in readiness and to take only things that cannot be repurchased with insurance compensation doesn't really work for us. There are too many things that are irreplaceable. There are things from our parents and grandparents that have managed to survive everyday handling, two World Wars, and many a transatlantic crossing. We wouldn't know where to start and what to select. It would have to be a matter of personal attachment guiding that decision.

Dear friends of ours had to evacuate twice already from their home close to the Missionary Ridge fire near Durango. We stayed in touch with them throughout the ordeal. Each time they had to leave with cars and motor home packed to capacity, they had to agonize for days not knowing what they would find upon their return. So far, their home has been spared. We cross our fingers and say prayers for each other.

For the past two weeks, we have been looking at the afternoon clouds, begging for the release of much-needed moisture. So often we have been disappointed. *If we only get a couple of good dousings once, the cycle of monsoon blessings will start. It simply is too dry right now to induce repeat performances of our typical summer afternoon rains.*

Last week it happened. For once, the weatherman was right on. We did get a few good showers late in the afternoon. For three days now, we have had some manna from heaven. The rain has refreshed the air, and once again the mountains appear clean and pristine in the early morning light. As the first cumulus clouds billow above the Continental Divide late in the morning, we plead for a merciful release of their much-wanted blessing. It is wonderful to see the tree trunks moist from the evening rain. My flowers seem to breathe a sigh of relief. As I walk around the lot, the softness of the ground caused by the recent dampness feels good on my feet. It even sounds better. The sound of dry pine needles and sticks can be frightening.

We are grateful for the moisture visited upon us during past afternoons. The thought often has crossed my mind that there are many precious things in our home we hold dear. Many of them could be replaced with similar things. The house could be rebuilt. But what if all the trees and bushes were blackened by the devastation of a fire? Who would want to build among charred trees that would have to be cut down? The answers to these questions are obvious. Everyone who lives at this elevation knows how long it takes for anything to grow, never mind trees.

We keep hoping for more manna and pray that all precautions taken simply remain that rather than become necessity. It will be a long, hot summer, a summer that will test our strength of character, fortitude, and our persistence of continuing to live in paradise—a paradise surrounded by towering green sentinels of time that could turn into walls of fire.

Memories of Else

WHEN I glanced at my desk, there it was. I don't know what possessed me to open the drawer since I knew everything it contained had already been packed for shipping in preparation for our upcoming move. Here, under a pullout shelf, I noticed something white just barely sticking out. As my hand reached for the corner of the white paper, I wondered what treasure had hidden itself. When I touched the white matter, I realized that it was an envelope. Carefully pulling it so as not to tear it or its contents, I retrieved the letter from its hiding place.

Immediately, I recognized the distinctive handwriting. It was a letter from Else, a dear, dear friend of ours still living in Germany. The letter was addressed to Herr Dr. Hektor Birken and Frau Laura Birken. I couldn't make out the postmark. As I removed the letter from its envelope, I noted that it was written on April 25, 1998, a few months before Else's ninetieth birthday.

If I am not mistaken, it was Else's last letter. While her handwriting was still distinct, it wasn't as clear and legible as it had been at one time. Furthermore, the physical act of writing had become difficult for her. Her mental capacity never diminished. Since phoning had become so ridiculously inexpensive in the past few years, we opted to call her frequently or she simply picked up the phone to stay in touch with us.

I had met Else and her husband, Walter, the great love of her life, in 1950. Else was a lifelong friend and confidante of Greta Beerenbaum. Greta was the mother of a classmate of mine in business school. Nick sat at the desk immediately behind me. Nicklaus Beerenbaum was jovial and fun loving while I took my studies rather seriously. I made the acquaintance of his parents when they attended a school play in which we both participated. It was an evening that would change and shape my last five years in Germany before I ventured across the Atlantic to the New World.

Within a matter of weeks, I received an invitation for dinner at the house of Beerenbaum and met some of their closest friends. It was there that I first made the acquaintance of Dr. and Mrs. Gunders and their son Rudolf. He was an only child and a couple years younger than I. I soon discovered that the Beerenbaums and Gunders were traveling in different circles than my own folks. These were professional and successful business people who had known nothing but affluence in their adult lives and were determined to resume that lifestyle once they had succeeded to rise from the ashes of World War II.

And then there were my parents, hardworking tradespeople who managed to eke out a living by running a sometimes-successful butcher shop. My mother had once belonged to that affluent class of the pre–World War II German bourgeoisie. Unlike my grandfather, my own dad was a real mensch but certainly no successful businessman. And thus, the constant battle of wanting to attain affluence and not being able to do so, created an atmosphere in my own home that I was only too willing to escape once the opportunity presented itself through the friendships I cultivated during my two years in business school.

Pretty soon, I merely slept at home and spent all of my waking hours at the house of Beerenbaum. I had a good head for numbers, a talent inherited from the Krämers, my mother's family. While still in school, I handled much of the accounting behind the scenes. Kurt Beerenbaum entrusted me with huge amounts of money and often discussed matters of important business with me in spite of my relatively young age.

Why do I bother to speak of all these mundane details of a developing and formative relationship that started all so serendipitously more than fifty years ago? It's because of the attendance of a school play by the parents of a classmate that my life changed. My own parents were too busy to become involved. It's through my friendship with the Beerenbaums that I encountered the Gunders.

Long before she was Else to me, she always was Mrs. Gunders. I never dreamt of calling her anything other than Mrs. Gunders until all of us had become a few years older and wiser. Long after we had shared precious moments, many a delightful dinner party, vacations, dancing and finishing school, and a transatlantic separation, did we eventually reconnect by chance in New York City. A letter sent to my home address in the summer of 1960 reached me via forwarding just in time to make contact with Dr. and Mrs. Walter Gunders. They had arrived on the *Hanseatic* a few days earlier and had given me the name of the Hotel Roosevelt where they were staying. We couldn't believe our good luck and arranged to meet in the city a couple days later.

They didn't know my wife and I had separated several weeks earlier and that I was renting a room near my place of business. It was a beastly hot day when we met in New York. All of us were thankful for air conditioning in hotels, restaurants, and theatres. After we caught up with the events of the four years since we had last seen each other in Germany, they decided it was high time that we dispensed with all formalities and started calling each other by our first names. They had adapted fast to the American way of informality.

Being in the doldrums post separation, I found that Else and Walter were the tonic I needed. I was their personal tour guide for the day, showing them the highlights of the magic city it was in the 1960s. They, in turn, wined and dined me, realizing that my purse wasn't exactly flush. It was a day none of us forgot in years to come. Whereas we had been very well acquainted up to this point, we were good friends henceforth.

When they met Laura in 1965, they fell in love with her right from the start. Else and Walter visited the United States for a second time in 1975. At that time, we met in Chicago; and they spent three weeks with us in the Midwest. After a few days in Hinterland, we shared an exciting long weekend in the Minneapolis/St. Paul area. Of course, I had to teach at the university, but Laura embarked on an extensive tour along Lake Superior that eventually took them back to Chicago. I flew there for the weekend and met Laura for the return trip to Hinterland. After that journey, Laura's nickname became *unser Engel* [our angel]. I don't believe Else or Walter ever called Laura anything else from that day forward.

As I reread her last letter to us, I can't help seeing her. She always was a grand dame—elegant, sophisticated, perfectly groomed, and full of zest for life. After Walter died, she had her moments of depression and sadness because he had been her whole world. When we would call her on special occasions such as Easter, her birthday, Christmas, and New Year's Eve or Day, we could always tell by her voice in what kind of a mood she was. We would smile when she was her spunky self, because we knew that she could be a steel magnolia. She had been through heights and depths in her life and generally focused on the positive aspects of it.

She often questioned why she was chosen to live such a long life. After Walter and so many of her good friends had left her behind, she didn't really enjoy her existence as much. But she made the best of it. She remained in her beautiful home, surrounded by her art and beautiful memories until the last few months of her life. Every day, come rain or shine, she would walk to the cemetery nearby and visit Walter's grave. She would do her own shopping and continued to prepare decent meals for herself. No meals on wheels for this lady.

After 1978, we spent time with family and friends in Germany every other year. We would see Else several times during our visits and treasured the years of an enduring friendship.

In May, we met for the last time. Else was beginning to show her age. At almost ninety-four she appeared frail and helpless. It was the only time that we didn't create photographic memories of our time together. I just couldn't do it. I wanted to remember her as the grand dame she always was and not what she had become as the result of the ravages of time.

None of us knew that day what would happen in a matter of months. When we spoke by phone on her birthday, she sounded like her old self. A few weeks later, she tripped over one of her Oriental runners and broke her hip and pelvis. Rudolf found her several hours later in the apartment. After emergency surgery to repair her broken body, she was diagnosed with advanced-stage cancer throughout her digestive system. Else was hospitalized post-surgically and eventually died in January of this year in a care facility.

Her funeral was very private. Rudolf opted not to place a traditional obituary in the newspaper or send out any formal announcements relative to Else's passing. We learned of her death when he called us. We had tried reaching Else and Rudolf numerous times but simply were unable to connect. He and a cousin were the only mourners that accompanied Else on her last journey to be buried next to her beloved Walter.

It was the end of a chapter in our lives. We still cannot believe that Else is gone. No matter how cold or how gray a day there may be next January, we will journey to the Ostfriedhof and pay our respects to Else and Walter, although she really didn't like gray and rainy days; both she and Walter were sun worshippers.

Missing in Action

GERMANA and her husband, David, recently spent a well-deserved vacation in Las Vegas. They were staying at one of the finest hotels and casinos on the strip. Not wanting to offend any of the illustrious establishments, the author refrains from giving the particulars since it makes little contribution to the telling of the tale.

After Germana and David had settled into their elegant suite, they ordered room service and toasted each other with champagne and caviar. Contemplating the hordes of people rushing in all directions as she was viewing the strip from the hotel windows, Germana called out to David, saying, "Darling, I want to put the jewels I'm not wearing into the safe. They tell you no matter how fancy a place you stay at, you better make use of their built-in safes. Here is my traveling jewelry box. Please put it in the safe right away. Oh, and don't forget to let me know what code you will be using. I should know since I may want to switch jewelry sometime when you are not here."

Thank goodness, she thought, the cabdriver had taken them right to the front door of the hotel. They were greeted by a dashingly attired doorman who had seen to it that a bellhop took proper and prompt care of the new arrivals. Germana was enjoying her thoughts as she was viewing the madcap activities taking place many floors below her vantage point while she was sipping the excellent champagne David had chosen for them.

"What would you like to do after dinner tonight?" asked David. "I'll be good and stay away from the tables this evening. It's too late to get tickets for a show. Personally, I would love to see *Mamma Mia!* at the Mandalay. I know you would like to see Celine Dion—but you may as well forget about that. The show is sold out for months in advance."

"Yeah, that is too bad," lamented Germana. "I would have thought by now it would be easier to get those tickets. Well, we'll catch her the next time we are here." She knew that there would be a next time in the not-so-distant future. They managed to fly into Vegas at least twice a year. And knowing David, she wasn't quite willing yet to give up on Celine Dion; she knew what a skilled finagler he could be.

They went to a charming French restaurant and had a delightful dinner. David excused himself and left Germana musing over the last sip of Crown Royal after he had signed for the tab. On his way to the restroom he couldn't help notice the convenient placement of the gaming tables. As he peered at the faces looking down at the action, he recognized an old friend.

"Hi, David!" said the familiar voice of Jerome Finkelstein. "When did you get here? Is Germana with you? Want to get in on the action?"

"Oh no, I need to get back to Germana. I promised her to stay away from the tables this one night. She is a little disappointed as it is. She had her heart set on seeing Celine Dion, but the show is sold out for months." Jerome looked up and smiled. "I suppose I can help you to get in her graces. Myrna decided to visit the grandchildren in San Francisco, kind of a last-minute change of mind. I have two tickets for the show tomorrow night. Personally, I don't really care if I go—certainly not by myself. I'd rather spend my time more productively at the tables. Write me a check for $250; I'll leave the tickets with the concierge at Caesar's Palace." They shook hands after David handed him the check. "Thanks a million. See you later. I better get back to Germana; I know she'll be thrilled. I'll call you tomorrow. Maybe we can have a drink before we go to the show."

David turned and headed back toward the restaurant. As he approached the table, Germana smiled at him knowingly, saying, "I know where you have been. Couldn't stay away just for one night, could you?"

"Actually, I was a very good boy. I didn't do anything I wasn't supposed to do. As I came out of the restroom, I ran into Jerome. He is here by himself. Myrna is with the kids in San Francisco. And guess what? You get to see that Celine Dion show after all. They had two tickets, but he doesn't care to go alone. It's your lucky night. We are going tomorrow evening; I suggested we have a drink with him before the show. Is that OK with you?"

Germana was indeed thrilled. Of course, it was OK to have a drink with Jerome. She was agreeable to almost anything. Things couldn't have worked out any better.

They had soaked up some rays at the pool. After lunch, David showered and dressed for the show and a late dinner. While Germana luxuriated in the whirlpool tub and enjoyed her bubble bath, David rushed off to the gaming tables. He just had to get it out of his system.

He spotted Jerome as he made his way to a blackjack table. David walked over and shook Jerome's hand, thanking him again for the tickets he had picked up earlier that afternoon. "How long are you in town this time?" asked Jerome.

"Just for five days—an extended weekend. We flew in yesterday and are leaving late on Monday afternoon. Why are you asking?"

"I'm sure you have seen *Siegfried & Roy* at the Mirage before. They won't be around too much longer. Try catching their show—it's more fantastic than ever. You told me about wanting to see *Mamma Mia!*, which is a fun show. But it will be around for a lot longer than *Siegfried & Roy*."

David tried his luck at a couple of hands but didn't do so well. Perhaps his mind wasn't on the action. He stepped away from the table and crossed the room to a courtesy phone. He called Germana. "Would you want to see *Siegfried & Roy* at the Mirage tomorrow night? Jerome thinks we ought to catch it."

"Sure, why not? It's been years since we saw them. We'll catch *Mamma Mia!* next time. Good luck. It may be tough to get tickets for Friday night, but try it anyway." He replaced the receiver.

When he called for tickets for Friday, October 3, he couldn't believe his good fortune. They would hold the tickets until the next morning; he had simply charged them to his card. *How lucky could he be?* Of course, he wished that some of that good luck would rub off while he was at the gaming tables.

The Celine Dion show was spectacular and much enjoyed by Germana. Some of it was too much over the top as far as David was concerned. He was looking forward to a rare steak and a stiff drink as he dutifully applauded at the close of the production. When they finally fell into bed after midnight, they concurred that it had been a pretty full day. They were looking forward to the show on Friday night at the Mirage.

David's luck had been much better that afternoon. Germana could tell. He was singing in the shower as they were getting ready for dinner. They decided it was better to eat before the show than so late. They could have a light dessert or a drink after the show rather than a big dinner before retiring.

After dinner at the Savannah, they grabbed a cab in front of the Tropicana Hotel and headed north on the strip to the Mirage. David tipped the cabby after he had helped Germana out. They strolled into the elegant theatre of the Mirage and quickly were ushered to their seats. Germana ordered Crown Royal on the rocks, and David decided to have a light beer. He felt thirsty after the rich dinner. The spectacular show started on time. Germana was peering over her glass as Roy Horn was putting a white tiger through his paces. Suddenly, the beautiful beast lunged at Roy's neck and dragged him off the stage like a rag doll. At first, Germana and David, like many attending the show, thought it was part of the act. Of course, they learned quickly that it was a tragic accident, as Siegfried, Horn's partner, stepped forward and announced that the show was over and cancelled.

Germana gulped her drink and asked David to take her back to the hotel. She was in complete emotional disarray. Before she slipped into her negligee, she took out her two and one-half carat diamond studs and set them on the vanity. After she brushed her teeth, she grabbed her assortment of pills off the vanity with one swoop and swallowed them with a generous drink of water. She coughed just for a second, but another drink of water did the trick. Germana then said, "David, please put my jewelry in the safe; I left it all on the vanity. I have to lie down. I can't get some of those images out of my mind." With that she hit the pillow.

David brushed his teeth and then gathered Germana's jewelry from the vanity. As he did so, he asked, "Did you take just one of your earrings out?" She reached up to her ears, quite certain that she had removed both of them. "No, they should be there on the counter top." She got out of bed and looked in horror at her jewelry on the vanity. There was just one of the diamond studs, and she realized instantly that the remaining earring was in very close proximity to the spot where she had gathered all of her pills.

"Now I know why I coughed when I took those damn pills." David looked at her in disbelief, and they didn't know if they should laugh or cry.

"What do you think I should do? Try to stick my fingers down my throat and make myself throw up?"

"I don't think that is a very good solution. Put some clothes on while I check where the nearest emergency services are available. I'm taking you to see a doctor."

A few minutes later, they were rushed in a cab to the nearest facility. The young physician in attendance had a hard time keeping a straight face. He had heard some crazy stories in the emergency room since he started working in Las Vegas, but this one topped them all. "As long as you are in no obvious pain, I recommend that you let nature take its course. I'll send you home with a few pairs of these surgical gloves. Every time you have a bowel movement, you'll need to examine your stools carefully. I would suggest you avoid using a regular toilet for the time being; a plastic dishpan might work better for you."

David cracked up. He knew how much Germana had enjoyed changing their babies' diapers. And he wasn't volunteering; this was one time where he would not get involved in Germana's business. And, of course, he knew how often she would go through the process in a given day. He never had known anyone who had more bowel movements in the course of twenty-four hours.

After Germana had gone through the search a total of five times, she became desperate. "I have been very carefully screening my poop without any luck. You have to take me back to the emergency room. They must have a way of scanning my stomach and my digestive tract. I cannot believe that a two and one-half carat diamond earring wouldn't show up."

Off they went. They were lucky. The young physician was on duty. Yes, they could scan her but couldn't make any promises. Actually, after five bowel movements she should have passed the earring. "Are you sure you examined your stools carefully enough?" Germana assured him she had done so and became very definitive in her explanations of the procedures she had endured without any assistance from her husband.

After the initial scanning, which showed nothing but an empty stomach and a clean bowel, a second attempt was made the following day with identical results. There was no evidence of the diamond, and the physician ruled that more likely than not she had somehow missed it in the action of searching through her feces. "More likely than not, you flushed your two and one-half carat diamond down the drain." Germana turned pale. As she tried to make contact with David's eyes she inquired, "You did have them insured, didn't you?"

Mission Hills Misery

HARRY and Daphne Sack sat wordless in their luxury Lexus as they took the crosstown to their fashionable neighborhood. It was a beastly Midwestern November night. Wet snow and gusty winds had taken down the last of the leaves. Without articulating it, they both knew what each was thinking. They were wondering what surprises were in store for them after they entered their home. Daphne finally couldn't stand it any longer. She glanced over her left shoulder at Harry. "What do you think Diefenblicker has succeeded in accomplishing today? I have gotten to the point where I hate going home in the evening. Whatever possessed us to hire this jerk to undertake redecorating the whole house? What I really resent is that we wind up doing much of the work we are paying him to do!"

"Now Daphne, it wasn't such a bad idea. We thought we were both working hard and should let professionals do the job for a change. I know, we did the fixing and the painting together for so many years. We could show that guy a few tricks. And remember—he came highly recommended. Of course, little did we know in August when we signed the contract, that we would be still living in a nightmare almost four months later. Well, one of these days we'll look back on this as an unforgettable experience."

They continued driving in silence as the wet flakes kept landing on the windshield. The only sound was that of the defroster and the constant swishing of the wipers. Daphne remembered how it all had started.

Earlier in the year, they had received an electronic transfer of Harry's inheritance from his mother. It wasn't a fortune, but a sizable amount anyway. They could invest it—as they usually did—or do something frivolous with the unexpected money. Harry spoke first: "Next year we'll celebrate our twenty-fifth. We have both worked hard to get where we are and have good jobs. I like our home, yet I know you have never been happy with the decorating job the original builder did. I recollect that you didn't even want to buy the place for that reason. Well, I think we should use some of Mom's money. Let's talk to the girl at the paint store at Crown Plaza. I bet she can recommend some contractor who could do the job well. They have pretty highfalutin' clientele; I would trust her recommendations."

"I suppose you have a point. Let's stop there on our way home on Tuesday. We both could leave a little earlier. Perhaps we can even look at their wallpaper and check out a couple of books. It sounds all so exciting. I have a pretty good idea what I want. I'm so tired of plain walls. I want to tie the two floors together by papering that steep stairway to the upstairs. What do you think?"

"Sounds like a plan to me. Let's do it!"

Erika Humpeldinck was the owner of the Decorating Emporium. The companies' headquarters were at Crown Plaza in downtown Kansas City, not far from Harry and Daphne's respective offices. Erika liked the setting. She enjoyed dealing with her upscale clients, although Harry and Daphne didn't exactly view themselves as belonging to that particular group. They were both professional people who managed their incomes well. Of course, none of that was Erika's business.

They walked confidently into the emporium. "We are interested in having some major redecorating done at our home. I'm talking a ton of wallpaper, a lot of painting, including all ceilings, and a few minor carpentry alterations. Can you give us some references for contractors with whom you have dealt? We need to rely on your experience with these people since we have not lived all that long in the KC area."

"Oh, there are a number of gentlemen I could suggest. Let me write down their names and telephone numbers. This one is particularly popular. Don't be put off by his crazy name. Doofus Diefenblicker does a lot of work in this town; I'll put you in touch with recent clients of his for references. Of course, you may decide to call Johnny Petrous. He is another good one. Johnny does a great job on wallpaper."

"Is it OK for me to check out these three wallpaper books?" asked Daphne.

"Sure, no problem at all. You may keep them for a week and then perhaps exchange them for others if you can't find what you really like. Keep in mind, we are having a big sale going on right now."

Harry and Daphne tucked the heavy books into the trunk of their car. As they slid easily into their cushy leather seats, they both burst out laughing. "Can you believe being stuck with that handle, 'Doofus Diefenblicker'?" howled Harry.

"Sounds German to me and probably was changed from 'Tiefenblicker'—someone who looks deep into things; perhaps looking deep into one's soul?"

Daphne caught her breath and said, "I almost wet my pants when she started talking about him." Harry coughed; still thinking about the guy. "But what's in a name? We'll call him and Mr. Petrous when we get home. She didn't sound that excited about the other people whose names she wrote down."

After they had their light supper on the deck, Harry picked up the phone. For whatever reason, he dialed Johnny Petrous first.

"Yes, this is Johnny Petrous. That's nice of Erika Humpeldinck to give you my name. The problem is I am solidly booked through the first of next year. Normally, I would love to take on your job. It sounds interesting. I love doing wallpaper. My crew is highly experienced. We do great work, if I may say so myself. If someone else doesn't work out for you and you can put it off until next spring, I'll be happy to talk to you again. You have a good evening, and thanks for calling." The phone clicked. Harry looked sort of disappointed. Johnny Petrous sounded like the kind of person with whom Harry enjoyed dealing.

"Too bad. We struck out on the first one. He's too busy and couldn't do the job until next spring. You don't want to wait that long! Right?"

"Not really. Now that I have decided to hire someone to do the job, I want to get moving. It would be delightful to have it behind us before the holidays. I'm planning on some entertaining this fall. It will be nice to share the new look with our friends. Call that Diefenblicker character just for fun. Who knows, we may wind up with him."

Harry dialed, mouthing Doofus Diefenblicker to himself,

almost laughing when Doofus answered the phone. "Diefenblicker Designs and Decorating, Doofus speaking. How may I help you?"

Harry bit his lower lip and replied, "Harry Sack speaking. Your name was given to us by Erika Humpeldinck of the Decorating Emporium. My wife and I want to redecorate our home. It's a major job and involves a lot of wallpapering. Might you be interested in doing the job?"

"Well, I am just finishing a big one. I expect to be done in two weeks. I could get started in mid- to late August. How about I come over tomorrow night and look over your place and see what you have in mind?"

"Daphne, are we free tomorrow evening? Mr. Diefenblicker would like to check out the layout and see what you want done?"

"Yes, that's fine. Ask him if he could come about seven thirty. We'll be done with dinner by then."

The time was agreeable with Doofus. Daphne was happy that they had a date and time to meet with the man. When he arrived on time and rang the doorbell, Harry and Daphne weren't so sure if they were seeing right. Doofus was huge. He must have weighed close to three hundred pounds. *How could he get up and down ladders?* Doofus looked like he had escaped from the Australian bush country. He was wearing a gigantic, dark-brown, leather-look, strangely shaped coat and a broad-brimmed leather cowboy hat. Little beady eyes were peering through thick lenses. Harry thought, *What do I care what the guy looks like? If he likes to dress up like a dude, that's his business. All I want to know is if he can do the job—and do it well. And if the price is right, all the better.*

Doofus walked through the whole house, carrying a yellow

writing pad. He was making some notes, recording measurements as he was moving from room to room. "You got a lot of things in these rooms. It probably would be better and more expedient for me not to have to maneuver around a lot of this stuff. Is there any way you can store things in the basement?"

Harry and Daphne looked at each other, thinking along the same lines. "Our basement is huge and completely empty except for a few boxes of Christmas decor, a mangle, the furnace, and a dehumidifier. It is basically dry. It would make good sense to move a lot of the furniture out of the way. Excellent suggestion," said Harry.

"I'll give you the name of the people where I'm about to finish a big job for a reference. In the meantime, I'll put my pencil to paper tonight and give you a call when I have some figures. Nice meetin' you, Mrs. Sack. You keep looking at them wallpaper books. I'm sure you'll find somethin' you like. Nice talkin' to you, Mister. You'll hear from me."—And he was gone.

Harry closed the door gently and turned around to face Daphne. "What do you think? He is a hoot. I still have trouble keeping a straight face when I need to address him. Doofus is just as bad as Mr. Diefenblicker, especially when I recall the German meaning."

Harry glanced at the name of the reference Doofus wrote down. "Don't call those people where he is working right now. He's a colleague in another department. I would feel funny about getting in touch with them."

"OK. I won't. Let's see what happens when he presents us with the estimate and a time line for doing the job," said Daphne.

Doofus called the next night. He was obviously anxious to get Harry and Daphne's signatures on the dotted line of a contract. "I have some figures for you. Can I come over right now? I'd like to get you signed up before someone else wants my services." They agreed to see him after supper.

Diefenblicker was well prepared. He had developed a time line and outlined the various costs for materials and labor for the complete job. Daphne and Harry were responsible for selecting, ordering, and paying for the wallpaper. Everything else was part and parcel of his contract. He wanted their signatures and expected half the money up front when work commenced two weeks hence.

"We'll look this over and give you a call tomorrow, if that is OK with you?" Harry winked at Daphne, letting her know that he wanted to cover all his bases. Three thousand dollars wasn't exorbitant, but it was still a tidy sum. Harry wanted to read the fine print, as did Daphne. They had little experience in such matters, having always done such work themselves.

And so they did. After studying the figures and looking over the amount of work that needed to be done, they agreed to give Doofus the job. "I'll call him from the office tomorrow. Let him stew tonight. I don't want him to get the idea that we are that desperate for his services. I have a few questions before we sign this thing. Otherwise, let's go with it, especially since he can start in two weeks."

They signed the contract in Doofus's presence the next evening. The following weekend, all hell broke loose. Harry and Daphne disassembled their cozy home. China, crystal, and silver were packed carefully in boxes. Everything was moved to the basement and neatly stored according to point of origin in the house. Every painting and wall hanging found its way to the bowels of the abode. Next came the furniture. By the time Sunday evening rolled around, the only thing left on the two floors were the mattress in the upstairs master bedroom; two hard, wooden stools at the breakfast bar in the kitchen; and the empty china cabinet in the dining room. The house was cleaned out. Drop cloths were in style and spread throughout.

"I can handle this for a few weeks. If he starts when he said he would and finishes the job in a matter of three weeks, that won't be too bad. Let's hope he is a man of his word. I almost wish you had not asked me not to get in touch with those people you know. I don't know why? Somehow I feel uneasy about this guy," said Daphne. Harry didn't want to agree with her, but he had similar feelings about Doofus Diefenblicker. Perhaps he was experiencing buyers' remorse.

Two weeks went by quickly since they had signed the contract. They expected Doofus to be there first thing Monday morning before they left for their respective offices. Harry had a spare key made for Doofus. Much to their chagrin, there was no sign of him by seven thirty. They had to leave, not wanting to be late for work.

Harry called the Diefenblickers' house. His mother answered the phone. "No, my son Doofus isn't home. He is on that job he is finishing—forever." Harry didn't like the inference of that last little tidbit of information so casually dropped by Mrs. Diefenblicker. *Living with his mother? He is a strange duck,* thought Harry. "Have him call me at home tonight. We were waiting for him to show up this morning. He told us he would start on our job this week."

"I'm sorry. I know nothing about my son's business. He just eats and sleeps here. When he ain't flitting around from job to job, he buzzes around on his Harley from bar to bar. I hardly see him long enough to talk to him about his jobs. Bye now!" She replaced the receiver, leaving Harry hanging on the dead phone. *God, what have we gotten ourselves into?*

Doofus did call that night. "Sorry, I didn't make it to your place this morning. I ran into a snag. I'll be there no later than September 15. Can't help it. Have to finish this job now. See you in two weeks." He hung up before Harry could say another word.

They talked it over and realized they were stuck. Although they had not paid Diefenblicker any money yet, he had their names on the dotted line. Breach of contract came to their minds; Doofus could sue them. They agreed to be patient.

The second week in September, as promised, Doofus was at their doorstep on Monday morning before 7 a.m. He moved in a couple of ladders, a toolbox, and two gallons of the white ceiling paint. He would start upstairs in the guest bedroom. Could he have the down payment of $1,500? He would like a key, allowing him to come and go as was necessary. They decided to acquiesce to his wishes. Their home, a disaster in progress, was wearing on their nerves. Neither Harry nor Daphne did disorder very well. The vacant-house-in-drop-cloths decor was not exactly what they envisioned to come home to indefinitely after hard days at the office.

And thus started their trials and tribulations with Doofus Diefenblicker. When they came home that night, they discovered that he had indeed applied the first coat of ceiling paint in the guest bedroom, although there was more paint on exposed areas of carpeting than on the heavily textured ceiling. After a major emergency clean-up job in the first room, Harry walked around the house. Doofus hadn't done anything else. They wondered how long he might have been on the job that day?

Harry called him. He learned that Doofus had been there for a total of three hours. "I'm working on another job a couple doors down from you folks. It's most convenient to have two jobs so close. I'll be back at your place in a couple of days." Doofus slammed down the phone; Harry thought he hadn't heard correctly.

"Well, if that doesn't rot your socks!" Harry blurted out. Daphne was almost in tears when he related his conversation with Doofus to her. "Guess we stepped right into that one. What are we going to do now?" said Daphne.

"Let's wait and see." That was all they could do. Doofus showed up a week later. He installed an additional shelf and a louvered door in the linen closet off the dining room. The shelf was so crooked, it could make you queasy contemplating it. The wallpaper had arrived. But first, walls and ceilings needed to be painted. Doofus was too involved with other jobs. He needed to hire some help. No way could he do all that work by himself as he had given them to understand before signing the contract. Daphne and Harry began thinking they had signed a pact with the devil.

Harry decided to take the bull by the horns. He picked up paint at Erika Humpeldinck's emporium. He and Daphne put on their paint clothes and started painting all the ceilings in the house. Next, they painted all the walls that were not to be covered with wallpaper.

And then the "expert paperhangers" made their first appearance. According to Doofus, it was an experienced father and son team. As it turned out, the father was in his mid-eighties, and the son was an imbecile. Harry decided to take the afternoon off to watch *this* operation. The senior was slopping on the paste rather thickly. The son was helping him rig up makeshift scaffolding in the eighteen-foot-high stairway. Harry was beginning to wonder about possible accidents occurring on their property. Did Doofus have insurance?

The wallpaper was striped. By the time several strips of elegant wallpaper had been affixed to the wall, Harry couldn't help but notice the terrible overlaps in the midsection and giant gaps between strips at the bottom. Not to worry, they would straighten that out. Junior, carrying an old aluminum ladder up and down the staircase, banging into the wet strips of wallpaper, managed to cause a few giant tears. Dad simply ran his large, fleshy, and wrinkled hands over the unsightly spots, attempting to fix the damage instantly. Harry had seen enough.

"What do you think you are doing? I have never seen such a Mickey Mouse job in my life. Is this what I am paying your contractor fifteen dollars a roll for? You must be crazy. No way are we accepting this kind of workmanship. I could hire someone off the street and might be lucky enough to have them do a better job."

"What do you think Doofus did? It's been many years since I have done anything like this. As you have probably figured out, my son isn't too swift. He's a good kid and tries real hard. And besides, when you hang this much paper, you have to expect a few glitches!"

Harry was dumbfounded. How would he explain all this to Daphne when he picked her up at the office later in the afternoon? She just sat quietly next to him as he related his observations and conversation with the old man. She dreaded going home.

"I think it's time for you to take some photos and videotape the shambles these people are making of our home. Also, let's stop and speak with Erika Humpeldinck about Diefenblicker and his crew. We need to think about ordering more wallpaper while matching dye lots are still available. I will never accept the job the old man is doing. And furthermore, I want you to call the people who we were supposed to call in the first place. I don't care anymore what they think or who they are. Just do it. I've absolutely had it with this guy!" screamed Daphne.

Harry dialed the number. A man answered the phone. Harry introduced himself and commenced with his inquiry regarding Doofus. "Oh, we heard he was doing some work for you. Yes, he is finally finished with us. He did a fine job, but it took forever. Our house was in turmoil for over two years. Sometimes, we thought he would never get done. I hope your outcome is more timely."

Harry swallowed hard and thanked the man before he replaced the receiver. He didn't want to listen to any more platitudes. He was sick to his stomach. *Why hadn't they called the guy before? Diefenblicker himself had given them the name as a reference. How stupid had they been? Of course, they might never have learned the truth about Doofus at an earlier point in time.*

When Harry confronted Erika Humpeldinck with their glad tidings, she agreed to inspect the job herself. A factory representative was in town; he could be an expert witness. Harry informed her that he had started to document the deplorable job Doofus and his crew were doing. When she got around to checking out the place, the wallpaper rep in tow, she was astounded—although she didn't say much to Harry. She could put two and two together.

After reordering certain papers for a third time, the dye lots were exhausted. They had to make do with what they had.

Grass paper to be hung in the kitchen was too difficult for the old man. Doofus hired a woman off the street to do the job. She bought her tools at a neighborhood paint store. Harry knew this because the bill for the tools greeted them on the breakfast bar in the kitchen.

"Have you ever seen a job like this? They started in that upper left corner and then moved to the opposite wall with the next strip. And then—look over there. The paper is thirty inches wide; they stuck three non-matching pieces together where a single piece would have done the job. It's going from bad to worse. Let's call Doofus right now—and let me handle it this time. The kitchen is my domain," said Daphne.

Diefenblicker could tell by her voice over the phone that she was seething with rage. "I'll be there right away," he said softly. He arrived on the scene in a matter of minutes. When Daphne confronted him, pointing out all the errors committed by the paper-hanging genius picked off the street, Doofus lost his cool. He jumped onto one of the kitchen stools and started tearing away at the grass paper. Before he realized it, he was tearing huge sections of drywall along with the wall covering. He had no idea that his crafty assistant had used super glue to affix the strips. The more he destroyed the walls of the kitchen, the madder he got before he fled the house—cussing Harry and Daphne and their damned job. They just stood there confounded, looking at what was left of their kitchen walls. Now it was really time for some serious documentation.

Harry called Doofus the next morning, threatening to fire him and his helpers for total incompetence. Two days later, they received a registered letter from the county clerk, informing them that Doofus Diefenblicker had filed a mechanic's lien against their property in the amount of $1,500—the balance they owed him on the contract. Harry and Daphne were bowled over by what they read.

Harry did some inquiring and learned that a mechanic's lien could only be removed through legal channels, involving an attorney. Small claims court would not work. His attorney assured him that he had been wise to document the unbelievably shabby job Diefenblicker had done.

That night, when they arrived at their mutilated home, they were certain that someone had been in the house. They found the place ablaze with lights. The old man and his son had apparently been there to finish the job of hanging foil paper in the bathroom off the dining room. It was never used as such, but they wanted it finished in case of selling the house in the future.

As they approached the bathroom, they noticed the fancy foil paper affixed to the walls. "Affixed" was actually a joke because the paper was literally floating on a sea of wallpaper paste.

They forgot about dinner. It could wait. Pizza later would do just fine. "Let's change our clothes. This will be a big and very messy job. We need to squeeze out all that excess paste and flatten out the paper with our wallpapering brushes." They worked diligently for a couple of hours, rescuing their fancy foil wall covering. When all was said and done, there was a five gallon metal bucket full of a mixture of water and wallpaper paste. The contents were thick, almost syrupy, gray and ugly looking. Harry carefully stepped off the rickety wooden ladder the old man had left behind. He moved the bucket of slime off the floor, placing it on top of the vanity before he slammed the bathroom door shut. Both quickly traded their grimy duds for comfy attire. "Let's get the hell out of here. I need some food—and a drink. This was the straw that broke this camel's back. Just wait until we are done with him."

Harry opened the front door for Daphne. As they stepped out, he carefully locked the house with his key. Daphne turned back and said, "Don't you feel creepy knowing that Diefenblicker still has a key to our home? I wish we had not given him free access."

"I'll call him from the restaurant and ask him to return our key in the morning. Obviously, he must have been here today to let in the old man and his son. Once we have the key back, I will have the locks changed—just to be sure. I feel the same way you do. He does give me the creeps. One hears and reads about such crazy things all the time. Now, I really need that drink. Let's go to Cappucis; we can't get drinks at the Pizza Hut."

They were both starving. Daphne rapidly scanned the list of different pizzas. It didn't take long for her to make up her mind—not tonight. Harry ordered two J&Bs on the rocks. Before the waiter could escape to the bar to place the order for the drinks, Daphne stopped him dead in his tracks. "Please, put in an order for a fourteen-inch pizza. Make it a supreme; I feel sinful tonight. We're starving. In the meantime, please bring us house salads and some bread sticks. Thanks!"

Harry excused himself to make the phone call to Doofus. He wasn't gone long. "I simply asked him in a civil tone if it was possible to drop off the key first thing in the morning. I had to bite my tongue when I let him know how we felt about our entertainment tonight, complements of his outstanding help. He mumbled some expletive but appeared to be agreeable to honor our request. I guess that is that. I can't worry right now about the outcome of any legal battles we may have to fight. For now, I will be glad to have him out of our home, not necessarily out of our hair."

Harry picked up his drink and toasted Daphne. "Here is to us and a happy home again—someday." He gulped his drink. When the waiter set down their salads and the bread sticks, he motioned to do another round of drinks as he hastily swallowed the last of his first J&B.

ЖX

It was almost ten thirty when they got back into the Lexus, heading for their home in Mission Hills. As they drove up to the garage, Harry noticed there were a lot more lights on in the house than when they had left a few hours earlier. Worse yet, he noticed right away that the front door was ajar. He knew he had locked the deadbolt with his key. They walked first into the kitchen. Harry saw right away that their house key was lying on the breakfast bar. Clearly, Doofus had been there. They walked through the whole house. Harry checked the basement. Daphne ran upstairs, finding everything in order. Descending the stairway, she noticed a stream of light coming from the slightly opened door of the bathroom by the dining room. She remembered distinctly that Harry had slammed the door shut before they left earlier.

"You go look. It's giving me the willies," she summoned Harry. He pushed the door open and gasped. "Holy shit! Come and see!" Harry couldn't figure out how it had happened, but Diefenblicker's massive body was lying on the floor, wedged between the bathtub and the vanity, completely entangled in the broken ladder. The bucket that held the mixture of gray, slimy water and wallpaper paste covered his head and upper body. He was obviously dead and totally saturated in sludge.

"Step back. Don't touch a thing or him. Call nine-one-one. It's a good thing we can account for our whereabouts for the last few hours. Just wait until the cops get here and find our fingerprints all over these bathroom walls. Of course, we can explain."

And explain they did. The cops were there promptly. Harry and Daphne related what had transpired earlier in the evening. They were given their rights but declined calling their attorney. It seemed too apparent what had happened. Doofus had lost his balance and fell when the flimsy wooden ladder broke into pieces, giving way under his enormous weight. It was speculated that he struck the sharp rim of the bucket, knocking it over with his collapsing weight. Harry was glad Daphne did not see Doofus's expression fixed on the dead face as the rubber-gloved hand of the cop lifted the now-empty bucket from the face covered in slime. His glasses must have fallen on the floor; his dead eyes were staring back at the cop and Harry. Doofus's head almost looked like that of a gargoyle dripping in gray muck. Harry Sack just about barfed as he turned away from the scene of total destruction and death. He had had his fill of the guy, but not in his wildest dreams could he have envisioned Doofus Diefenblicker being sacked by the tools of his trade.

Doofus's body was taken to the morgue. The inquiry was relatively brief. The autopsy revealed that he smashed his larynx in the fall and aspirated some of the ugly ooze from the bucket that had been filled to the brim, apparently causing him to choke to death. The mechanic's lien became a moot point; its removal was a minor technicality handled by Harry and

Daphne's attorney. The decorating job was finished by Johnny Petrous after all. When they ran into Erika Humpeldinck at Crown Plaza, she avoided eye contact with Harry and Daphne. Perhaps she was worried about legal action they might take. After all, it was she who had opened the door of their home for Doofus Diefenblicker. She was lucky Harry and Daphne were not of the sue-happy ilk. They rejoiced; by early March, sanity and peace had finally been restored to the house in Mission Hills. All Harry could say was, "That was one hell of a redecorating job." They sold the house seven years later and lived happily ever after.

Paradise Lost

IT was during Spring break, exactly twenty-seven years ago, when we discovered the Fraser Valley and its awesome beauty. We fell in love with the little town of Hideaway Park and its friendly people. Three months later, we became the proud owners of our first property in Winter Park Ranch. Then we would acquire the land two years later where we ultimately would build our retirement home.

As the years went by, we became an integral part of the community and learned to cherish the friendships we made with countless people. We enjoyed our work in Iowa but always looked forward to our frequent escapes to our love nest in the sky. Here we could forget the troubles of everyday existence and relish the beauty and splendor of snowcapped mountains and fields of white dreams.

While it was the winter scenery that initially captured our hearts, in time we learned to appreciate and fall in love with the beauty of the high-country summers. There was nothing like it. We discovered that the winters were long and the summers rather short. That made the living here from May to

September all the sweeter. I will never forget the fall of 1996. It was the first time I experienced with my own eyes the spectacular annual color show of the aspen turning to shades of gold, orange, and rust. My work had always forced me to be away from the Fraser Valley during this annual event; it was only after I retired that I could experience nature's splendid gift of beauty.

As the years went by and we chalked up one birthday after another, particularly I had to cleanse the lenses of my rose-colored glasses. It was still paradise, but now certain caveats would enter my mind. I used to say, "When the winters become too difficult for us, we'll go south for a few months. When I can't rake the snow off the roof or shovel my decks and walkways any longer, I'll hire someone to do it for me."

Of course, we know that reality can be extremely harsh. Leaving a place for several months during winter can be harmful to the health of your home. Yes, our house can handle plenty of snow loads, somewhere around one hundred fifty pounds per square foot. That's a "ton" of snow. Having to rely on others to make the determination of shoveling or not shoveling one's roof is a challenging proposition. To find someone to take care of other chores of winter can be a formidable task in a resort town. Everyone young enough to do so wants to be schussing down the mountain rather than toiling in other people's fields of snow. That's no fun at any price.

As we get older we also become more aware of needing access to qualified medical facilities. No question about it, our emergency services had improved through the years. However, in extreme and life-threatening situations, transport to Denver for diagnosis and treatment is usually the answer. And as we all know, help isn't just around the corner. We must go over our beloved Berthoud Pass and travel close to two hours to get down to the big city. That's just manageable in many situations during less-inclement periods of the year. But what would have happened during our most recent storm of the century? Not only was the pass closed for days on end, but the Interstate to Denver was as well.

Laura discovered several years ago that she has rather severe osteoporosis. Not worrying about her abilities to ski safely but very much concerned about being hit by others, she made the ultimate sacrifice and gave away her downhill equipment. My left knee has never been the same since I had to have a medial meniscus repaired. That took away part of the charm of the long winter. Yes, we enjoyed cross-country skiing and snowshoeing. But it wasn't the same. And there were the annual mud seasons, the fifth and sixth seasons in any mountain community. We all laugh about it, but it really isn't fun.

More recently, we became frightened by the danger of fires. For the last two years, I wouldn't dream of both of us leaving the house for any length of time during the hot days of summer. I'll never forget returning from a shopping trip to Denver one day last August. As we crossed the top of Berthoud pass, the sky was bright red and mountain peaks barely emerged; the valley below us was filled with smoke. "It looks like we have a fire in the Fraser Valley," I said to Laura. We couldn't wait to get to the bottom of the pass, trying to get a handle on one of the local radio stations. We soon learned that there wasn't a fire in our beloved valley. Strong winds had blown the smoke down from fires devastating the surroundings of Steamboat Springs.

And thus it went. The perfect view of our paradise became

somewhat tarnished and distorted. More and more ideas buried in the subconscious mind moved into conscious territory—perhaps not so much for Laura as for me. That may have something to do with our age difference. I never vocalized my concerns to her as we embarked on our most recent adventures in the American Southwest.

We marveled at Monument Valley and enjoyed our return to Betatakin. Seeing the Grand Canyon emerging from lifting fog, covered lightly with a dusting of snow, also was an experience not soon forgotten. Sedona in heavy, wet snow didn't ensnare my hidden feelings of looking for a new nirvana.

As we headed down toward Phoenix, the skies turned to blue and temperatures became pleasant. No, the Phoenix area wouldn't do for this kid. Too much traffic! Yes, there are mountains in the distance, but basically the terrain is rather flat. The palm trees swayed lightly in the breeze, different from lodgepole pine gently moved by the winds of an approaching storm. And speaking of the approaching storm—the one alluded to earlier as the storm of the century—it dumped more than eight feet of snow in Winter Park while we were away.

I washed my car in Mesa, and it remained clean for the next ten days. What a miracle!

We traveled to Tucson, and I could see the beauty in the desert landscape, envisioning what all those cacti must look like in full bloom. I loved getting up shortly after six and going for brisk walks without concern for snow and ice under my feet. Of course, we had to keep an eye open for rattlesnakes. Darlene said, "Carry a big stick—just in case." A couple days later, we started looking at resale homes. None truly appealed to me; Laura was even less enamored. For her, it was just idle curiosity.

She didn't grasp that I was looking for a new and different place to settle. Eventually, we wound up at Canoa Ranch, a new community being developed in Green Valley. We toured all nine models and I found one that I liked. We went to lunch with our friends and went home with them to get our own car and returned to the sales center. We signed a contract for the purchase of a new home several hours later.

Neither one of us slept well during the ensuing night. We talked a lot, with Laura not believing what we had done—or better, what I had done. We had made a life-changing decision. The next day we spoke with friends in the valley who are in the real estate business. We learned that we were dealing with reputable people and a reputable builder. Further, we learned that we could finagle our way out of the contract and get our money back if that was what we wanted to do.

There were hours of soul-searching and revisiting the site where the new home was to be built in the coming months. Gradually the reality of it all began to sink in. We met with a large contingent of the Fraser Valley South community in Green Valley. Everyone welcomed us as the newest future neighbors. The next morning we saw the interior design staff for eight hours and made all the necessary selections. It started out to be a traumatic experience for Laura. Eventually, she was pleased with her thoughtful choices. She still couldn't accept the fact that we had done what we did. Walking away from the sales center, I could hear Laura mumbling behind me. "What are you fussing about now?" I said.

"I don't know how I ever will learn to live with all sorts of bugs and rattlesnakes."

"What about tarantulas and scorpions?" was my comeback. I could have shot the interior designer when she told Laura that she had bugs big enough to put a saddle on. Realizing what she had done to Laura, she voiced a disclaimer, saying, "Of course, I have dogs and all sorts of critters around the house attracting bugs."

We made our good-byes with our dear friends and stormed out of Green Valley toward Albuquerque. After sleeping for a few hours, we were back on the road, heading home at six fifteen. Approaching Colorado Springs and seeing the splendor of snow-covered mountains made me choke. I consoled myself with the thought I would enjoy them in June, July, and August in years to come. We pulled into the driveway by four thirty, glad to see that the house still stood and was waiting for our return. So were feet and feet of compacted and frozen snow. Laura was the one who eventually shoveled the decks and carved a walking path to the front door. I had decided to let the sun melt it all away instead of incurring a heart attack.

In a span of ten days, we settled on nirvana in the sunny southwest and sold our home in God's country. Both of us began to believe that it was all meant to be. We would miss our friends in the Fraser Valley—that was for sure. But we were not going away for good. There would be annual pilgrimages to Paradise Lost and a renewal of friendships that both of us held very dear.

Rites of Spring

A few days ago, I saw a few robins hopping around on relatively scarce bare spots in the yard. The days are getting longer, and there are definite signs of spring in the air. Our fine-feathered friends are beginning to entertain us with their annual early morning concerts. I don't know if it is my age, but I seem to be waking up earlier all the time. The sound of birdsong is pleasant to greet one upon awakening. It sounds a lot better than traffic noise or howling storms.

While our yard is still largely covered by the residue of mountains of snow, in town we have spotted tulips and daffodils trying to burst into bloom. Spring is definitely on its way. It was great that the early morning of Easter held the promise for a sunny and pleasant day.

After hearing about Spring Splash for twenty-seven years, curiosity got the better of us. We decided to discover for ourselves what it was all about. We often read about it in the local papers and heard people discuss and laugh about the shenanigans that go on during the much-touted event.

So, shortly after attending the early church service, which

was rather long, we hightailed it back home to change into some more casual attire. Easter clothes definitely would have been out of place. A friend gave us a lift in his four-wheel equipped vehicle. Good thing! We might have broken an axle on an ordinary car trying to maneuver the gigantic potholes in the parking lot and approaching roads. We wondered how they could have had the nerve to charge for parking in such deplorable conditions. At least on this day, the final day of the season, parking in the pay lot was free of charge. It was small consolation though, if one managed to inflict major damage to one's vehicle.

We were grateful for old jeans and heavy shoes as we traipsed across the muddy and slushy lot at the foot of the ski area. The place of action was not difficult to find. One just had to follow the blaring music and aim for the huge crowds gathered at the base of Larry Sale and in front of West Portal Station.

The announcers were getting the crowds all fired up about the impending event. Soon we spotted the large pool of ice-cold water that had been created for the purpose of the happening. We seemed to recall that it used to be a natural pool of water collected during spring melt at the base of Lower Hughes. Perhaps that wasn't so safe. In this day and age of sue-happy people, the area might take certain precautions to reduce the chance of harm to any of the participants.

It was well known that those who wanted to be part of the fun had to register and pay for the pleasure. A lift ticket was the basic requirement. In addition, a twenty-five-dollar registration fee was necessary. As the crowds grew larger and rowdier with the consumption of alcoholic beverages, the announcers' inane commentary and the blaring music were raised a few decibels.

Shortly after we had finally made it to a good viewing spot at the venue of the event, the entertainment of the day began to commence. Ladies went first. "Ladies" is an overstatement—most of them were young and very young chicks decked out in crazy and rather skimpy attire. The commentators provided the audience with pertinent and not-so-pertinent facts about each of the contestants, such as an interpretation of the costumes worn or the location of visible and not-so-visible tattoos.

First came the lady snowboarders, then the lady skiers. Many of them had difficulty getting through the gates or managing the obstacle course. It was obvious that some of these individuals were novices on either snowboards or skis. Their primary objective seemed to be to make it to the jumping-off point near the pool of water and landing as far across as possible, trying to miss the pond of ice-cold water. Thank goodness for the rescuers standing in the icy waters and wearing insulated waders while helping all of the contestants—female or male—to free themselves of snowboards and skis after successful and not-so-successful jumping attempts.

Eventually, it was the men's turn—also a very young crowd. *You have to be nuts, or at least half-nuts and extremely young and competitive, to participate in the Spring Splash.* And that was the case. Mature people were seated or standing having a drink while watching the unfolding spectacle.

The guys were even more daring in the selection of the costumes, or lack thereof, flashing their heavily tattooed bodies to the yelling audience. I decided that those on boards were clearly inferior in tackling the terrain and had to be novices who were trying to show off their stuff. Skiers of both sexes were far more adept at handling Larry Sale and the obstacles of the Terrain Park.

After watching the event for almost two hours and tolerating the so-called humorous commentary of the announcers, we decided we had seen enough. *Maybe we are getting too old for this sort of thing*. Personally, I thought what we saw was highly overrated. I had pictured it to be much more fun and spontaneous than something so totally fabricated. I have an idea that it would have been a lot more enjoyable had we attended one of these bashes in the seventies when we first started skiing in Winter Park.

For us, it was a rather sentimental goodbye to a spot that we loved. Since this will be, more likely than not, our last winter in the Fraser Valley, we took a good look around the base area. Our eyes took in the changes that had taken place in the course of the years since we fell in love with downhill skiing in 1976. We glanced at the bottom of the Practice Hill where we first raced across to be placed in an appropriate class of the ski school. We looked at Larry Sale and pictured it the way it was all those years ago. The snow of Lower Hughes looked absolutely perfect for this late in the season. *Such a shame to close the area this early*. Once we walked around the ugly buildings now dominating the base of Winter Park, we gained a view of Parry Peak in all of its heavily snowcapped splendor after receiving its most recent blessing of white gold.

We said our quiet farewells to a place on this earth very dear to our hearts. It was the beauty of the valley and its mountains that attracted us to Winter Park in the first place. In the years that followed, the people who live here made what the Fraser Valley became to us—not the hoopla as manifested by today's

Spring Splash. Poignantly, it was seeing one of our dear friends that put the finishing touch on the event. We were delighted to see Eddie greeting us as we got on the bus. His face beamed as he spotted Laura and greeted her with a big hug.

The years to come will be different. Summers in the high country will be glorious. Reunions with dear friends will be cherished. Memories of treasured times during twenty-seven marvelous winters in Winter Park will be rekindled as we leaf through albums of photographs taken throughout the years. They simply will have to suffice, but they will never take the place of the real thing.

Salute to Technology

HAVING been raised in a country were building a house is a really big deal, undertaking such a project in the good old USA seems to be a cinch by comparison. In years past, when homes were built in most European countries, and particularly in Germany, they were always built to last a millennium. At least it seemed that way because of the manner in which the builders would carry on and take their sweet time with every step of the process.

Perhaps things have changed there to some degree as well. Building technologies certainly have changed all over the world. And ease of communication has made the world a much smaller place, allowing the exchange of ideas and concepts more readily.

I have to admit that we have certainly benefited from the existence of twenty-first-century technology during our most recent experience in building a home. My family in Europe thought—and still thinks— that it is utter folly to build a new home one thousand miles away from our present residence: "How can you sell your beautiful home in Colorado? Why would you want to move to the heat in Arizona? How can you build a home when you live that far away from the construction site? How do you know that they are doing the right thing? How can you decide to build a new home in a matter of hours one afternoon and then make major decisions relative to each and every detail of the new house in a matter of eight hours? It takes detailed planning and documentation before one enters into such a project. We just don't understand how you can do all this and then just take off and leave everything to the fates of the building gods."

Well, I guess that is exactly what we did. Maybe I have become a bit more American and adventurous in the course of having lived here for almost fifty years. One learns that sometimes it is necessary to take certain chances and just hope for the best.

After initial recriminations and buyers' remorse, we felt pretty confident about the builders and the staff of the large concern with whom we were dealing. As time moved on and the project literally got off the ground, we felt better all the time.

Technology played a major part right from the start. Years ago, contracts and documentation would have to be typed with many copies—often subject to many typing errors—making careful proofreading mandatory. Word processing and computer technology increased the ease of personalizing and customizing building plans and sales contracts.

My digital camera allowed me to photograph the model inside and out and from every angle. When selecting decor and details of the house with the design staff, I could capture colors and items selected to help us refresh our memories once we were one thousand miles away from the building site.

Subsequently, telecommunicating, faxing, and e-mailing enhanced the culmination of a final document, allowing progress toward starting the building process. Who would have thought of all of these elements of modern communication twenty years ago?

There is no question in my mind that the whole process of building our present home would have been far more traumatic had it not been for all that was available to us. After we had gotten over the trauma of the folly we had visited upon ourselves, particularly myself, we were in touch with the building process from week one thanks to technology and an extremely cooperative and helpful staff near the building site.

Digital imagery was transmitted to us on a weekly basis. We could follow the process as the lot was reworked and footings were designed and poured. Next we got the pictures showing the pouring process of the slab. As framing of the house took place, we could picture it far better in our mind's eye. And thus, we were participating in almost every step of the adventure of building a new home in spite of being almost one thousand miles away.

The crowning touch of the adventure occurred just this week. Our favorite rep, who had sold us the house, was in the process of building her own. Fortunately for us, it was the exact same model, and she shared in the excitement of building this particular house. So periodically, she would send us a picture of her new home, allowing us to anticipate what ours would be like a few weeks later. Her house had been started about one month ahead of ours. It was indeed great and we could far better conceptualize our future abode.

Ten days ago, she and her husband had moved into their

house, and she transmitted to us a photo of her kitchen. Although totally different in color scheme and decor, we both noticed right away the difference in the manner in which the large tiles had been laid. "Did you notice the diagonal placement of the tiles in the kitchen?" asked Laura.

"Yes, I was about to comment on that myself. Do you think that is a special option? I don't recall the designer asking us about it. Why don't you give Jane a call and find out if that is still an option for us."

And thus it went. Laura called early on Sunday morning. Yes, it was a special option and perhaps it might be too late to add at this stage of the game. "Leave a message at the design center and have them call you first thing in the morning. I'll go over to the house right now and see if they have started the tiling of the floor. I'll do anything I can do at this end," was Jane's comment.

They had not started the tiling but were ready to do so first thing Monday morning. The diagonal process would be slightly higher in cost. They would need more tiles, which hopefully would be readily available for shipping. A delay in finishing the house was out of the question for them and for us. There would be a late charge for changing and updating the contract.

Umpteen faxes, telephone calls, e-mails, and FedEx mailings later, the project was a done deal and in the works. It would never have happened even ten years ago.

The proof was in the digital photographs that arrived exactly one week after the initial telephone inquiry had been made. "Hope you like it. I think it looks beautiful," Jane wrote. We couldn't agree more. If it hadn't been for that serendipitously transmitted digital image of Jane's kitchen, we would never have known about the possibility and never would have had an opportunity to act upon it. Hektor lifted his glass: "Here's to technology, as much as we despise it sometimes, especially when it summons us to respond to an unwanted telemarketer."

September Mystique

I don't know what it is, but there has always been something special about the month of September. When I was a child, it generally meant the return to school after lengthy summer vacations, although our summer vacations in Germany were never as long as those observed in the United States. In later years, September, and particularly Labor Day, heralded the beginning of the busiest period in retailing, culminating in the traditional Christmas rush.

There were autumns in New York; some more memorable than others. Some, I'd actually rather forget. My first Labor Day in New York was the welcome end to a beastly hot summer. The heat had almost done me in. I had never experienced such temperatures in my entire life. If it had not been for air conditioning, I might have decided right there and then that the good old USA wasn't for me.

The second Labor Day in New York was downright fatal; I made the acquaintance of my first wife. The liaison led to a disastrous and stormy relationship that ended in divorce a few years later.

Politicians often kick off their campaigns in September leading to triumph or disaster at some distant election day. Of course, that is a kettle of fish I don't wish to touch with a ten-foot pole.

Actually, what prompted my writing about this subject on the auspicious first day of September 2003, coinciding with Labor Day, are rather pleasant thoughts. As far as nature's calendar is concerned, fall was always one of my most favorite seasons. I loved fall even as a child in Germany. The annual color show turned myriad deciduous trees in our woods to a blaze of bright reds, orange, and various shades of yellow, which always captured my imagination. The stately pines and firs of the Black Forest were particularly pretty when snow-laden but couldn't rival the spectacle of color observed in areas with so many different leafy trees.

The same was true in the East and the Midwest of the United States. None of the seasons ever matched the beauty of autumn with its spectacle of colorful displays. I'll never forget the fall of 1973. I had just finished writing my doctoral exams, and Laura and I decided to drive to Florida in mid-October to visit her grandfather. The glorious touches of brilliant coloration of the trees followed us from Michigan and Ohio into Kentucky and Tennessee and finally into the Deep South. By the time we returned in November, the magic was gone, and winter had arrived. The wind was toying with the last of the leaves, which had turned to an ugly, lifeless brown, tearing away at the stems, leaving the giant trees in our neighborhood staring barren at the gray skies.

Oh yes, and there was that spectacular fall of 1963 when I asked my sweetheart on Sunday, September 15, if she would consider marrying me during her lunch hour on my day off the following Thursday. We were indeed married at high noon on Rosh Hashanah, September 19, by Judge Former at the city hall in Detroit. It was a glorious, sunny fall day as we stepped out into the bright sunshine with our witnesses. After a quick lunch, Laura went back to the office of her unsuspecting employers—I went to see *The Great Escape*. That night we supposedly had dinner with the family of my Jewish boss. Our family had no idea what we had been up to. I guess it took; we are celebrating our fortieth this glorious September. Where have all those fabulous Septembers gone?

When we started spending our summers in Colorado in 1976, I always wondered what fall would be like. I saw many photos and videos of the spectacular color show of the aspen but never could experience it for myself. Come the middle of August, it was always time to return to Hinterland, Iowa, and to resume my teaching responsibilities at the University. Mind you, our campus was beautiful, especially at that time of year. But I felt cheated that I could never see the aspen turn to gold.

At the time when I planned my phased retirement, I decided to have the best of both worlds. I arranged my early and partial retirement so that I could experience autumn in the Rockies and taught during both mud seasons. By the time we left Winter Park in mid-October, the aspen spectacle was over and the trees in the Midwest were headed for their peak.

We were building our retirement home in 1995, and Laura stayed behind to add the finishing touches to the project while I returned to Iowa and kept the financial ship afloat. We talked a lot on the phone. Now and then I would ask her how she was enjoying the fall scenery, and particularly the colorful aspen.

"Honey, I am so involved with the house, I haven't really had a chance to look at the leaves," was her typical response. I couldn't wait to experience the scene for the very first time in fall 1996. I have been enchanted with it ever since.

And now it's another September, one that brings a wonderful chapter in our lives to a close. We are leaving the mountains of Colorado to move to our new home in Arizona. The cacti won't turn to gold but will remain green under the bright blue skies of the Southwest.

It is the beginning of a new chapter and adventure in our lives. The consolation prize is that we may be able to return to the high country for many summers to come. The high point of each of these visits will always be the annual color show of the aspen before we head back to the sunny South. As so often in our lives, autumn will spell the end of an era and herald the beginning of a new and different one.

Slender Fella

MY wife's mom used to say, "Sonny, it's hell to get old." In the early years of our marriage, I wasn't sure what she was trying to tell me. For a few years now, I have learned to appreciate that comment of hers. I remember the days when I could eat anything in sight and never gain an ounce. Those were really the golden days. I could come home at one or two in the morning and raid the cooling house—a giant walk-in refrigerator—and cut down ten or twelve of my dad's very best hotdogs, throw them in a pot of boiling water, dip them one by one into the mustard jar, and enjoy every morsel. I never got sick, and I never needed to have my pants let out.

My mother knew of my sweet tooth. For my thirty-first birthday, she baked six of my very favorite cakes and tortes. We flew into Germany the evening of the event. Mother was prepared. She had the coffee table set when we arrived. There was a cheesecake, an apple cake, a strawberry flan, a cherry flan, a gooseberry torte, and some kind of chocolate torte—probably a Sacher torte. Of course, there had to be a large bowl of whipped cream to top off those delectable concoctions and the coffee. "I baked these especially for your birthday and your homecoming. Laura ought to know the things you like. Before you leave, I will bake again and then I can show her how. How about trying the cheesecake first?" With that she proceeded to cut gigantic pieces of the calorie-laden bomb. She had imagined that we would have at least one piece of each of her creations.

When we asked her to cut tiny slices of subsequent selections, her typical German mother's nose was slightly out of joint. It was the beginning of twenty-one days of being stuffed like geese. There were sumptuous breakfasts, followed by cognac and finger food as we visited friends and relatives in the course of the morning. Of course, mother expected us to be punctually at her dinner table at one o'clock. By four it would be time for Kaffeeklatsch; at seven, there would be drinks and sandwiches, cheeses, hams, and cold cuts served on rye bread to die for. Finally, there would be the inevitable late snack served around ten p.m. No one wanted to go to sleep on an empty stomach, right? Stout German beers or delightful wines and champagne always accompanied all of these wonderful treats. By the end of the three-week visit, I had gained twenty-three pounds.

Within a few days, I managed to shed the extra poundage in those long-gone days. The battle of wanting and denying began in my early forties. Sedentary living set in, and with that came the gradual expansion of the waistline.

Yesterday would have been Mother's ninety-fifth birthday; she made her grand exit sixteen years ago. Now it's my dear sister-in-law who doesn't pay attention to our pleas of cutting down on the portions placed on our plates or the number of refills visited upon our glasses. We have learned to just leave things on our plates or not to keep drinking. They can't add to a full glass.

In spite of our strong protests to family and friends, we managed to add a few dreaded pounds to our svelte figures during our most recent visit with the family. The frequently heard admonition. "You can diet again when you are back home." did not ease the blow once we stepped on our ever-truthful digital scale. The evidence was incontrovertible. Although my weight gain was not as dramatic as in past years, the zippers on my pants didn't close as readily as they had before we departed for Europe.

"We have to get these pounds off now. I am not buying a new wardrobe. Been there, done that. Let's just cut out any alcoholic drinks and sweets and go really easy on the carbohydrates," admonished Laura. We did, and I managed to lose most of the extra weight I had gained during our four-week sojourn in Europe. "I don't know why it is so much easier for men to shed weight! No matter what I eat or do, I cannot get rid of five extra pounds. I believe we need to go on the infamous three-day diet," announced Laura.

As the pronouncement was made, I had visions of water, herbal tea, and tuna fish. I have never been one to drink excessive amounts of water. Germans believe that water rusts your "pipes" (stomach and intestines). At least the herbal tea has some flavoring to it; I can handle it. I like good tuna, but eating it without anything in it is more of a challenge. The dinners for the first two days aren't bad. I can handle the well-seasoned broiled chicken breasts and don't mind broccoli, carrots, beets, and even spinach, if it is prepared well. The last dinner is the absolute pits—one half cup of plain tuna, beets, spinach, and cauliflower. Dessert constitutes one half cantaloupe and herbal tea. Sticking to this baby by the letter is supposed to allow you to shed ten pounds.

My nutritionist spouse does not believe in such radical regiments. Therefore, the tuna is dressed with low-fat mayonnaise and some herbs. Instead of having one hardboiled egg for breakfast, she presents it in scrambled form.

We have just finished our first luncheon. It wasn't bad. I am still struggling with the first bucket of water; can't wait for the second dose. My stomach is squawking at me; it wants more food. As I am typing this little story, I am already thinking about the gourmet dinner in store this evening. I simply can't wait for the herbal tea. Slender Fella is turning into a mirage.

Snorkel Mania

FIVE years ago we enjoyed our first cruise through the Caribbean. Our first port of call was Aruba. As most novices to cruising, we decided to avail ourselves of the shore excursions by the cruise line. The snorkeling venture sounded most exciting to us. Just getting to the site of the adventure was a trip and a half. First we boarded an antiquated bus that took us to the outskirts of town.

An even more antiquated barge carried the happy snorkelers across an inlet to the beachhead, where we were to be indoctrinated into the fine art of snorkeling in one very easy lesson. As we were shillyshallying across the muddy waters, we couldn't help but laugh at the primitive conveyance that was transporting us to the blue lagoon. Half-rotten beams were held together by rusty chains and wires. All of us were wondering to what ominous adventure we had committed ourselves. Of course, all the participants had paid their good money up front. There was no turning back.

Pretty soon we had sand under our feet and were directed to collect our snorkeling equipment. We were issued masks, snorkels, and fins. None of the people dealing with us had any fluency in English, German, or French. Even sign language didn't do the trick. We had to rely on gestures and facial expressions.

We discovered that there is no difference in left or right fins; no one told us how difficult walking would be for mermaids. We gathered that the masks would be put on the head, covering up eyes and noses. No one mentioned that persons with glasses should not wear them while snorkeling and that mustaches could be detrimental to one's lungs. It was logical to put one end of the snorkel in one's mouth and to be sure to keep the other end above water.

No question about it, the blue lagoon was blessed with water as clear and pristine as one could wish for. "Honey, come over here and see all of these beautiful fish. Look, there are whole schools of them. Let's try what everyone else is doing; let's use the equipment we rented. And we did. No sooner had we dunked our heads below the surface of the clear water, we came up quickly, trying to expel the saltwater swallowed. Naturally, we didn't realize that our masks didn't fit properly, especially mine handicapped by my glasses and mustache—there was no seal at all—and no matter how often I tried, I continued to ingest enough saltwater for a lifetime.

My wife, Laura, didn't do much better. As a superb swimmer, she had envisioned snorkeling to be a very simple task. Not so. We were terribly disappointed watching others enjoying themselves. What we didn't realize then was that most people who were experiencing the pleasures of the blue lagoon had brought their own equipment. We just sat under the roof of a straw hut and chalked the whole thing up as a once-in-a-lifetime experience.

Before landing at the next port of call, we met three couples from Minneapolis. We pooled our resources and simply rented a van and driver. It was cheaper and more exciting than any excursions organized by the cruise line. Needless to say, no one was interested in another snorkeling adventure.

We are about to embark on another cruise. I mentioned to our friend Joyce that we were sailing to Belize in November. She inquired if we were going to do some underwater explorations. I didn't hesitate to inform her that we had been there and done that—obviously not too successfully. I related our disastrous experience in Aruba.

"Don't let that discourage you. You just didn't have the right equipment. You need to visit Underwater Phantaseas in Lakewood. They'll sell you the equipment you need and train you in the use of it. When they are done with you, you'll be ready to luxuriate in the waters of Belize. Take my word for it."

We took her advice and did buy good masks and snorkels, fins, as well as protective lightweight suits. I learned that I couldn't wear my glasses under my mask, and, if I wanted to see anything under water, I needed to get a mask with corrective lenses. Not exactly what I had bargained for, but certain pleasures don't come cheap. As suggested, we signed up for a two-hour lesson to become familiar with masks, snorkels, and fins and how to maneuver with these underwater contraptions.

We went to our underwater indoctrination and learned a great many things. Laura will probably make an excellent snorkeler while I, most likely, will remain primarily a surface explorer. But who knows, with greater exposure, I might learn to dabble into finer aspects of mermaid existence.

"The reason for wearing some sort of protective suit is to keep your body temperature up and to protect your backs and the backs of your legs from getting sunburned," said Storm. "Also, you may be less likely to be bitten by sea creatures such as jellyfish. Be sure to put some sun block on the tops of your ears. Whatever you do, do not wear makeup or cream on your face. Eventually, it will work itself under your mask and cloud your lenses," continued our teacher.

Storm, our instructor, invited one other couple and us to join him in the pool. We were standing in the shallow end, learning how to treat our lenses and how to put on our masks. "First, if you have not done so, you need to remove any protective film from your lenses by scrubbing them with toothpaste or plain soft scrub," said Storm. The latter was not necessary for my prescriptive lenses. All I needed to do was to give them a light squirt from the defogger, smearing it to the edges, and then rinsing the mask in the pool. That part was easy.

"How do I adjust the tension on the mask and is there a special way of putting it on and taking the mask off?" I asked. All of us learned how to tighten our masks. The mask is placed so that it fits below the nose comfortably, and the back of the mask is seated obliquely to the head. Taking it off works just in the reverse. At the same time, we learned that wearing the lenses on the forehead constitutes the international distress sign. Seeing anyone wearing a mask in that position should prompt an inquiry as to that person's well-being. By the same token, were I to wear a mask in that fashion, someone might ask me if I am all right.

"The snorkels are designed to be attached to the left of your mask in the following fashion." Then Storm assisted us in properly attaching our snorkels. The bottom of the snorkel has a relief valve in case water gets into the device; the top is always open and serves to expel water forcefully after a dive. Of course, its main purpose is to supply the snorkeler with air. Later, when I kept swallowing water, Storm discovered that the bottom of my snorkel was not properly closed. Once this discovery was made, things went a lot better.

Maneuvering with fins was another kettle of fish. The good swimmers had no difficulty keeping their legs straight and flipping their fins up and down. That was a real challenge for me. I tend to rely on my arms and had a hard time holding them useless next to my body. Storm suggested I buy myself some "gilled gloves" that would give me more power with my hand and arm movements.

We learned how to properly get out of the water at the ladder of a boat. Rather than holding on to the steps of the ladder, we were taught to hold onto the rods of the ladder while taking off our fins. In a bobbing sea, bouncing steps could make getting out of the water a greater challenge. Also, we learned that we should mark our fins with our names since they are fitted to each person's feet, and many of them look alike—kind of like picking up other persons' suitcases at baggage claim.

Both Laura and I found the fins to be rather uncomfortable. Only after our lesson did we discover that the new fins come with a stiff, plastic insert from the factory that is designed to retain the shape of the foot piece. Those awkward things ought to work a lot better without the inserts. And, of course, we learned that walking backward works much better when pretending to be a mermaid.

I never did try the underwater diving. That just looked too complicated for me—especially when I continued to swallow water with the snorkel wide open. We learned to jump off the side of the pool. Actually, I did OK with that. I watched Storm and the others closely as they followed him one by one. I stood close to the edge of the pool, my fins almost parallel. Then I extended my right foot as far as possible almost in a "split formation" as I leapt into the pool, holding my right hand in front of my mask for the big splash. Perhaps the safety vest kept me from doing a real dunk. Anyway, contrary to my expectations, the big leap went OK.

Soon the two hours were over. We didn't come away expert snorkelers, but we knew a heck of a lot more than we did after our experience in Aruba. We even learned how to use a camera under water. For example, when snapping pictures of a face it's best to aim at the neck rather than at the face because of the visual distortion introduced by the water.

We have decided to do a couple more practice sessions at a local swimming pool and hope to be more comfortable with our planned underwater adventures in Belize. *Thanks, Joyce, for steering us in the right direction.*

The Bed

THE bed, as we know it in western society, has a long history. I knew it had been around for a good while but didn't realize that the idea was first conceived during the early Bronze Age. I guess that is quite a stretch. Further, I do not intend to turn this into a research project, although the idea is titillating.

Before your wheels start turning, I also do not want you to get the wrong idea why I am discussing the bed on this early Monday morning. The topic has nothing to do with sex. However, at our age, I consider it the only place for making love; backseats in an old Chevy, tops of kitchen tables, sand dunes, etc., are highly overrated!

Having traveled a bit, we have slept in and on all sorts of beds. I presume that I slept in a crib when I was a baby. My memory doesn't go back that far. What I do remember is sleeping in a bed when I grew up in Germany. My brother and I shared a bedroom with twin beds. I also recall that sleeping in clothes and shoes wasn't very much fun. We were always ready to run off to the next bomb shelter when the alarms sounded. Oh, the pleasures of war!

At one time, when Laura and I were visiting my parents early in our marriage, we wound up sleeping on a sofa bed that was only slightly wider than a twin bed. Lord, we did that for a whole month. I don't know how we lasted. Home never looked so good!

In our camping days, we discovered sleeping on the ground in our four-season tent designed for three people. I don't know how a m*é*nage *à* trois would have worked in the Igloo Inn, as we had baptized it. With the proper ground protection it was OK. We spent seven weeks in Alaska with the tatami-type arrangement. It was an unforgettable experience, one I would not want to have missed. Sometimes I did have to convince myself that it was healthful for my aching back. Most nights I was too tired to even give it a second thought. I literally hit the sack and fell soundly asleep even if it was still daylight outside; the cries of the wolves signaled that it was time to go to sleep.

Funny, I can't remember the type of bed we slept in at the motel where we spent our wedding night after we were married secretly that afternoon. Perhaps I forgot, since sleeping wasn't actually on our minds that evening. Maybe it was a queen-sized bed. I do remember sleeping in the four-poster at Laura's parents' house. Mother insisted on us sleeping in their bed after we had let them in on our secret. It was full-sized.

Our first bedroom set we bought second hand. It was a full-sized version with an excellent mattress. It was comfortable and lasted for thirty-eight years. We, ourselves, didn't sleep on it that long. After twenty-five years of sleeping around, we had decided that a queen-sized bed was just the right size for us. Our first bed was turned over to visitors.

Some people have to have a king-size bed and nothing else.

We decided a long time ago that they are OK on occasion, but for us, they are just too big. We grope and look for each other half the night and wonder if one or the other has taken off. That's just too much bother.

Although we never owned one, we discovered that waterbeds are highly overrated and too uncomfortable. We were visiting a friend in Anchorage who had nothing but waterbeds in his house. When we sat down on the thing, it felt too warm. Smarty decided to turn the heater completely off. By three in the morning, we were both shaking like aspen leaves in a late-September windstorm. The water had turned ice cold and was sucking the body heat right out of us. We learned to never turn the heat completely off on a waterbed. Maybe turn it down, but never off. Right there and then, aside from the motion problems, we knew that waterbeds were not for us.

One thing we have discovered. We love cruising; at least we have the same bed every night. And the beds we have enjoyed on our cruises so far have been exactly the right size and firmness of mattress.

When all is said and done, a queen-sized bed with a good, firm mattress is decidedly our choice. Of course, we love our bed but can't drag it around with us. I suppose what brought this whole thing to mind is the fact that once again we are about to depart from our beloved bed for a couple of weeks. I estimate that we will sleep in at least nine different beds in the next two weeks. I'm sure we'll have a great time seeing friends and family. I'm not so sure about the beds. That is to be seen. I'll fill you in after we get back.

We arrived in Fort Myers almost two hours later than anticipated. The flight was uneventful but delayed due to weather conditions in Denver. The sunny and warm days had given way to thick fog and drizzle. It was twelve thirty Eastern Standard Time when we arrived at Caitlin's house. Needless to say, we had to have a tour of the place. Tino, their one-hundred-pound Benji dog, a cross between a white standard poodle and a golden retriever, had sufficiently become acquainted with us. We headed for bed about two thirty in the morning. At this point, I didn't care what the bed was like. It was a queen, covered by a colorful quilt. We literally fell into it. We decided to close our door tightly since Caitlin had advised us that Tino tended to wake up any visitors with friendly licks of his giant tongue.

We were wearing turtle necks, sweaters, and jackets almost all day. The ride in their new boat was pretty rough—even in the canals. Never mind the Gulf! All of us were glad when the boat was safely anchored again under its canopy. After an early dinner, all of us headed for our respective beds. Tino had been taken to the kennel. I am not so sure who was more traumatized by the separation, the dog or its owners. Laura took Caitlin and husband to the airport at four thirty. I climbed back into the queen and watched the women's final from the Australian Open. Not much sleeping that night although the queen was pretty comfortable and one of the few places I kept warm. *Aren't we in Florida?* came to mind.

We had an early breakfast and took a hot shower to warm up. After changing the sheets on the queen, we turned the Chevy toward Pine Island. Our friend Bob and his wife Josephine greeted us warmly. Bob was my store manager who stood up for me when Laura and I were married in Detroit. He lost his first wife to cancer almost ten years ago. He has been married to Josephine for seven or eight years. They summer in Michigan and winter on Pine Island.

Disappointed that he could not take us out on his boat, we shared stories of the past and the distant past between sumptuous meals. There was always much too much food. And then there were their pet cranes, egrets, and flamingos. They all had their names and practically ate out of Josephine's hands. Funny—and very entertaining. When we retired, we slept in a tiny room that held a comfortable full-sized bed covered with a white chenille bedspread. It almost reminded us of the bed we slept in when we were first married.

Today, we are off to Jupiter. We can't really complain. It has been sunny right along. No lie. It is the Sunshine State. But the wind blowing from the north is not exactly bringing the kind of breezes people look for when they winter in Florida. It's a relatively boring drive across the center of the state. We arrive at Cousin Roy's place about one thirty. He and Laura have always been very close. His wife Sharon is a peach. All of us love her. We talked endlessly and feasted on treasures of the sea and killed a few bottles of good wine. Their place is brand new and very comfortable. None of us were feeling any pain when we fell into bed. Ours was a queen, covered with a down comforter. We slept like babies.

After breakfast, we headed for the West Coast. Our next stop was Boca Grande. We crossed the causeway and easily found Margo and Paul's palatial house situated right at the shore of the Gulf. Katie, a bearded collie, and Zeus, a Bichon, made up the noisy greeting committee. Once they settled down and became friendlier toward the invaders of their territory, we received the extensive tour of the mansion. Each room was more spectacular than the last. We watched parts of the Super Bowl between cocktails and hors d'oeuvres and dinner at the yacht club. While most Floridians were glued to the boob tube rooting for the Bucks, our friends, being from Indiana and Iowa, were only slightly interested in the event. We finally retired to our king-sized bed at eleven thirty. The bed was fit for the large room, decorated with beautiful art collected during travels to the African continent and parts of Asia. The window and terrace gave a splendid view of the Gulf. The rustle of palm fronds and sea grapes in the hefty breeze from the north lulled us to sleep.

Our next stop was Venice. If we were forced to move to a warmer climate, we might consider this place. It is a charming little enclave that is a real town. There is a cultural and business center and all within walking distance of the beach. We met our friend in the afternoon. She gave us a guided tour, showing off the trophy homes of the rich and famous along the shores of Casey Key and the Gulf. We had an excellent dinner at the "Crow's Nest." When it was time to retire, we discovered twin beds fashioned from wicker in a modern design. The beds were comfortable enough, but Laura and I didn't particularly enjoy the arrangement since it continued to be rather cool outside, to say the least.

Our next stop was Sun City Center. Temperatures were still cool but warming up a little during the course of the day. Betty and Bob have a large and comfortable home. Its extremely contemporary appearance is striking. We dined elegantly and played a few hands of bridge. For the next two nights, we slept in a comfy king surrounded by a black-and-white decor of wicker and down.

We were well rested as we turned north toward Port Richey.

Our friends of more than forty years were anxiously awaiting us. As had become the case everywhere we went, we caught up on old and current events over a meal. Eventually, we played a few hands of pinochle for old times' sake. When we retired, we discovered that we would be sleeping in a white French Provincial queen. It was our resting place for two nights.

It was February first, and we were off to Sarasota for two nights. As we were cruising down I-75 and listening to Scott Simon on NPR, we learned of the Columbia disaster. It gave us the creeps. Deln's place, overlooking one of the keys and onto the Gulf from her seventeenth-floor vantage point, was spectacular. We had a delightful lunch at Plymouth Harbor; paid a visit to the Ringling Museum; met Deln's future husband, Marty, over drinks; and went to dinner at a lively Greek restaurant, featuring a terrific jazz quartet. In the back of our minds were the events of the day that overshadowed everything. When we finally retired to the queen hide-a-bed fashioned of elegant rattan and cream damask, I fell into a restless sleep. I couldn't get rid of the images of a deteriorating spaceship hurdling through the atmosphere and the remains of seven humans and their "marvel of technology" scattered over several western states.

I awakened frequently, not being able to shake the images from my mind. When I finally rose from the bed, the glow of the sunrise cast an eerie, reddish light over the bay and the Gulf. A single white egret rose into the air. It reminded me of the symbolic dove flying off into space at the conclusion of each episode of *Touched by an Angel*. For a moment I thought that the egret rose symbolically for the lost seven souls in space.

The visit to the Marie Selby Botanical Gardens was a delightful diversion. The brunch at the Yacht Club was elegant.

Visits with mutual friends were heartwarming. But no matter how we tried, the events of the previous day and the talk of impending war dominated the conversations. Exhausted, we retired to the hide-a-bed shortly after ten. We fell into a sound sleep, which allowed us finally to hide for a while from the thoughts occupying our minds.

This was our last full day in Florida. We met with John and Elaine for an hour over breakfast at Perkins. John was president of the university when I first arrived in Iowa. One hour turned into two and one-half as we were trying to catch up on events of our lives since we last saw each other fifteen years earlier. It was a wonderful reunion. Then we were off to Sanibel Island. We stayed at a bed-and-breakfast. Charming. But we again had twin beds fashioned from wicker. Well, just one more night in strange beds. We went for a walk in the sunshine through an eerie park and eventually on the famed beaches of Sanibel. Not too many shells; too many seekers had been combing the beach ahead of us.

Had dinner with a friend of Laura's whom she had not seen in forty-five years. We met her most current husband—a biker—decked out in Harley Davidson attire. He would have liked to volunteer for services in Iraq and kick butt. We got the drift. They had to head home after a couple of hours of lively conversation. We met for an hour with long-time friends from First Congregational in Waterloo, Iowa. They have wintered at Sanibel for many years. And then it was time to cuddle up with our twin bed at the bed-and-breakfast.

We got up at six o'clock and flew off into the wild blue yonder at ten. It was cold and snowy in Denver. We caught up with our friends and enjoyed a good dinner and an excellent performance at the Ricketson theatre. We were finally home by eleven fifteen. The house looked like a castle. We couldn't wait to cuddle up in our familiar queen. It felt great to sleep once again in our own bed. *Thank God the trip wasn't any longer than two weeks,* the reader must be thinking.

The Betrayal

A familiar figure in her neighborhood, Else made her way to the nearby cemetery shortly after breakfast. She always made sure she had a good first meal of the day. Starting the day without eating anything was to her like trying to start a car without gas. Walter's birthday was in a few days; to be specific, it was November 10. All too soon, he had been taken to his final resting place. She missed him terribly. Walter was her one and only great love in life. Else had to make sure that Magyra's had done a suitable job of preparing the gravesite for the fall season.

As she was headed down the hilly street, she held firmly onto her large umbrella. Strong gusts of wind would periodically try to snatch it from her hands. She was wearing tailored wool slacks under her stylish fox jacket. Ostrich-leather gloves complemented her large brown felt cloche that she wore rakishly pushed into her face. She had sort of a Garbo-like appearance. Else had always retained her slender silhouette. Despite the fact that she had recently celebrated her eighty-eighth birthday, she made a striking figure as she marched onto her destination with a firm gait. Else never slouched; she walked perfectly straight with almost military stiffness.

She stood in front of Walter's grave and conversed with him. There was no one around to hear her, and she really didn't care if they did. "Well, Walter, looks like you are presentable for your birthday. I had them wash and polish the granite marker. It was high time. After all the rain we had this year, the stone needed it. Looks so much better. I know you would approve. Just wanted to make sure the caretakers did a good job. I won't stay too long today. Mustn't be late for my weekly hair appointment. On the way home, I will shop for some things for lunch and dinner. I'll see you tomorrow. Bye for now. Looks really nice." With that she turned and waved as she walked away.

She used to shed a couple of tears after she had her little chats with Walter. It had been too many years by now. Else often thought, *It can't be too much longer before I join him.* The wind had picked up; once again, it was raining. The big umbrella swayed in the breeze, but she held firmly onto it. Clutching her purse under her left arm, she strutted along the sidewalk. Now and then a familiar face greeted her with "*Guten Morgen.*"

There weren't too many of those faces these days; she had outlived most of them. She almost hated to peruse the obituary page in the daily paper, so often had she caught a familiar name among those who had departed from this earth. "What a nasty day," she mumbled to herself. *If this wasn't my regular day to have my hair done, I sure wouldn't bother. Lord knows what I shall look like by the time I get home. This rain and this wind—it's just awful.*

She stepped into the beauty parlor, glad to be out of the ugly weather. "*Guten Morgen,* Frau Gunders," said her regular beautician. "I was wondering if you would make it in today.

The weather is so nasty. Of course, I knew better. No matter what, you would be here on time—especially today, since it's time to freshen up your tint."

"You are right. I need to look my best for Walter's birthday." With that she slipped off her hat and jacket, declining with a subtle gesture to be assisted by the much younger hair stylist. It was nice that someone was trying to be accommodating. Nevertheless, Else liked to let others know that she was still totally self-reliant.

When she emerged from the beauty salon, there was a touch of elegance about her. She felt good about the color and styling of her hair, and for the moment she didn't care what wind and rain might do to it in a matter of minutes. Else retrieved her sizable cloth shopping pouch from her jacket pocket as she entered the bakery. After the exchange of vigorous "Good Mornings" with the clerks behind the counter, she selected a hearty rye bread and declined to have it sliced. She liked cutting her own bread; it kept fresh so much longer. Next she stopped at the regular butcher shop and got some fine cold cuts and a couple of lean pork chops for her noonday meal. Her last stop was the florist shop, where she selected a few bright yellow chrysanthemums. The owner, Herr Müller, tied them with a few greens, and handed the handsome bouquet to her with a flourish. "Looks like you have your hands full today, especially needing to carry the umbrella."

"I'll manage. I just have to get across the street. and I'll be home. Of course, I don't have to tell you. We have been neighbors for fifty-one years." With that remark she marched out of the shop. She deftly opened her umbrella and pushed the button for the crossing light. Else had learned to walk carefully on the wet cobblestones and to pay particular attention to the slipperiness of the metal rails of the streetcars embedded among them. *Well, I'm almost there and in one piece. It is a nasty day, for sure!*

The house she and Walter had called home for most of their lives, was the second from the corner. It faced the historical *Wasserturm* [water tower]. The ground floor had been occupied by a fashionable pub, which she and Walter had designed. It was a place oozing with charm and *Gemütlichkeit.* Now it had stood empty for many years; she couldn't find a suitable innkeeper after their original tenant decided to move to another city. The second floor occupied the offices of the dental practice. It was here that she and Walter had worked side by side. He came from a family of eight boys; every one of them had become a successful dentist. Their widowed mother had earned her living by doing laundry and ironing for neighbors. Rudolf, Walter and Else's only child, was now carrying on the family tradition. After his father's death, he took over the practice, and the dental emporium was completely redesigned and moved into the twenty-first century.

Else and Walter's elegant quarters were located on the third floor. Neither of them ever minded climbing the lengthy flights of the marble staircase. In years past, the two floors above them were rented out or were used as guest apartments at one time or another. As of late, they remained unoccupied. Not too many people were interested in climbing all those stairs. Now Else wished they had considered putting in an elevator when they rebuilt the house after the war.

As she approached the locked front door, she juggled all the things held in her hands: her handbag, the groceries, flowers, and the umbrella. She managed to open her purse and reached for the keys. A young woman came out of nowhere and kindly offered her assistance. "May I hold your flowers and this bag for you while you open your door?" she asked in a most friendly manner. Else, who was normally inclined to reject such overtures, especially from total strangers, decided to take her up on the offer. *I do have a lot of things to manage this morning; perhaps it doesn't hurt to accept such kindly offered help* ran through her mind. "Well, thank you. That is very nice of you." With that she handed her the bouquet and the sack containing her purchases from the bakery, the butcher shop, and the grocers. She unlocked the front door which could only be opened with a formidable key or by someone inside pressing a buzzer after ascertaining that it was someone known to Else or a patient for her son's dental practice.

Well, this has been quite an outing this morning. I guess I got my exercise for the day. The two flights of stairs will be a nice finishing touch, mused Else. As she reached to retrieve her flowers and the grocery bag, the young lady offered to carry them for her. Again, hesitatingly, Else acquiesced to the young person's kind gesture. She headed up to her apartment followed by the young woman. Else unlocked both locks on her door and entered the elegant foyer of her home.

The young lady looked around and noticed the antique pieces of furniture and stunning oil paintings gracing the walls. All the doors had stylish arches trimmed out in ebony. After entering, she noticed that the door to the right was open, giving her a look into Else's boudoir. The bed was made and the large picture window emitted pleasant light on this gloomy day. *Quite the place*, she thought as she followed Else into her kitchen. "Where would you like me to put these things for you? May I help you put flowers in a vase and your groceries in your refrigerator?" she inquired.

Else wasn't quite sure how to handle such courtesies. Most young people today weren't interested in helping an older person. For years, she had kept Walter's car and engaged the services of a chauffeur for her long-distance travels. In town she would walk or simply call a cab. She hated to use public transportation in the last few years; young people so often were rude and far less courteous than in her younger days.

"There is an appropriate vase in that cupboard up there. You can probably reach it; I would have to get up on my footstool. That's a big help. The groceries I can put away myself." As soon as the flowers had been trimmed and arranged in the vase, Else reached for her purse to retrieve a five-mark bill. As she handed it to the young woman, she expressed her appreciation by shaking her hand. "Thank you so much for helping me. You have been very kind."

Walking the girl to the door, she realized that she had not closed it behind her when entering, something she normally would never have done. But all seemed to be in order. She thanked the young woman again and peered down the stairway as she descended rather quickly. Else moved just one step forward, allowing her to gain a full view of the banister winding down the two floors to the entry below. She was going to wave to her kind Samaritan but discovered that the girl was actually making a rather hurried getaway. On the last turn she noticed that there were two people charging down the stairs. One clearly seemed to be a male. *Perhaps someone who had just come from Rudolf's dental practice?*

She reentered her apartment, this time closing the door firmly behind her and making sure both locks were secured. Else put her groceries away and heated some water for a cup of tea. This had been a rather full morning. *I hope I didn't catch a cold being out in that weather,* she thought. She walked into her bedroom to retrieve a fresh hanky from her night table. As she bent down, she noticed that the top drawer was wide open and pulled completely out. *I know I never would have left it that way this morning. I never do.* Else knew instantly what had transpired: she had been the victim of a robbery. Her jewelry box was open—only empty compartments stared back at her. In years past she had kept many of her beautiful jewels in a bank vault. Lately she had decided to wear the things Walter had given her through the many years of their happy marriage. Whenever an opportunity presented itself, she wore some of the stunning pieces Walter had fashioned for her. *What good does it do to keep them in a safe all the time? I'm heavily insured. That should be good enough.*

Not only had she been robbed of all her jewels, but a few thousand marks she had on hand were taken as well. She picked up her phone and called the police. She didn't bother to involve Rudolf since they weren't on speaking terms at the moment. The young police officer rang her doorbell, and she admitted him into the apartment. She answered all of his questions, and he completed the report. "Please notify your insurance company of the theft as soon as possible. We will send them a copy of my report pertaining to this investigation." And he was gone.

Else called and reported the theft. The insurance agent with whom she spoke was rather noncommittal. Much would depend on whether the thieves were caught. The likelihood was slim since her description of the young woman was rather sketchy and even more so of the likely accomplice whom she had only seen from the back as they made their speedy getaway. She still could not believe her own gullibility. *How could I have been so stupid as to have fallen for this ploy? I must be losing my marbles,* she thought.

Else got busy at her trusted typewriter and fired off letters to the insurance company. Already in her early communiques with the insurance agent, she discovered that the company declined paying her the eighty-five thousand marks at which her jewelry was appraised. She received a check in the amount of two thousand marks toward the cash she had lost. And that was it.

She took the insurance company to court and initially fought her own battles. Else was well-versed in legalese and actually enjoyed going into battle with anyone trying to cheat her out of what she believed to be rightfully hers. By the time the case had gone to appeal, she engaged the services of a shrewd lawyer. Else was well into her ninetieth year when she had exhausted all appeals.

The final ruling: *Yes, she had been betrayed and robbed, but the thieves had not broken into her apartment. She, herself, had admitted the thieves into her home; and therefore, she personally was responsible for her loss.* She didn't get another pfennig from the insurer and was stuck with all court costs and attorney's fees.

While Else was well known all of her life for her resoluteness and strength, some referred to her as a steel magnolia. It was with bitterness in her heart that she accepted her fate. She never quite recovered from the episode of utter betrayal. Else had lost all faith in mankind and remained on her guard for the rest of her days.

The Fine Art of Barbecuing

AFTER lengthy travels through the American West with family visiting from Germany, we were all glad to be finally back home and able to do as we pleased. Each of us was tired of studying menus at least three times a day. Aside from sleeping in our own beds, being able to sit down to a home-cooked meal brought as much pleasure as anything we could think of.

Laura decided to make it a typical American holiday meal to celebrate the end of my family's visit. Her choice was a standing rib roast with all the trimmings. Normally, we would have baked the roast in the oven, first searing it at a very high heat to seal in all the wonderful juices and then roasting the meat until finished at a somewhat lower temperature.

My dear wife had cleaned her stove just before we departed for the Wild West, and it had remained perfectly clean in our absence. Knowing what a mess preparing the rib roast could visit upon the clean stove, she decided to have me do the roast on our outdoor grill. Neither one of us had ever done a roast in this manner but thought it should work just fine. *People do whole turkeys on their grills. Why shouldn't one be able to do a standing rib roast?*

Since I don't do messy very well and always use a foil liner or foil wrapping whenever cooking anything on the grill, Laura had prepared a good-sized heavy-duty foil tray upon which I was to place the meat. I dutifully preheated the grill to bring its temperature up to snuff. Then I placed the foil tray directly above the coals and situated the well-seasoned roast in the pan. *Voila!* The roast was on its own and cooking away.

We decided to have a glass of wine before dinner and were enjoying our chitchat in the living room. The sliding door to the deck was closed to keep any possible smoke out of the house. *That was the whole idea of cooking outdoors anyway. Who wants to have the cooking smells in the house when you can keep them outdoors?* And a timer was set according to the weight of the roast, allowing the grill to do its proper thing.

After about thirty minutes, my cousin was peering across his wineglass and noted puffs of smoke blowing past the glass of the sliding door. "Do you smell something burning?" he said as he turned to me.

"Must be the roast," I replied.

"I think we should check it—you just never know." And so we got up and walked out to the deck. Good thing I had moved the grill as far away from the house as I had. The entire grill was engulfed in flames, fire emanating from every tiny opening between the grill and its hood. We knew we were in trouble the second we looked at the inferno facing us.

Trying to open the hood made the flames go even crazier. So we slammed down the thing and thought quickly. We can't use the fire extinguisher; that would ruin the roast. Perhaps we should not worry about the roast and worry about the house instead. "What about some soda water?" said my cousin. Luckily, because of our German company, we had enough of that stuff in the house. Germans don't like to drink tap water and don't like bottled water without gas, as they say.

Laura got us a quart bottle of club soda and we went to work. As someone gingerly lifted the hood of the grill, I generously doused the flames with the soda water. And lo and behold, the grease fire was put out. The roast was a tad singed but none the worse for wear. As we sat down to our special American barbecued dinner, all decided that it had turned out just fine. I conveyed to Laura and our guests that it was *einmalig,* meaning that it was a one-time adventure in preparing a standing rib roast on the grill. I hoped they all enjoyed it.

As we were relating this tale of woe to Laura's sister the other day, she shared a similar experience she had had a number of years ago when she was a young bride. She turned to her husband: "Do you remember my experience with barbecuing when we were first married?"

"Do I?! You almost set the house on fire."

Elaine continued. "We bought this ninety-nine dollar grill; and to protect our major investment from walking off the deck, Charles decided to chain it to the house with a heavy steal chain that could be locked. I decided to cook a pork roast on the rotisserie spit, using some fabulous barbecue sauce I had read about. Charles wasn't home, and I experimented with getting the roast going on my own. I didn't know the combination of the lock on the chain. So I just moved the grill away from the house as far as I could—which wasn't very far.

"Being a young bride, I followed the cooking instructions closely. When I was satisfied with my efforts, I started up the grill and turned on the rotisserie. I checked the roast after forty minutes and made a similar discovery as you did with your standing rib roast. The only difference was, I couldn't move the grill further away from the house. I did have a fire extinguisher and knew how to use it. I didn't give a hoot about the roast. I just didn't want to lose my happy home. After the first dousing with the foam, I grabbed the spit with a heavy mitt and tossed the whole flaming thing over the edge of the deck. And would you believe? It burned a hole in our lawn. I'm telling you, that was the last time I used the chained-down grill to barbecue anything." All of us had a good laugh while eating steak that had been grilled to perfection indoors on the George Foreman Grill.

The Marvel of Human Language

LINGUISTS, anthropologists, and other scientists studying human behavior and traits have wrestled for years with questions pertaining to aspects that distinguish man from other creatures in the animal kingdom. Most believe and still hold the view that one of these is language. It has been demonstrated that primates can be taught American Sign Language, albeit on a very elementary level. However, most humans hold the view that the mastery of language, allowing us to share, communicate, and preserve ideas, is the one element that clearly separates and distinguishes us from the other animals on this planet.

All of us are fascinated with babies. Modern technology and current philosophies regarding the creation of babies and their grand entrance into this world have shaped our views of these helpless little creatures. Less than fifty years ago, no man in his right mind would have gone to classes with his pregnant wife in preparation for being actually and personally involved in the birthing process. That was all women's stuff.

Isn't it great that most men today are physically and emotionally present during this event?

Babies of almost all of God's creatures are fascinating to us. Zoo attendance has a tendency to increase dramatically when the arrival of offspring of one critter or another is announced in the media. I am no different from most humans. Baby animals are cute—and many human babies steal your heart as they snuggle up to you in their search for warmth and the touch of loving hands.

I speak from recent personal experience. During the holidays, we spent time with our grand-nephew, David, a wise old boy of thirty-three months, and his sister, Colleen, a cuddly seven-month-old charmer. I had been forewarned that she would indeed steal my heart upon meeting her. And she did. Colleen didn't have to say anything; just looking at me with those big blue eyes and giving me one of those irresistible smiles did the trick. Of course, it didn't hurt that she is almost a carbon copy of her mom, whom we have had the pleasure of loving for thirty years.

Not having had children of our own, we are fortunate that our siblings have allowed us to be surrogate parents to their children. Our nephews and niece, and now their children, brighten our days as we move into the autumn of our lives.

But I am digressing, which is easily done when thinking and talking about babies. They are such spontaneous and lively creatures. As you can probably surmise, both my wife and I are completely taken by the latest additions to our extended family. There hardly has been a conversation of any sort in the last few weeks that does not involve some reference to David or Colleen.

Colleen is indeed a beautiful baby and a real love. But I

honestly have to say, and I have always felt this way, that I am absolutely done in by toddlers who are experimenting with human communication. In another two years, it will be Colleen's turn to make her grand entrance on the stage of language. Of course, if she runs true to form, it will be much sooner. For now, her older brother, David, holds forth in that venue.

Not only does he hold forth, he dominates it; he is a walking and talking machine. Indeed, he exhibits some very minor articulation errors that undoubtedly will receive the professional attention of his mom. After all, she is a speech-language pathologist. But the thing that knocks all of us for a loop is David's uncanny language ability. You would not dare utter anything around him that you would not want to be repeated elsewhere. He seems to be a regular linguistic sponge, absorbing, digesting, repeating, and using appropriately what has been within earshot just a few minutes ago.

There is no question about it; he is a very smart boy. Parents, grandparents, and uncles and aunts are in full agreement on that. Based on some of David's linguistic prowess, some might say that he is a little smart-ass—and sometimes he is. But his abilities to comprehend and use language have shaped his behavior. No, he isn't a perfect little angel. Let's face it; he is only thirty-three months old. However, a child who, when wanting to act like a typical toddler, is asked, "Do you want to be a happy or an unhappy child?"—and then responds with appropriate behavior—underscores the marvel of human language ability. He knew exactly what his mother meant, he understood the consequences, and he acted accordingly and appropriately.

It was an absolute delight to sit down for Christmas dinner and have little David lead us in prayer. He didn't even have to be prompted—he simply did it and did it with style and linguistically correct. Of course, humorous scenarios please us adults the most.

The other day he got in his grandfather's way while he was attempting to vacuum. "David, would you mind moving over there while I finish my job?" elicited the following from David: "Oh Poppa, I didn't wealize I was in your way." Grandpa mumbled to himself, "I didn't wealize that you knew the word 'realize'."

While playing with his Auntie Laura in October, he told her she was "Gordy the Worker" and he was her supervisor. When asked what that meant, he told his aunt she had to do the job because he was her boss and he could tell her what to do. By the time I was Gordy the Worker at Christmas time, he advised me that he was the head man. I didn't even bother to ask him what that was supposed to mean. I knew the answer in advance.

Sitting securely strapped into his car seat, David observed his grandfather making a right turn on red, which promptly elicited this less than three-year-old young man to exclaim, "Poppa, you just went through a red light." What could Poppa say in reply?

Yes, all of these anecdotes are cute and charming, and we love to share them with friends and family. But the truth is, David's communication abilities are indeed a marvel of human brain power. They demonstrate in a most profound way that our lives as humans on this earth are shaped by our unique ability to use and manipulate language, an ability that clearly separates and distinguishes us from all other animals.

The Good Samaritan

AFTER an early appointment in Winter Park, my wife and I had to make a quick getaway to Denver. She was to be at a surprise birthday party for a friend at a restaurant near the Tiffany Plaza Mall. We just made it down there with a few minutes to spare after we had maneuvered through the construction site between town and the ski area.

I dropped her off in front of the restaurant. We agreed that the luncheon would probably take two hours. I would wait for her in the air-conditioned lobby starting at a quarter to two. With that, she made her entrance into the place.

It looked like it was going to be a hot day. So, I searched for a shady spot to park the car. I was lucky. Not really too far out of the way was an ideal bank of parking places that had been sought out by only one other person. Actually, the area looked like it would remain shady for most of the day. *How lucky could I be?*

As soon as I got out of the car and locked it, I noticed an entrance to the mall. In search of a restroom, I found one right away near a movie theater that appeared to be operational but wasn't opened yet. Too bad! That might have been a good way to kill a couple of hours on a hot day. However, in the first place they weren't open; second, none of the movies on the bill had any appeal to me.

Having taken care of business, I strolled through the mall. *What a dismal place*. Most storefronts were vacant. There was a crummy-looking fur storage place with ratty-looking specimens in the windows offered for sale at markedly reduced prices. *Not very enticing*. I could have bought myself a wig or have one restyled. I decided to stick with what's left of my natural hair. There was a plethora of not-so-appealing restaurants just opening for the luncheon trade. I had spotted an "Old Chicago" pizza place at the mall across Hampden Road. I would head that way in due time.

As I emerged from a different entrance to the Tiffany Mall, I spotted a Walgreen's to my left and turned in that direction as soon as I had shielded my eyes with sunglasses. Passing the store, I heard a woman yell at an elderly gentleman who just parked his car across from hers. "Honey, do me a favor. Get me one of them shopping carts from Walgreen's. I need it to hold onto."

She was about seventy-five feet from where I stood. I could see the carts right by the door inside the store. I decided to get the cart for her since I had plenty of time and nothing specifically planned. Cart in hand, I emerged from the store and told the elderly gentleman to go ahead, I would take the cart to the lady. "Thank you, sir. That's nice of you. I was in a hurry to get to the pharmacy."

I pushed the cart down the parking lot and confronted my helpless little Jewish lady.

"Oh, thanks for getting me that cart, honey. Darn, I just dropped my cane."

"May I pick that up for you?"

"Oh, that would be kind. I can't let go of this. I don't want to fall again. I'm just getting over a broken hip."

I got the picture. "How are you going to maneuver the walker, cane, and the shopping cart all at the same time?" I asked her.

"Oh, dahlink, I will just need to put the cane in the cart. The walker will stay in the car. Now, I need to find something in my purse. I know I had this coupon for Walgreen's." With that she started digging in the bottomless pit of a satchel attached to the walker that she had referred to as her purse.

It seemed like it contained hundreds of coupons. I was beginning to wonder what I had gotten myself into and kept telling myself to be patient. *Someday you might be like that.* She placed her wallet and keys in the basket of the cart. Along with those she had a few coupons that apparently were not the one for which she was searching in her treasure trove. A sudden gust of wind began to play with the coupons and wallet placed in the basket.

"Is it OK for me to hold onto these before the wind blows them away?" I asked her, thinking of protecting myself. I didn't want her to get the idea I was trying to rob her. I could just see her suddenly screaming for help. *What the hell did I get myself into?*

"That's OK, honey. It is really nice of you to help me. Now here is that coupon I was looking for. Could you get that steamer out of the backseat of my car? Also those plastic tubes? Put them into the cart; I need to take that contraption back to them for a refund. This coupon is for a better one that they have on sale this week."

I was getting the idea of what she was trying to do. I got all the stuff out of the car that she had requested to be placed into the shopping cart. "May I close all your car doors?" I asked.

"Yes, you may. But you need to fold up my walker and put it in the backseat behind the driver's seat," she instructed me. So, after closing both doors on the passenger side, I walked around the back of the car to attend to the walker.

"I will need to lock the car with my key before I can go to Walgreen's," commented my little lady.

I had folded her walker together and was ready to place it in the car when the lady decided to cut me off by stepping in front of me in her attempt to lock the driver's door. The woman was wearing some old-fashioned glasses with absolutely gigantic lenses. She ran into the back of my right shoulder with the edge of her left lens and frame.

"You stupid man! Look what you have done? You bumped into my glasses and poked my eye. Now I have to see the doctor again!" she screamed loudly at me, calling attention to us.

I quickly placed the walker in the car, closed the door, and checked to see if she was all right. She was still fussing about her glasses when I made sure she was holding onto the shopping cart I had gotten for her.

"I'm sorry, Ma'am. I didn't do that on purpose. I was just trying to help you." I decided there was no point in letting her know that she had been the one who had walked into me and caused the unpleasant collision. She marched off, pushing her cart up the slight incline, mumbling some terms of endearment as she turned away from me. I stood there for a moment in the blazing sun. *That's what you get for trying to be a Good Samaritan.*

I crossed Hampden to Tamarac Square, bought myself a *USA Today*, found a comfortable chair in the air-conditioned pizza parlor, and lost myself in the front-page saga about the 2003 blackout involving fifty million people in the East. Having taken a deep breath and positively delighted in the consumption of the Old Chicago pizza, I assessed my experience with the old lady: *Count your blessings, bud; your problems were not* that *bad. All things considered, she could have accused you of trying to rob an old, helpless woman.*

A Night to Remember

LAST year, dear friends told us about a venturous and charming few days they spent in the big city between the holidays. "We stayed at this fabulous old hotel in the downtown area of Denver. We had Christmas dinner with the family and then checked into the hotel early in the evening. It was so much fun playing tourist right after the holiday! Our accommodations were fantastic, actually quite elegant. We just loved being in Denver between Christmas and New Year's."

Hearing this story, I turned to my wife: "If we don't have any house guests for the holidays, why not plan on a visit to the city next year? It sounds like a lot of fun. As I always say, 'Nothing ventured, nothing gained!'"

The holidays approached, and we learned that our friends, two couples, also had plans for a repeat performance of their post-Christmas city fix. We made our reservations at the hotel independently, since all of us would arrive at different times. We also ordered tickets for a matinee performance of the "Nutcracker" for the six of us. Dinner plans were left open and subject to discussion while having breakfast at Dixon's the day after Christmas.

We took our time and enjoyed our festively decorated home on Christmas morning. There weren't that many presents to unpack. For the two of us, we have learned not to dream up too many surprises. Now and then we manage to come up with an original idea. After lunch, we headed down toward Denver. It was a glorious, sunny day in the high country. We almost hated to leave it.

The drive to Denver was uneventful and pleasant. We arrived at the hotel shortly before four o'clock. The lobby was splendidly decorated with an absolutely gigantic natural tree. It was like walking into the opening scene of the *Nutcracker*. The warmth from the open fireplace felt great. There was little staff on hand. The doorman who greeted us was almost a little bit too friendly. He took charge of our suitcases, walked us over to the concierge, and informed us that he would park our car in the garage after he had shown us to our room.

The concierge was a young Japanese man, still perfecting his English skills. "Do you have leselvation? Undel what name?" He found the reservation promptly. After filling out the registration, he handed me the key attached to a giant key ring. "When you try open rock, turn key in rower rock to light and in upper rock to reft." I got his drift right away but decided to have him repeat the instructions for good measure. All of us smiled and we followed the doorman and our luggage to the elevator.

I opened the hotel room with the key, following the instructions of the concierge. It worked. As we walked into the room, both of us thought we weren't seeing correctly. Neither one of us said a word, but we knew what was running through our minds. *Why the hell did we leave home for this?* I tipped the doorman. As soon as he had closed the door behind him, I walked over to the small window and lowered the venetian blinds, not wanting to stare at the brick wall facing me. *This is not what we had in mind,* we thought but did not verbalize it.

My wife began to unpack our suitcases and tried finding places to put things. There was a small coat closet and a large armoire with one shelf, largely occupied by a TV. There was no place to sit but on the bed. By the time she was finished with the task of settling in, it was getting dark and our stomachs signaled that it was perhaps time for Christmas dinner.

We took the elevator downstairs to the elegant lobby. As we stepped off the elevator, I spotted a bench and asked my wife to have a seat. I had decided to be a squeaky wheel. I walked over to our Japanese fellow and inquired, "Is that the best you can do for accommodations? Our friends told us about fabulous suites and not some dingy old room. We are utterly disappointed. We are both wondering why we left our comfortable home for this."

"Ret me see what I can do. Would you rike loom with view? Me have one on fourth floor. Would you mind moving flom other loom to this one?"

"How about letting us look at it before we decide to move. We are completely unpacked." I took the key and fetched my wife. "Why didn't you think of this a little earlier before I unpacked everything?

"I agree with you. I was terribly disappointed in the looks of our room, but I didn't want to say anything. You know me, I don't like to make any waves. Well, let's go and look at this other room." Laura was undoubtedly pissed.

We followed the specific instructions on how to open the

door. "This is a lot more like it," we agreed. The room indeed had a nice view of the town; it was spacious, furnished with lovely antique pieces, and was more what we had envisioned. "You go upstairs and start packing. I'll let him know that we are moving."

As I walked up to the large desk, my Japanese friend beamed at me and said, "You rike new loom?" and I answered in the affirmative. "Yes, my wife is already packing up in room 801."

I helped Laura gather up our belongings, not that it was all that much. Soon everything was properly put in its respective drawers and on the right kind of hanger; we decided to make a second try at going out for dinner. We turned in the keys for both rooms and asked the concierge what time the restaurant in the hotel would open.

"Oh, lestaulant not open today. Vely few open on Chlistmas. You rike rooking at our rist of lestaulant open?" We were both terribly disappointed, but what could we do? We looked down the list and discovered the Ship's Tavern at the Brown Palace was open for dinner. I noted under the comments that we should expect a long wait. We emerged from the lobby and decided to walk up the 16th Street Mall. The decorations were lovely. There were hardly any people on the streets. "I really can't blame people for not wanting to leave their homes. If we do this again, we'll come down the day after Christmas. That would be OK, but on Christmas we'll stay home unless we are visiting family." I agreed with her.

When we got to the restaurant, we learned that we had a one-hour wait. We sat in the opulent lobby of the Brown Palace and ordered a drink. Fortunately for us, the waiter brought us a dish of nuts along with the drinks. We ate those nuts as if they were going out of style. It was fascinating watching the different people seated around us. Before long we were paged. Dinner and our waiter could not have been better. We decided to take the trolley back to the hotel; that is, we got off a block from where we stayed.

Smiling faces and glasses of sherry by the fire greeted us upon our return. I retrieved our key and thanked the concierge once again for letting us move to the nicer room. Not knowing if our friends would try to locate us by the time they arrived later, we decided to lie down on the bed fully dressed. In typical male fashion, I operated the remote control to the TV, grazing the offerings of the day. Among them, I noted Deborah Kerr and Cary Grant in *A Night to Remember*. I gave the remote a rest, and we watched for a very short time before both of us fell sound asleep.

We woke up shortly after eleven o'clock. The movie was long over. "Let's get ready for bed. Lord knows we have a full day planned for tomorrow." We had gotten completely undressed and had everything neatly hung when Laura turned to me. "You won't believe this, but I left our night clothes under the pillows in the other room. Would you mind seeing your little friend downstairs and retrieving my nightgown and your pajamas from room 801?"

We stood there and laughed our heads off. When I recovered, I threw on a shirt and some jeans and proceeded to head downstairs. With a sheepish grin on my face, I approached the concierge. "I hope you didn't give the other room to anyone. We left our nightclothes under the pillows."

"Oh no, I not give loom to other peoper. You rucky. Here key. You lemembel how unrock?"

"Yes, sir. I'll be right back." I retrieved the items in question and promptly returned to the desk. As he saw me coming, he gesticulated to a young woman standing next to him—apparently his relief. He was holding one hand in front of his face, the other in front of his fly, giggling like a young girl. It was obvious that I had them in stitches. As I handed him the key, I said, "Now don't you wet your pants. I know it is very funny. I write little ditties. [I wasn't sure he understood what that meant!] I believe this will make a cute one. I'll call it 'A Night to Remember.'"

A Question of Balance

MOST everyone has heard the expression "It's like riding a bicycle," which implies that once you have learned something, you never forget how to do it. It's a cliché like "Use it or lose it." We live in a world of clichés; we are surrounded by them every day. One that drives me absolutely crazy is "It's déjà vu all over again"; it's completely redundant. The ignoramuses, especially the talking heads in the media, don't seem to realize they are saying, "It's happening all over again all over again." Sometimes I feel like screaming at them. Of course, they wouldn't hear me.

The funny thing about "It's like riding a bicycle" is that it assumes you must have mastered riding a bike to begin with. For most young children, it's a rite of passage. We start off with a tricycle around age two and can't wait to progress to a two-wheeler by the time we reach age three or four. Learning to master the bike is the second step toward independence. The first one is to use those things we call legs; that is, we learn to crawl and then to walk. It allows us to move away from those who have birthed and fed us. On wheels, of course, we can get away even faster and further.

Then there's me, who never learned how to ride a bike in the first place. I really don't know why. I suppose it might have had something to do with the availability of a bike. But my brother, less than two years older than I, managed somehow to get hold of a bike and learned to ride it just fine. I vaguely remember being put on a bike when I was quite young. Maybe I wasn't ready for such independence yet. I truly don't know. But for whatever reason, I just didn't get it. Not quite like the current Subaru commercial, it also drives me up the wall, hearing it again and again.

Just the other day, Laura was discussing with a friend their most recent adventure to Europe, which included hiking and biking in Italy. I couldn't help overhearing my wife's responses: "That sounds great. I would love to do that some time. But, of course, I would have to do the biking by myself. Hektor doesn't ride a bike. He never did learn how to master two wheels. Oh, he has tried, but to no avail."

Looking back, I had to agree with her that I did try. The last time was in my fifties. When we visit my family in Germany, Laura loves to go for bike rides with my sister-in-law, Margarethe, who is an avid bike rider. They live near a lake that is surrounded by a bike trail. Lake Baldeney, or Lago Baldino as some locals say jokingly, makes for easy biking of ten to twelve kilometers—a nice ride on any sunny morning. The family had kept their canoes—and later their bikes—at the Yellow-Blue Canoe Club for fifty years. I remember watching my brother refinish a wooden canoe with his then girlfriend in the early 1950s. Their son learned to use a canoe there, and later Margarethe tried to teach her granddaughters the joys of riding the waves of the river Ruhr. The girls never did learn to like canoeing; all they used the boathouse for was their early birthday parties. Just a couple of weeks ago, Margarethe told us on the phone that their last canoes were sold. "Soon we will have to find a different place to store our bikes; the canoe club is dissolving. The young aren't interested in it, and we are getting too old to keep it going. We are using up our kitty to make some trips with the remaining club members. When the treasury has been exhausted, we'll call it quits. If we don't spend the money ourselves, the funds will have to be turned over to the city. That's the law."

Well, in 1987 the four of us walked down to the infamous boathouse and picked up four bikes. "This is a great place for you to finally learn how to bike. You'll see that there's nothing to it. All you do is get your butt on the seat and start peddling," said my sister-in-law. "I'm so tired of you having to walk halfway around the lake to meet the three of us for lunch. Just try it, you'll like it." Talk about clichés!

On a sunny Sunday morning in early summer, it seemed like hordes of people had crawled out of the woodwork. Not only zillions of bicyclists but all the roller-bladers had emerged as well. Pedestrians have their own trails, but bikers and bladers share the same track. Off we went. As long as there were no oncoming riders, I was OK.

I did exactly as I was told; I got my butt on the seat and started peddling. At first I kept looking at the front wheel instead of ahead, trying to stay on the straight and narrow. "It's like dancing—you don't look at your feet," said Laura. "And remember, you have two kinds of brakes. You can brake with your pedals, and you can brake when you squeeze those things on your handlebars." That was useful information.

When I had tried biking years and years ago, brakes were activated only when you did something to the pedals. Obviously, we had come a long way, baby.

And then we hit the first really big snag of oncoming traffic, a large mixed group of bikers and bladers, zipping in and out of each other's way and coming straight at me. I didn't know where to go or how to avoid hitting some of them. I decided to use my brakes. *Which ones was I supposed to use? The ones on my feet or the ones on my hands? Maybe both? Oh, to heck with it, I'll just put my feet on the ground. That will stop this thing for sure.*

Of course, I should have remembered the old inertia trick. A body in motion stays in motion. As soon as I tried stopping my bike by putting my feet on the ground, I took a flying leap over the handlebars and landed on my knees in a puddle of mud. I was so embarrassed I felt neither pain nor the blood trickling from my scraped knees. Like a good fifty-three-year-old kid, I got back on the bike as soon as the snickering group had passed by. I think my brother was more embarrassed than I was.

I thought, *I'll lick this thing yet. I have started very few things in my life that I didn't finish very successfully eventually.* Well, we went along for a ways, with everyone, including myself, thinking, *I think he's got it.* Be darned if another large gang didn't come straight at us again. You can probably guess what happened. Yes, I did it with aplomb. This time, I did a number not just on my knees but also on my elbows. But as they say, all good things happen in threes. Back on the bike I went. The third episode took place less than halfway along the trail. My palms took the brunt this time. My sister-in-law looked me over carefully and threw her hands up in the air: "Now I believe it; you are not meant to ride a bicycle. You stick to four wheels. Maybe a bike with training wheels would work for you. You know, the kind old people use."

I looked like a little kid with my bloody and scraped knees, elbows, and palms and covered in mud from head to toe. I decided to push the bike back to the boathouse while Laura and my family finished the trek to the luncheon place across the lake. I found some bandages in the first-aid kit at the Yellow-Blue boathouse and washed myself. I dried the mud on my shirt and shorts with a hairdryer and brushed out the damage as well as possible. After this major overhaul, my appearance was markedly improved—not perfect, but somewhat presentable. As I was walking to the restaurant where we were to meet numerous old-time friends for lunch, a Sunday ritual, my bones began to ache. I was longing for some extra-strength Tylenol or its German equivalent. "This too shall pass," I said to myself as I was limping along. *There's no fool like an old fool* entered my mind a few times.

Of course, I was the center of attention as I greeted our old friends around the table. Everyone had been forewarned by the time I arrived on the scene. Actually, they had expected me to look far worse, not realizing that I would be slightly dusted off. Needless to say, I was the butt of everyone's jokes. I could take it.

Never again did I try learning to ride a bike. I decided that there must be some things in life we weren't meant to master. For me, it was biking.

Four years later, Mayo clinic discovered a pea-sized lesion deep in the right hemisphere of my brain, likely of congenital origin. When I spoke with my brother by phone, I told him that the doctors speculated that it might have affected my sense of balance, implying that this thing in my head probably caused me not to have the ability to ride a bike properly.

He fell for it hook, line, and sinker. I thought he would swallow it, since he has a tendency to get much of his info from German tabloids. He swears they always get it right. I never did have the heart to tell him that the speculation was mine and not that of the doctors at Mayo.

Anything but Fish

SHE has been gone for a number of years now. When she died, she was well into her nineties. Helen was a delightful woman. She was the mother of one of our dearest friends. Shirley and her husband had to be away from Winter Park for a weekend. I can't remember exactly what the cause was, but it had to be a good one. We were pleased to have Helen with us for the day.

She made her home in McCook, Nebraska, and liked living in the small western town—most of the time. The one-hundred-degree days of July and August didn't particularly agree with her. It was then that she would come for a visit to the high country.

We made it a point to see her often. She loved playing cards and was just plain fun to be around. Helen always was so positive. I have never forgotten the intriguing story she told us when she kept company with us on that particular weekend.

As my wife was getting ready to plan dinner for Saturday night, she casually turned to Helen: "Is there anything you can't eat or don't like to eat?" To her surprise, Helen had a quick answer: "I'll eat anything but fish!"

She had a funny expression on her face that was just begging for an explanation why she definitely disliked fish. "Of course, there was a time not so long ago that I would not have said that. Allow me to share a little story with you. It's a rather long tale, so please indulge an old lady."

Helen was four score and a few years in age but very young at heart. We gladly indulged her. We knew it would be a most interesting account.

"For my eightieth birthday, my girls and their husbands came to McCook for the celebration. When you get to be my age, you have grandchildren and great-grandchildren. I was looking forward to having so many of them sitting around my table for this auspicious occasion. My sons-in-law and some of the other menfolk decided to go fishing. They went to the Swanson Reservoir. Had a hell of good time and caught a lot of fish. They were good about cleaning the fish right by the water. No mess in my house. I thought what a great treat for the whole family.

"The guys cooked the fish on the grill outside; there wasn't even any seafood restaurant odor in the house from cooking all those fish. The girls made wonderful potato salad, fresh corn on the grill, and all kinds of special side dishes. Shirley made these great-tasting beans. It sure was a feast for the gods that was laid out on the sprawling table.

"I sat at the head of the table since I was obviously the matriarch of the family. One of my daughters said grace, and the meal was off and running. Shirley's husband spoke up: 'This is the nicest looking fish of them all. I thought it was perfect in size. We cooked it especially for you, Mom.' With that announcement, he elegantly placed the fish on my plate.

It really was pretty, although I would not have minded had he removed the colorful skin and the bones. I guess I was lucky they hadn't left the head on the creature.

"It took a few minutes for all the dishes to be passed around the table. Finally it was time for me to touch my fork to the chest of the fish. Once I laid back the skin, exposing the meat, I noticed that it was pure white, flaky, and cooked to perfection. 'You boys did all right catching this fish; such a treat to get it so fresh.'

"As I was taking my second bite, I thought I wasn't seeing right. It looked like something gold was blinking back at me. I took my fork and tried to expose the golden object just a little more. To my astonishment, I discovered that my fish apparently had swallowed a wedding band. All the womenfolk around the table sat there looking positively aghast.

"My daughter who lives in the area spoke up. 'Mom, I can't believe this. Do you remember, a few years ago, when we had that double murder in that little town near the Swanson Reservoir? It might have been Trenton. Some guy was two-timing his wife. When she found out, she decided to take matters in her own hands. She shot them in bed and then hacked them into pieces small enough for her to feed them to the fish in the reservoir. Her trial was all over the papers. You remember that, Mom, don't you? Do you think maybe your fish feasted on one of their corpses?'

"I almost threw up. I pushed away the plate with most of the untouched food. Shirley's husband, sitting next to me, pointed at his ring finger. What I saw was the white ring on his darkly tanned hand where he normally would have worn his wedding band. That devil knew about the murders in Trenton.

He and the other boys decided to pull a fast one on me. Now that the cat was out of the bag, they all laughed uproariously. I don't have to tell you, since that eightieth birthday celebration dinner, I have never eaten fish again."

Are You Buzzing Me?

I have known Bob for over forty years. We worked together at getting a new store operation off the ground in the early sixties. We shared our common miseries over a drink at the end of day. Often we ate our dinner together, compliments of the per diem arrangement with management. For Bob it was not fun to be separated from his wife and two children. They were biding their time a few hundred miles east. To top it all off, he had recently learned from his wife, Lora, that they would be blessed with a little surprise package in the months to come.

Myself, I was still dealing with the aftereffects of legal separation from my own family. It had been almost three years, and I hated being so far from my children. But a job was a job. The money was good, and it helped to pay the bills. Bob saw me go through the divorce process and eventually stood up for me when I was remarried. Even after I left the business world and went back to school, we always maintained a special bond with Bob and Lora.

Lora has been gone for almost nine years now. She fought a

valiant battle with cancer for a long time. I'm not sure of the exact number, but she and Bob were married for over forty years, a considerable length of sharing and becoming used to and dependent on one another. He was devastated and lost. His story unfolded as we were sitting around, catching up on old times.

"You know, I inherited this place from my mom. The family used to love to come down here to Pine Island. It never was fancy, but everyone could let their hair down and do exactly what they enjoyed. I loved the fishing and always had a little boat to take me around the area. More often than not, I'd manage to catch me a bunch of fish.

"I came down here after Lora passed on. I sat around in this place and cried and cussed a lot. I didn't think it was fair for me to be left alone in my retirement. I was firmly convinced that God did not do the right thing by me. In other words, I was feeling sorry for myself. I was drowning in self-pity.

"The only person I spoke to was my neighbor across the street, so to speak. He could tell how miserable I was. One day he lit into me. 'You need to get out of your place and think about living. Lora would want you to do that. Your wallowing in self-pity is the last thing she would have wished upon you.'

"I guess he was suggesting that I start looking for another mate. Just the thought of meeting women and the dating game scared the heck out of me. Somehow, I couldn't face the whole issue. My neighbor talked about this widow a couple of lanes away, the other side of the canal. She seemed to be a pleasant sort, perhaps a few years older than myself. 'We know her well. How about if we arrange for you to meet at our place? There is no harm in getting out and making the acquaintance of a neighbor.'

"I finally gave in. We met. Knowing what the purpose of the arrangement was, we kind of looked each other over. Josephine is a very tiny woman. During the course of the evening, I discovered that she was a little spitfire, full of life and in good spirits. She had many talents and interests, many totally different from mine. When we parted company that evening, I went home and began thinking about something other than myself.

"It was a step in the right direction. A couple days later I had the gumption to pick up the phone and called her. Before long, we had our first dinner date on our own. We talked about our children and grandchildren. We touched on our backgrounds and what had brought us to this point in our lives. Somehow the age difference was inconsequential. *Who was counting?* Josephine was someone pleasant to talk to and most enjoyable to be around. After dinner, we stopped by my place, and I showed her some of my family photos. Eventually, I took her home, and we parted company on a handshake. I wasn't quite ready to kiss her on our very first real date.

"'I'll give you a ring. Next time we'll have dinner at my place, if that is OK with you?' was Josephine's parting shot.

"'Of course; I'll look forward to it.'

"A few days went by, and eventually Josephine called. The date was set. Normally, I don't get dressed up down here. For the occasion, I decided to wear a suit and tie. I also remembered to buy her some flowers. You can't forget about these niceties when you go courting.

"Josephine had fixed a nice dinner and set a pretty table. I was impressed by her domestic skills, and she was clearly taken by my chivalrous attempts. The evening was a success. After dinner, it was my turn to glimpse into Josephine's family by looking at photos of her husband of over fifty years and their offspring, now already in their fourth generation.

"The evening was decidedly a success. I learned so much about her. Among other things, I discovered that she was a talented artist in various media and that she enjoyed pursuing her interests. Life was not boring for her at all. One thing she shared with me was her lack of companionship, someone with whom to appreciate life's daily events. And so we continued our courtship for a couple of months. We informed our children of our mutual discovery. Before long, we decided to terminate a beautiful friendship and got married. We celebrated the event on a cruise ship.

"Josephine sold her home in Florida; I sold mine in Detroit. We have been spending the summers in Manistee, Michigan, where Josephine has a lovely home near a lake. We enjoy being in my place here at Flamingo Bay during the winter. It usually takes us a couple of months traveling comfortably with the motor home between south and north and vice versa. We stop and smell the roses along the way and check on the kids as we mosey along.

"Thinking about our first trip north brings back some special memories. I asked Josephine if she would mind if we stopped by the cemetery while we were in Detroit. 'Of course, I wouldn't mind. You and Lora were married to each other for almost fifty years. I would expect you to want to check out her gravesite.'

"'Oh, I didn't think you had any objections to my wanting to go, but I wasn't so sure that you wanted to go with me. I'm pleased that you are willing to join me.' And so one sunny day in early June, we made our way to Forest Lawn Cemetery. I parked the car, and we walked hand in hand to Lora's grave. It wasn't long before we stood in front of her final resting place. It was in pretty good shape. One of the kids obviously had visited their mother's grave for Memorial Day. The flowers placed there had wilted and the vase had been blown over by a gust of wind. As I reached down to retrieve and upright the vase, we both heard an unusual sound emanating from the grave.

"We stood back and listened. It sounded like an angry buzz. I turned to Josephine. 'That gives me the creeps. It almost sounds like a voice from the grave. You don't suppose Lora is trying to communicate with us? Maybe she is angry with me for getting married again? Maybe she is mad because I married so soon after her death? I've never believed in such things. But this is really weird. What do you think?'

"'I'm not sure about weird, but it is unusual. I don't believe in ghosts either. There has to be a simple explanation. Let me look at it closer.'

"Josephine bent down and picked up the dead flowers. Next, she tried reaching for the vase. As she touched it, the noisy buzz became even angrier. 'Whatever is buzzing is caught under the vase. I'm going to lift it. Curiosity has gotten the better of me.'

"With that she picked up the vase and we discovered the biggest, black bumblebee either of us had ever seen. Apparently it had gotten caught underneath the vase. As soon as the noisy critter saw daylight, it took off like a bat out of hell.

"If you don't think that gave us something to think and

talk about for a few days. Who knows, might it have been Lora? You know, she could get awfully mad with that Russian temperament of hers."

We didn't know what to say to Bob in response to the story he had shared with us. One thing we could not recall was Lora's temperament—Russian or otherwise. To us she had always appeared to be a most docile and laid-back personality.

"Well, that's a side of Lora we never knew. Interesting!"

Bob had to have the last word. "Let me assure you, she was what you seem to recall. But when something got under her bonnet, she surely knew how to buzz!"

Stranger in the Yard

DORA and Randy Robin were busily hopping among the pine needles on the lot at 665 Hughes. They were searching for the ever-elusive breakfast treat for their young. Danny, the haughty young buck, had decided to sample the delectable, delightful delphiniums gracing the flower garden in front of the box. Much to everyone's annoyance, the squirrel tribe belonging to Sandy and Sylvester were fussing at each other vociferously.

As Dora looked up momentarily peering across the yard, she spotted the creature who had come to their rescue so often this year. Whenever possible, he had been activating those snakelike water-dispersing devices all over the yard. Despite the very dry summer, Dora and Randy had managed to find food for their young and themselves. In the coolness of the morning and evening, the pine needles were lush and soft with the moistness the creature had brought them with those black snakes crawling all over the woodsy lot.

"But what is he doing now?" chirped Randy busily hopping alongside Dora. Before she had a chance to respond to him, Charlie the Chickadee replied, "He's carrying a bench out into the woods. And guess what? He's setting a cute little girl on it."

"She is cute. I like the hat. It will shade her face from the hot summer sun. Do you think she will sit there all the time? She doesn't seem to move at all." Dora kept right on hopping and rambling as she kept a close eye on the little girl and the guy in the yard fussing over her.

When the mistress of the box joined her guy in the yard, they were chitchatting about the placement of the pretty little girl. "I love the basket she is carrying. Maybe a plant might look good in it. We will have to look for something that will thrive in partial shade. Impatiens don't do well here because of our frosty nights. It's too bad. They do so well in shade elsewhere. Well, we'll have to look for something else," said the one wearing an apron.

The guy came up with a different idea: "I think she could carry some water in that basket. I bet the birds and squirrels would love it."

"Dora, look what he is doing. He's getting one of the black snakes. Oh, wow; he's putting water in the girl's basket! We need to check it out as soon as they disappear into the big box," chirped Randy.

"I'm not going to wait for that," said Charlie the Chickadee. "Those creatures don't scare me at all. They're perfectly harmless. All they do is water the blooming things, move the black snakes about, pull a few of the weeds, and drive in and out of that thing that keeps sliding up and down. They never hurt us.

"See that bluebird box over on that big tree? Clarinda and I raised our young in there a few weeks ago. He knew we were occupying someone else's abode, but he didn't care.

Furthermore, when he sprayed with those black snakes, he always made sure our brood didn't get wet. Like I said, that guy is very friendly. Sometimes he even tries to talk to us. Of course, he speaks a different language. Not only that, he even sounds different from all the other creatures whose paths we cross around here. Well, I'm going to see what this girl and her basket are all about."

With that, Charlie swooped down from his perch in the nearby aspen tree. As he landed on the hat of the little girl, he could see his reflection in the mirror-like surface of the water in the basket. "Funny, the girl didn't budge when I landed on her hat. Maybe I am so light that she didn't even feel me or know I was there. She appears to be so quiet. She doesn't seem to converse with those creatures who carried her out into the woods. Usually creatures always chatter. It's almost like they're trying to compete with us. Very different though. Well, I'm ready for a good drink. Perhaps a bath? Why not, before the other critters discover this brand-new fountain."

Charlie landed on the rim of the basket and repeatedly dipped his beak into the cool and refreshing water. "I wish Clarinda would get back soon. She'd enjoy a good drink. By gosh, we might even take a bath together. That hasn't happened for a long time. Guess we've just been too busy feeding and raising those kids. It took quite an effort to get them their flying licenses. Finally, they are off and on their own. It's great! We love them dearly, but it's always nice when it's just the two of us again for a little while. And, of course, there's always another spring."

"Hey, Charlie, are you going to get out of there soon? Dora and I would like to take a nip and then a refreshing dip in the water."

"All right, I'll get out of here. I was hoping Clarinda would get back to join me. No such luck!" With that Charlie flew up into the aspen and busily looked around for Clarinda, who was not to be seen.

"Come on Dora, let's sample the fresh water. I see Danny, the deer, approaching from over there. Once he and Diana and little Duffy discover the basket, they'll slurp it empty right down to the last drop. Then we'll have to wait for a refill from our friendly guy. You know how those deer are. They eat and drink everything in sight. Sometimes I wish they, the bear, and the moose would stay out of our civilized neighborhood. I know we shared the land with them once upon a time; but back then, they were happy to retreat to the wilds for most of the summer. It's become so dry that they visit us a whole lot more and don't seem to go away at all in summer. I guess hunger and thirst are terrible for everyone. Uh-oh, here they come."

In the meantime, the two-legged creatures retreated into their box with the sliding things. They were looking down at their peaceful yard. Hektor said, "I think the birds really like the little girl. She is cute and fits right in. Oh look, there's Danny and his family. Once they discover the water in the basket, I'll have to fill it often. Otherwise, our fine-feathered friends will be mightily disappointed. That was a wonderful present Elaine and Charles gave you for your birthday. The little girl won't stay a stranger for long. Everyone will learn to love her when she sits in the garden every summer. We'll have to think of a name for her. How about 'Joy'?"

Generation Gap

CHARLIE and Clarinda were easily flitting from branch to branch, now and then shaking off some of the fluffy snow. "Wasn't it nice that we had such lovely weather for Valentine's Day?" chirped Clarinda.

"Never mind Valentine's Day. It's a long weekend as well with President's Day. You know what that means, don't you? Hordes of people will be up here to glide around on those long boards. Well, it's OK. They'll all be gone again by Monday afternoon. Hope they enjoy all this nice white gold. Have you taken a look around this yard? Looks like Morris the Moose has been here."

"Looks to me more like Morris and entourage. They sure leave some very distinct calling cards. Take a gander over there. It's not Morris, but Mara, his spouse, with last year's baby in tow. The youngin looks just like her. Couldn't be more than a year old."

"I don't understand. To me, they all look alike. I can't see any family resemblance. Well, females are just better at figuring out such things. Now watch this, how they work their way through the yard, checking out one willow patch after another. What's she calling her offspring? I swear she just snorted 'Myrna'."

"Mara is much taller, so she can crane her neck and reach up with her snout and drag down those really tall branches. With her strong teeth, she can handle the thicker, older branches. Myrna on the other hand sticks to the low stuff. She seems to prefer nibbling away at the younger and thinner sprouts of willow. Mara has taught her well. The youngin seems to be doing just fine."

"I guess the folks in the box have discovered their friendly visitors. Can you see him opening those lacy things hanging in their glassy openings? He's got that clickedy thing in front of his face again. Watch this. Those big moving things keep slowing down on the road. Creatures are walking toward Mara and Myrna. More clickedy gadgets. I understand they capture permanent glimpses of us with those things."

"How come, we never attract all those folks? Must be because they are so big and we are so little. And, of course, we also hardly ever sit still. It's the only way for us, especially in the cold of winter. Our little feathers don't keep us as warm as those thick hides and fur the big critters have. Oh, what's the use of complaining? We are what we are—just little chickadees." And with that parting shot, Clarinda flew off to a neighboring yard, Charlie following her closely.

The occupants at the box on 665 Hughes were watching the spectacle unfold in their yard. All sorts of people were walking into their driveway to catch a shot or two of Mara and Myrna. Myrna, the yearling moose, had actually taken the lead at this point. Having nibbled her way within twenty feet of the box, she discovered the walkway the guy had shoveled, allowing him easy access to the bird feeders. *Now this is just dandy. I don't have to use my long legs to maneuver these high drifts for a while,* thought Myrna. She handily stepped into the path and walked right up to the front door of the box. She took a healthy lick on the shiny glass door and a quick peek inside, but no one seemed to be looking back at her. They were all upstairs with their clickedy gadgets.

Yuck, these potentilla sticks don't taste very good. Should have paid better attention to mother. She always tells me, 'stick with willow, or later in the spring, with aspen.' I must remember that. And then Myrna stalked her way up the walking path, crossing the driveway into new and unexplored territory.

It was fun getting away from mom. Then Myrna froze muttering, "Uh-oh, here comes another guy with one of those clickedy things. He's got a lot of nerve. He is right in my face. How dare he get so close to me? Good thing I'm a little older, and Mom's around the bend. She wouldn't be too happy to have him get that close to me or her, for that matter. Oh my, and now he has that big black dog in tow as well. That one doesn't scare me so much. I have heard Freddy, the fox, talk about Byers. He says she is a friendly black lab. Her sister, Niva, was said to be a real wild one. She moved away. When those two were together, they were quite the pair, from what I understand. They must be getting older. Older dogs are not so frisky, like all older creatures, I guess. Look at Mom, how slowly she is moving around the snow. I, on the other hand, I love to move about and discover new things. Uh-oh, here comes Mom now across the driveway. I better watch my Ps and Qs. She must have heard Byers before that guy shooed her back into his box."

"Myrna, I don't want you to get that far ahead of me. I

like to keep an eye on you. You are still my baby, and I like to see what you are doing at all times. Would you mind telling me why you were licking on that thing sitting in the drive? That had to be nothing but dirt. What did you think you were doing?"

"Mom, all it took was one lick, and I could taste the salt in the mud caked onto that thing. It actually tasted pretty good. You should try it sometime."

"Don't get smart with me. I tasted that stuff long ago. It's not as good as it used to be. Now, they mix something else into the salt. It's supposedly new and improved but not necessarily better. I understand it isn't very good for all sorts of things in nature. I suggest you stick with tasting from the willow and aspen. It's all natural and much better for you. I don't want you to get sick on me. You hear me? And stay close so that I can keep an eye on you at all times. You are not quite ready to be on your own. When the time comes, your father and I will turn you loose."

Of course, that went in and out of Myrna's ears. She nodded her head, indicating understanding and complying with Mara's wishes. After stomping through the deep snow and stuffing themselves with willow for hours on end, Mara finally decided she had enough. She needed to rest and chew her cud. She gracefully seated herself into a pile of deep snow close to one of the old lodgepole pines. Myrna looked over her shoulder, seeing her mother taking a rest. *Guess I am supposed to do the same thing. I'm not tired yet. I could keep right on going. But I better pay attention and do what she does. If I don't, she'll lecture me, and I'll never hear the end of it. Worse, the old man might poke me with that ungainly rack of his after she tells him about my bad behavior during our outing this afternoon.*

And so Myrna finally settled down as well, not close at all to her mother. While still in sight and earshot, about fifty yards separated them easily. Myrna had her backside to Mara, staring into space. She began to chew her own cud as Mom had taught her. A few months ago, they would have been much closer together. Mara never would have allowed her offspring to be that far away from her. How things change as we get older. Unquestionably, we were seeing a case of generation gap.

In the glow of the late-afternoon sun, Mara and her calf, Myrna, rose from the fields of snow and moseyed once again through the woods, nibbling on willow in passing. As dark settled on the forest, they disappeared. The guy at the big box on 665 Hughes wondered where and how they spend the night. "Do you think they stand and or lie down during darkness?" the guy asked his spouse.

"I'm sure they lie down and stay close together. They'll keep warmer that way, just the way we do." He nodded in agreement, closed the curtains, and put his camera away.

Early Returns

"RANDY, I never should have let you get that laptop computer Charlie talked you into buying. Sometimes I wonder if that silly chickadee has any brains. If you weren't able to get his weird messages from up north, we wouldn't be in this fine kettle of fish." Dora, Mother Robin, was absolutely incensed by her predicament. In her little pea-pickin' mind, Randy Robin, her spouse, was completely to blame for their desperate situation at the moment. If it hadn't been for Randy's gullibility, she might still be enjoying the big, fat worms of Padre Island. Even Crawford had been rather nice. She continued her tirade aimed at Randy: "I just don't know how I let you talk me into flying back north so early. I would have much preferred to stay for a while longer in Crawford. It was perfectly safe with no one being there. You knew they were all in Washington, beating the war drums. There were plenty of bugs and worms. Just look at all of this snow—feet and feet of it. It will take forever until we'll be able to find a single worm, never mind bugs. You expect me to sing on an empty stomach? You must be kidding. I'm not in the mood for singing. All I can think of is food."

"Dora, you are being very unreasonable. You can't blame Charlie for this debacle." Clarinda was so happy with all the sunshine they'd had in the last few weeks. After that big storm in March, most of the snow had melted. They had seen so many bare spots and didn't think there would be any trouble for us to find food. She thought we might get an early start for a change and raise our first brood of youngins. She was all excited and looking forward to seeing Joy back in the yard. Perhaps she was just a bit too optimistic, but Charlie should not be blamed for it all."

"I don't care who gets the blame. All I know is that I'm very hungry, cold, and tired. And if you think you can persuade me to fly back with you to some warmer place, you have another thing coming. I'm dead tired from flapping my wings for over one thousand miles. I see the guy put out another feeder after he and his woman shoveled all that snow. My—they worked really hard! You don't suppose he might put out a bone with some meat on it? Perhaps even some bread crumbs? I can handle them a lot better than those seeds all our friends seem to like so much."

"I'm sorry, Dora. You'll just have to sit close to me under those pine branches. It will keep both of us warm during the night. I talked with Charlie earlier. I flew into him as the sun was trying to come out. He was happy to see me. Of course, he apologized for luring me up here this early."

Charlie had spotted Randy as he was trying to get away from Dora, who was obviously bitching at him. "I gather Dora is as mad as a wet hen. Can't blame her at all. We've had too much snow this late in the spring. I just can't believe it. I suppose she is criticizing me for telling you it was OK to come north. Who would have thought we would get another big storm? You think this is bad. You should have been here a month ago. We got more than eight feet of snow in less than two days. There were mountains of snow—everywhere. I had never seen that much snow at one time."

"Well, I'm glad we missed that! Can you imagine how Dora would have handled it? She was all prepared to build a new nest, wanting to get started with sitting on the first brood. Of course, now she isn't even talking about breeding. All she wants is some food, and there is none to be had. You know we can't eat the seeds that you and Clarinda enjoy so much. I suppose the sun will have to come out again one of these days. As soon as some of this snow starts melting, we'll be able to get a drink of water. I'm almost more thirsty than hungry. Can't wait to get some of that good Colorado water! Do you think that guy will put out the little girl again? What did they call her? Joy? Well, she sure was cute sitting there in the yard. All of us loved the fresh water she carried in that flower basket of hers."

"Not to change the subject, but do you see all those tracks in the snow? Looks like Mara Moose and her calf, Myrna, have been around. I wish they wouldn't leave those smelly calling cards of theirs. All they do for hours on end is nibble on the willow and aspen, poop all over the place, and then lie around and chew their cuds. I haven't seen Morris for a while. I suppose he is roaming around in other parts of the Ranch. He always has been sort of a solitary fellow. You should have seen what happened a few weeks ago.

"Mara decided to chow down on the guy's Fraser fir. First, she chomped down the crown of the tree, and then she decided to give it a proper pruning. I've never seen the guy so mad. He came charging out of that thing that slides up and down.

He wielded that orange shovel and was shaking it furiously at Mara. She just stood there and glared at him. Finally, he got so mad he walked right up to her, still shaking that orange thing in her face. And then he kept striking it forcefully against one of the lodgepole pines. The noise spooked both Mara and Myrna, and they took off in a gallop. Foxy Freddy was watching the whole thing as he was cutting through the yard to look for his supper at their back-door neighbors."

"I bet that was a sight to behold. I can't blame the guy for getting mad. I know he doesn't care about them trimming the willows, but he is fussy about those fir trees and spruces. He babies them all summer long. And with all the willow around, they didn't need to massacre his tree. Well, what are you going to do about it? We have to teach Mara and her offspring some forest etiquette."

"You think *they* need teaching? Just wait until Danny the Deer and his entourage shows up again. They really could benefit from some serious teaching. They decimate all of his beautiful flowers. Of course, he has gotten smart. He sprays them regularly with stuff they don't seem to like. I've seen Diana come around sniffing on his roses, delphiniums, and columbine after he's doused them with some strong-smelling stuff. She doesn't care for it one iota and moseys on to another yard. Glad we don't have to deal with sprayed seeds."

"Well, Charlie, I better start looking for Dora. Sure have enjoyed tweeting with you. We'll see you around the neighborhood in weeks to come. Say hi to Clarinda." With that Randy flew off, searching the snow-covered tree limbs for signs of Dora. Suddenly, he saw her. She had found a spot on a wooden beam beneath the deck at the front of the big box. "Oh no, not that again. You are not planning to build a nest in that same spot, are you? You know how that guy hates it when you do that. I remember how you two fussed at each other last year when he kept pushing the branches off the beam every few minutes while you were trying to build your nest. Let's not go there again."

"Stop fussing! I'm just trying to warm my tush while you were flitting about, Lord knows where. I suppose you ran into Charlie and Clarinda? I hope you let him know how mad I am. If you didn't, I will the next time he flies across my path. I'll let him know what I think of these 'early returns.' And as far as you are concerned, you can forget about any breeding. I'm in no mood for that." And with that parting shot, she plumed her feathers and turned her back in his direction.

Heading South

RANDY Robin was sitting on the edge of the water basket, trying to see his reflection in the water. He kept pecking away at the image but couldn't seem to get a satisfactory drink this morning. "Dora, come over here. Take a look at this. See if you can get a drink. No matter what I try, I can't see myself as I usually do. I really would like to wet my whistle and get in a bath."

Dora flew over and settled herself right next to Randy. She peered into the basket the little girl was carrying. They both had enjoyed a refreshing drink and a cool bath several times for the last few weeks ever since that strange guy had placed the lovely figure of the girl into the yard. "What did I tell you? There isn't any water in the basket," said Randy.

"Come on now, you know better than this. Of course there is water in the basket. You have been here often enough. Didn't you almost freeze your tail feathers off last night? That's the problem. The water is frozen. As long as you insist on staying here for now, you better get used to the idea of getting your morning water fix and your bath a little later. You'll just have to wait until the rays of the morning sun warm things a bit. Remember, you have to be patient in spring and fall. I know patience isn't one of your virtues. But as I said, if you insist on hanging around here much longer, you better get used to changing your ways."

"You don't have to be so uppity, Dora. Time has just gotten away from me. It's been such a nice long summer. We hardly had any frosty nights after we arrived here in mid-May. Where did the summer go? It's been so nice to get a good drink from this birdbath whenever we felt like it. Ah, and the baths have been so refreshing every day. That place we go to in the South doesn't offer such amenities. We always have to go looking for some decent water. That's another thing. I love the way the water tastes around here. Down south, it always tastes like a swimming pool. I'm not fond of all those chemicals those creatures use to treat their water."

"Take a look around. Just notice how most of this guy's flowers have gone to seed. The aspens are beginning to turn color, and most of the willows are bright yellow. And then, the days are getting shorter all the time. I really don't like pecking around for worms in the dark. And the nights are so long. I'm getting older and my wings hurt in the morning after sitting still for so long. Randy, I wish you would consider leaving in a few days. After all that rain we had last week, it was easier to find some fat worms. But now that the weather has cleared up, it would be nicer to start our journey south in sunshine. It sure will be easier to see where we want to land for the winter months."

"You have a preference, Dora? I thought we might try Texas this year. Crawford is quite fashionable these days. We could stay at the President's ranch. I understand they irrigate the meadows and water their trees really good. Victuals ought to be plenty. And maybe the water from the presidential well doesn't smell so bad. Lord knows, they might put bottled water in the birdbath. What do you think?"

"I wouldn't mind Texas. But I'm not so sure about the president's ranch. I don't care for all that political chitchat. The other thing is all that security. I'm not crazy about the Secret Service. You know, they always carry guns. And sometimes, out of sheer boredom, they may just take a shot at us. No, no, Randy. I don't want any part of that. I have never argued with your political leanings. And I know how you would enjoy touching base with all the politicos who fly in and out at taxpayers' expense, seeking the wise counsel of their leader. Absolutely not, Randy—let's just go a little further south. I would feel more comfortable just north of Padre Island. We can visit our friends, the Sealys; they are some of the friendliest gulls I have ever met."

"Next Monday is the autumnal equinox. If the sun is shining, let's head south early in the morning. If we don't stop too often and visit all sorts of friends on the way, we should get to Padre Island by Wednesday or Thursday. You'll just have to flap those old wings of yours a little faster. You better not keep complaining about your aches and pains. Otherwise, I may scout around for a younger mate while we are relaxing in the sunny south."

"You have a lot of nerve to complain about my references to getting older! You are not so young yourself. Remember, I could look for a younger mate myself. Furthermore, my work is much harder each summer. When we first get here, I have to build the nest. You help very little. Then I have to lay the eggs and sit on them for days on end. And finally, when the youngins come along, I have to feed them, keep them warm, and give them all those flying lessons. Yes, you help, but not that much. After all these seasons in Colorado, I have a right to complain about aches and pains. You put that under your cap and think about it. Such audacity! I have half a mind to leave right now. As often as I have done it, I can find my way south. Who knows, I might find a younger travel companion along the way."

Randy looked stunned as Dora turned tail and headed in a southerly direction. He had not banked on her taking him that seriously. He thought he better follow her right now. It had been too many great years of togetherness. Why spoil a good thing at this stage in their lives. *Texas, we's a-comin'!*

White Gold

"THEY are still flying that silly flag with the pumpkins and witches. And now look at this white stuff all over the trees and, worse yet, all over the ground. I just don't understand it. Do you, Clarinda?" said Charlie Chickadee to his spouse of many moons as they were ducking the snow falling from branches above their favorite perch.

"I don't know why you are so upset about the white stuff. It happens almost every year at this time. Try to remember that it has been weeks since Dora and Randy Robin took off for Padre Island. I understood Dora to say that they were flying via Crawford after all. Once Randy convinced her that the president wasn't gonna be at the ranch, she was OK with the idea. Guess the prez was hopping all over the country drumming up support for his cohorts in the house and senate. You know how these politicians are. Of course, what's much more on my mind today is if we will find some food. Certainly pickings will be slim as long as the ground stays covered like this. Sometimes I wish we were smart enough to go south for the winter.

We wouldn't have to rely on the charity of the creatures living in these boxes."

"Look down, Clarinda. Here comes the guy now. What's he doing with that bright orange thing in his hands? Ah, I see, he is moving some of that white stuff to the side. Maybe if we flit about and let him know that we are searching for food, he'll be kind enough to put some out. I finally figured out why so many of these creatures are not feeding us anymore all through the summer and often wait until snowy November to put out some seeds for us."

"How is that, Charlie?"

"They used to feed us all the time until Barkley Black Bear tore down the feeders several times a couple of years ago. Now they wait to give us feed until they are sure that Barkley and his ilk are taking their long nap for the season. That's what that is all about."

The guy at 665 Hughes couldn't understand their conversations but noticed them flitting from branch to branch as they were having their bird talk. He wondered what they might be saying to each other. The yard and the trees with more than two feet of fresh snow looked so peaceful and quiet. There were all kinds of tracks among the trees. He wondered if Danny Buck or Foxy Freddy had been visiting. He knew it wasn't Morris Moose and his harem. They leave very distinct tracks in the yard. Perhaps it was a little too early for them. They usually don't show up until the snow is really piled deep along the road. Somehow, Morris and his tribe feel safer and protected by the high wall of snow along the road. Perhaps the snow blocks the noise of vehicles and people moving along their way.

"I wonder what happened to the cute little girl that sat in

the yard all summer? Do you suppose she went south for the winter?"

"Come on now, Charlie. You know better than that. That wasn't a real little girl. It was just a statue, as we discovered. No person could sit still for that long and hold that basket of water. I agree, she was cute. And, I must say, I loved the fresh water in the basket all through the hot summer months."

"You are right. We did discuss her at the homeowners meeting. All of the birds decided she had to be a statue. And no, she didn't go south. A few days after Dora and Randy took off for Texas, that guy worked in the yard. He put away all the black snakes and carried the girl and the bench to the big box. I saw him put her in a carton. He kept calling her 'Joy' and handled her with much care. I thought that was a good name for her. She sure brought all of us much joy. That stuff they put out a few weeks ago is colorful but of no benefit to us. The girl sitting inside the wreath has a nice smile, but that witch on the flag is ugly. I think she needs to see an orthodontist."

"Stop using those big words, Charlie! I can't handle you showing off like that on an empty stomach. I wish that guy would get a move on with his work around the box. Look! Now he is pulling the white stuff off the roof. That must be hard work. First he shoveled the decks, then the walkways, and now this pulling off the roof."

"Clarinda, you are not as smart as I thought you were. Haven't you heard the people talk about snow and white gold? They like it. Not only will it provide us with water next summer, but now these creatures walk through it with their big feet or glide on it with those long boards. They seem to have a great time playing in the snow. Sometimes I have seen kids build little creatures out of snow. They stick around as long as it is cold. Only when the days turn warmer do these little figures seem to melt away."

"Hey, Charlie, look. He's cutting a path through the snow. And guess where he is stopping? Right under those brackets he mounted on the trees. And here he comes with our late breakfast. I like this feeder. It has lots of perches for our friends and us. Looks like it is filled with sunflower seeds and birdseed, all the stuff we like. As soon as he disappears behind the sliding doors, let's fill up."

"Guess we'll have to wait a few more minutes. He's taking the witch down. He's replacing it with the red, white, and blue thing. He's been flying it for the last year. I wonder why? He never used to fly anything on that pole. Well, I like it. It looks great against the whiteness of the snow."

"OK, Charlie. He's gone for good. He's done shoveling the white gold. He's finished clicking that thing he is holding in front of his eyes. I wonder what that machine does? When you find out, let me know. But right now, I don't care. All I want is food. I'm famished."

Summertime

"CHARLIE, I don't know what's the matter with those creatures in that box of theirs. There is so much activity in that place, and things are different out here in our domain. Have you noticed they still haven't put that little girl with the water basket back in the garden? Sure could use a good drink now and then! Good thing he is still watering regularly. Good of him to keep the ground nice and moist. It's easier on my feet. Also, when our brood is taking to flight, it will be more pleasant for them during their take-off practices. You know how often they manage to just let themselves fall when they don't gain enough lift. You better stick around when they start practicing. Speaking of sticking around, I would appreciate you taking over on the nest for a while. I need to stretch my wings a bit."

With that, Clarinda lighted on the nearest aspen branch; Charlie made a perfect dive into the opening of the bluebird box, being greeted by the happy "tweet tweet" of his young ones. After checking that all was copacetic in his present headquarters, he stuck out his head and looked in all directions.

Soon he spotted Fedora, the wife of Freddy the Fox. "What are you doing back in the neighborhood? I heard Freddy the other night. Was that you screeching back at him? You two sure made a racket. Practically woke up everyone in these woods."

"Yes, Freddy and I had a fight. He was giving me a hard time about our four little vixens I practically raised by myself this spring. You know how it goes. First he gets me pregnant, and then he takes off for some other little Foxy. Then I have these four cute little kits in the middle of winter, and he is nowhere to be seen to help me take care of them. Good thing I found this nicely protected den under the shed of this guy's neighbors. I used the same place last year. Of course, last year I had only three kits to raise. This year it got to be a little tight, especially when they started to grow. The best part about the place is that the creatures that live in the big red box keep supplementing our diets. I know, it makes me lazy, and the vixen get totally spoiled by having all those delectable treats put regularly in front of their snouts."

"How does Freddy feel about that? Doesn't he come around checking on you and the kits?"

"He is terribly jealous that we are living on welfare and getting a regular handout from the creatures. On the other hand, he is telling me that I am becoming spoiled and dependent on the help. Our fight was about the kits learning bad habits. He thinks that he should have a say-so in their rearing at this stage in their lives. He imagines that he needs to teach them how to hunt. At least he wants his sons to know how to catch fresh prey. I believe that is very chauvinistic."

"What do you mean by that?" said Charlie.

"I'll tell you what that means. He wants to teach the boys

to become independent and self-sufficient. I think it's just as important for the girls to start fending for themselves. If I had to rely on Freddy, the brood and myself would have starved a long time ago. After he has fathered them, he takes off and leaves me in the lurch. Good thing my mother taught me how to take care of myself and any offspring I might have every year. I think it's nice that you give Clarinda a break from her duties now and then. She deserves it, especially since this is already your second set this spring. You're not planning on another brood so soon, are you?"

"We have tweeted about it. Since we have had so little rain in the last few weeks and things are getting pretty dry, we believe that ten new chickadees from our loins are more than plenty for this year. Of course, you realize that we lose two or three every season. For one thing, that nasty cat, that big white one living in the box over there, is always on the lookout for an easy meal. It's the first thing Clarinda and I teach them after they have mastered their flying lessons. 'Keep your eyes and ears open at all times, especially when you are sitting on the ground pecking away at seeds. You always have to be alert for predators. And watch out for that white cat. She's really sneaky.' I don't know how often Clarinda and I tell those little ones to be on the lookout. Well, nice talking with you, Fedora. Here comes Clarinda. I'm sure she is anxious to get back to her wifely duties. In the meantime, I'd better find some lunch for the family and myself."

With that, he emerged from the bluebird box, letting Clarinda achieve a perfect landing. For a moment, she disappeared into the dwelling, making sure all was OK within. As she stuck her head out the tiny opening, she spotted Fedora still sitting beneath her on the damp ground. "Well, hello there. What brings you back to the neighborhood? Where are your four youngsters? They haven't left you for good yet, have they?"

"Oh no. The girls, especially, still stick around most of the time. Freddy and I had a big fight over their rearing just last night. I'm sure you heard the racket that went on. He wants to have sole custody of the boys and teach them all the bad tricks of the trade—kind of remaking them in his own image. A little bit of his philosophy goes a long way. Well, you have some idea of how it is. Of course, you realize Charlie is far more supportive of you and the youngins than Freddy will ever be. Not to change the subject, but what's going on with them in the big box. Things seem to be different this year. He's still watering his flowers and trees. You suppose he forgot to put out the little girl in the yard?"

"I don't think he forgot. They didn't put her out on purpose. He doesn't want her to get wet and muddy. We'll never get to see her again in these parts of the world. I overheard them talking. They are moving to Arizona in the fall. He is saying he has had enough of all that snow. I suppose Robin and Randy might run into them in Green Valley. Sometimes she likes a change from Padres Island. They might just pay them a visit after they are all settled into their new place."

"Well, if that doesn't rot your paws. Just up and leaving us here high and dry! I thought they were never going to leave these parts of the country. Guess you never know. I better be off looking for the girls. Don't want them to get in trouble! Freddy will never give me peace if something happens to one of them. Have a good summer." Fedora strolled across the driveway and disappeared in the woods. Just then, the guy opened the windows on the front of the big box, watering his flowers. They could hear some lovely tune emanating from within—Jessye Norman was singing Gershwin's *Summertime*.

Humming Along

HARDY and Hanna Hummer reluctantly had gleaned their last breakfast at the red strawberry in early September and fluttered their way south. Hanna was breezing so much easier as they swooped past the Santa Rita Mountains and passed Madera Canyon. She said, "Hardy, I love spending our time in Green Valley and look forward to the warmer days and nights in this part of the country. It will be fun to check out our old haunts and to see how many new red berries have been hung to make our stay so much more enjoyable." With that, she fluttered and buzzed off toward Canoa Ranch, following Hardy like a dutiful wife.

"Hanna, look! I don't believe what I see. There is Joy sitting in the backyard of that new box. Isn't this box next door to the one where the lady often sits outside with her headset on listening to music?"

"Yeah, that's right. She and the guy are off playing with those little white balls early in the morning. Then they fuss around the backyard, make sure that our berry is filled, and finally rest their bods and listen to music and read. I can always spot this place by the colorful bougainvillea along the wall facing south. Oh look, the guy that owns Joy planted some pyracantha along his backyard wall. They will look pretty in a few weeks when those berries begin to turn fire-red. It's so colorful. I like to look at them, but they are not particularly good for my diet. Some of our fine-feathered friends go gaga over the berries and maneuver just fine around all those prickly thorns hidden among the leaves and berries of the pyracantha.

"Did you see Randy Robin get drunk on those berries last year? We ran into Dora and him when we were down here a year ago. It was just a few boxes down the street. I can still hear Dora buzzing about him eating too many of those red things and getting giddy and inebriated. Guess he just doesn't know when to stop. I'm so glad that all you are interested in is the elixir of the hanging giant strawberries. Come. Look. There is a waterfall just down from Joy, and the water looks nice and clear. Remember how she used to carry water in her basket when she was sitting in the shade of the aspens in Grand County? I like the bright-red begonias our friend planted in her basket down here. Doesn't she look pretty sitting there in the sunshine?"

"Good heavens, Hanna, the way you keep on chattering about all the things you see. I don't have that much air. I can't eat and talk at the same time. It's not good for my digestion. Furthermore, I'm just starved after that long flight and am much more interested in checking out all the strawberries swinging in the southern breeze. Now, that feels a lot better. Yes, Joy does look pretty sitting there. It looks like she survived the long trip from up north just fine. Do you remember the day they washed her and packed her in that big carton? None of us knew what was going on."

"Do I remember? I still can hear Dora Robin and Charlie and Clarinda Chickadee go on and on about it. Randy was incensed about the disappearance of his favorite bird bath. Just wait until he gets down here in a few weeks. When he and Dora discover the little girl sitting down here, carrying begonias instead of water in her basket, he will have another bird. Of course, he doesn't have to hop very far to take a nice drink right over there at the waterfall. I can see it already, how they will fuss with Deedee and Denis Mourning Dove, who seem to enjoy taking their libation regularly at this new watering hole. Look over there; isn't that Harry Hawk?"

"Yes, how can I miss him," said Hardy. "He must be on the lookout for Peppi and Paula Javelina. Some think they are wild pigs!"

"Do you mean to say that those javelinas are back in the area?" Rolling her eyes, she continued chattering away at Hardy. "I hate to see them invading this neighborhood. Paula is always so busy feeding her own face and never can keep an eye on her squadron," buzzed Hanna.

"Well, maybe Harry will shoo them away. I can see why he likes sitting on this wall. All he has to do is shift his eyes from left to right and make a sweep of the open territory. As soon as he spots something moving, he just swoops down and grabs it. I love the wide-open view from this spot, don't you?"

Hanna had to agree. It was a pretty spot and had such a commanding view of the Santa Ritas to the east and the Tumacacori Mountains to the south. "The sunrises and sunsets from this vantage point are spectacular. And Elephant Head looks majestic when a few clouds enhance the glow of the setting sun. Those sunsets get more and more sensational as the days get shorter a little later."

"The way you go on, Hanna. It's the same every year, although I do have to agree with you about those spectacular sunsets. I just love the way those mountains glow almost awesomely red by the fading light of day. Of course, it is our favorite color. Look at all these cacti the guy has planted. Just wait until they bloom next spring. Looks like Roger Rabbit and his friends have been paying a visit to the guy's backyard. I can tell by these distinct nibbles on these lower paddles of the prickly pears. He particularly likes this Burbank prickly pear—it doesn't have any sharp spines to fear. And the new growth is tender and especially succulent. With the hot and dry weather they have had here, I can see how Roger was attracted to these juicy eats. Uh-oh, I see he actually managed to knock off one of the paddles. Just wait until the guy comes back and sees this."

"Oh, Hardy! You chide me for going on and on. But you should just hear yourself. I don't think the guy is going to be that upset with Roger. He'll probably pick up that broken paddle and stick it in the ground. With his green thumb, that thing will grow into a brand new cactus in no time flat. He has such a knack for getting things to grow. It's just amazing what they have done in such a short time. Did you hear the gal next door talk about that cactus. He found it lying in the middle of the road on La Canada. He stopped and picked it up with his bare hands when he realized it didn't have any sharp spines. And just look how the prickly pear has grown in those few months. Well, I'm gonna hum along to the folks next door. Need to check out a few more new boxes. I'm so glad that we found Joy's new home. It's always good to rediscover old friends." And with that parting shot, they buzzed west of Canoa Ranch.

Never Too Old to Learn

ON this bright sunny day, the first of Grand County's Concert Series took place at East High. Planning, selecting, and contracting with entertainers can be a true challenge for the organizers of these annual events. Sometimes artists can be exasperating, as our good friend Joyce would be more than willing to testify. But now, the day of the first event arrived.

As we drew near the venue of the show, *Inside the Orchestra,* presented by the Junior Symphony Guild, it was a pleasure to see so many young people. Obviously, Joyce and her crew had succeeded in getting the word out to music teachers and schools in the county. This was to be a concert with a different twist. It wasn't designed to be strictly entertaining; it was meant to be a learning experience for the young and the not so young.

Expectations were heightened as the audience entered the auditorium. Representatives of the various sections of an orchestra were stationed, or should I say sprinkled, among the audience throughout the hall. Only a grand piano and a harp were positioned on the stage. The first and second sections of strings were in front and to the right of the conductor, who beheld the eager faces of the participants—young and old. To his left were the cellos. Violas, percussion instruments, woodwinds, brass, and bass sections were facing him from their varied positions among the audience. It was great for the audience to be facing the conductor rather than looking at his back and arms flailing in the air.

Within minutes, it became evident that we were seeing a charismatic teacher in action. I clearly could relate to the man, as could everyone in the audience. Personally, deep down, I have been a frustrated actor all my life. For me, the classroom became my stage. I have an idea the conductor is of the same ilk. The playing of his audience became his performance.

Teaching all of us the aspects of concertizing was accomplished with aplomb. He drew in his very young and eager participants by casually mixing teaching and testing as well as instantly reviewing just-learned concepts. By the time the first musical selection enchanted the audience, they had learned the names of the various members of the string section, knew who the concertmaster was and his or her role in making good music, and understood that the oboe provides the tone to which the entire orchestra is eventually tuned. And should the conductor have failed to do his job, the members of the orchestra could take their cues from the concertmaster without ever missing a beat.

It was pointed out that composers write music in different rhythms and tempi, which require differentiated movements of the conductors' arms to convey such variations to the musicians and the audience. We were given elementary lessons in

"Conducting 101" with the warning that one of the very young participants would soon be randomly selected to demonstrate what was just learned.

The young lady selected was delightful. She had mastered the right movements of the baton and indeed executed according to the timing prescribed. However, her tempo periodically varied just a little, and the music produced by the various musicians reflected the conductor's slight "offness." It was hilarious and enjoyed by all.

It was a joy to see how easy it can be to teach the young an appreciation of music and the making of music, not necessarily just classical, but good music, and certainly not noise. The examples chosen by the master teacher came partly from the classical repertoire as well as from the contemporary scene and the world of film, television, and stage.

As familiar as I am with Beethoven's famous Fifth Symphony, I had never realized that there is no break between the third and the fourth movements of the work. As our conductor was teaching us that it is impolite and in poor taste to applaud between movements of a singular symphonic piece, he let us know about the subtle changes that take place between the third and the final movements of Beethoven's Fifth without the customary cessation of sound.

Among the highlights of the afternoon were the performances of E.L. at the piano and harp. Not only did the eleven-year-old young lady shine with virtuosity at the two totally different instruments, she also was extremely pleasing with picture-perfect poise—a wonderful example for our young people in the audience. One could only hope that her presence would encourage others to emulate her conduct.

As this most delightful opening act of the 2002–2003 Grand

County Concert Series drew to a close, we could only show our appreciation with applause for our performers. Special thanks to our organizers, Joyce and her committee. Indeed, they pulled it off once again. And they were right. It was a concert with a different twist. It was a great learning experience for all of us and one in which it was wonderful to see that learning can be fun at any age if the lessons are taught by a teacher who clearly has mastered and enjoys his craft.

The Portrait

I recently visited an artist friend of mine. While I was waiting in her studio, I noticed an unusual portrait glancing down at me. It was almost like the face had come alive and was looking me straight in the eye.

"Whose portrait is it and where did you get it?" I asked her when she returned.

"You like him, do you? He is very special to me. He is my guardian angel. I got him some time ago. A patron asked me if I could take some old frames off her hands. I told her I would put them in my used-frame bin and might be able to sell them for her. As I was sorting through the frames, I noticed that one of them held the portrait that caught your eye. She told me I could keep it. It would save her storage charges. And thus, the handsome young man in the portrait became mine."

I could see why she had fallen for him. It appeared to me that he sat for the portrait sometime during the nineteenth century. One could certainly deduce that from the garb he was wearing. The most striking part of the painting was the handsome, bearded face. The eyes were captivating and seemed to follow the beholder. I just couldn't take mine off his peering down at me.

"Let me tell you about the painting," my friend proceeded.

"When I received it, it was in pretty bad shape. I have no idea when it was painted or who created it. It doesn't bear any signature, at least none that can be detected by the naked eye. Perhaps restorers working on it in the future might use X-ray technology and shed some light on the master who painted him. At some point the owners decided to cut the painting down in size. The canvas was damaged in the process. Whoever tried to repair the ravages of time didn't do an expert job. Notice how clumsily the paint-over was done on his right shoulder. The color doesn't match the rest of the painting. It's a dull black instead of a very subtle deep green. The coat and the shoulder just do not look right."

"You see it correctly. I have to agree with you. At first I didn't look at the whole painting. I was so taken in by the eyes and the expression on his face. It's a magnificent painting. I can see why you fell in love with it. Now, I also notice the difference in the shirt collar. The right side looks old, the left looks like a badly done paint-over."

"Look at the subtlety of the paint on the right, and the amateurish touch-up job on the left. Not only did they wreck the collar, they also destroyed the appearance of the young man's beard. It's a shame. I have already invested a tidy sum in having the painting restored. The main objective of the first attempt at restoring it was stabilization. As soon as I can see my way clear, I will have further work done to it. Any of the overpainting has to be carefully lifted. Depending on what they find, the original appearance of the painting will then be expertly restored."

The more she shared with me about the portrait, the more intrigued I became with the whole process. I remembered seeing a restoration studio at the Ringling Museum in Sarasota, Florida. It was fascinating to observe how removal of, or looking through layers of undesirable paint by means of X-ray technology revealed the artist's original concept.

Returning to the present scene, I said, "Wouldn't it be great if X-ray technology could ultimately reveal the creator of the portrait, and perhaps even the date when it was done?"

"Yes, it would be. But, for now I am perfectly content to have him just looking down at me from the wall. It's kind of mysterious, and I love it. I wouldn't part company with him for any amount of money."

"True, true. Money isn't everything, to use a cliché. And some things in life cannot be bought for any amount. I am so glad you allowed me a glimpse into the history of 'the portrait' on the wall."

Things

BEING threatened by war, hurricanes, or possibly floods or forest fires, we are sometimes forced to think about the things we possess. Pharaohs and kings have been buried with earthly treasures to ease their existence in the afterworld. Christian teachings advise us to work toward treasures in heaven rather than on earth. Nevertheless, all of us accumulate possessions in the course of our lives that we view as precious.

I guess making a list of invaluable belongings is alright. But as a friend of mine suggested, one should explore the reasons why one considers certain items to be worthy of rescue in emergency situations. Obviously, prioritizing the significance of one's earthly treasures becomes critical.

There is the green marble fern stand. It was a wedding gift from a colleague of mine. Coy surprised both of us with the unusual present. We questioned her about the appropriateness of giving us this beautiful antique. She let us know it had been in her family for generations, and neither of her adopted daughters gave a hoot about it. Coy summed up by saying,

"My days are few on this earth, and they would probably have it picked up by Saint Vincent de Paul."

We loaded the precious gift carefully into our car and still didn't know what a real treasure we had just been given. It was accompanied by a rococo-looking bisque lamp, a coach drawn by four horses. Not exactly our taste. We kept it for years on our night table. Eventually, it wound up in a garage sale before we moved to Iowa. We learned later that the marble table was brought here from France and is two or three hundred years old. It was never touched by professional movers; we always transported it ourselves with commensurate care.

A large oil painting by a Swiss artist depicts an Alpine scene. We had seen it in a fine gallery on Grand Boulevard near the GM Building. I admired it. When we drove by the window a few days later, the painting was gone. "Guess we weren't supposed to get it," was all I said. Laura didn't even respond. A few days before Christmas, when Laura was lying in Harper Hospital after a stroke, she informed me to stop by the gallery on the way home. "They are holding your Christmas present for you." Sure enough, it was the painting. I had it framed for her birthday the following June.

Several years later, Laura was at Schoitz Hospital in Waterloo for a mammogram. Rather than sitting around in the waiting room, I told her I would visit the gallery across the street. As I walked in, I immediately noticed a beautiful oil painting on an easel. I was so intrigued by the piece that I inquired of the owner as to its price. It was extravagant but still affordable for us at the time since we were both working. I couldn't wait to drag Laura into the gallery. The minute she walked in she spotted the painting without my having said a word. We bought it and hung it in our living room. Only then did we remember we had not obtained an artist's profile. Garrett, the owner, mailed it to us. We were both surprised to learn that the artist was German; even better, he lived and painted in a suburb of my hometown.

I treasure two original watercolors by my first and favorite teacher, Bill Alexander. These were demo paintings he did in the workshop that influenced my painting style henceforth. I was lucky to bid high enough in a true silent auction—meaning I had no idea what the competition was offering.

Unlike many people, we have very few limited-edition prints among our art collection. A number of years ago, we spotted Les Didier's *Winter Grotto II* in a Hinterland gallery. We had been searching for a male cardinal; this was a beautifully executed work of a female. We decided to buy it and had it framed to our liking. Supposedly, the male version, *Winter Grotto I*, was no longer available. A year later I pestered the owner of the gallery to search the net for the male cardinal. A few days went by, and I received a call at the office. Gordon had found the print in question; he framed it exactly the way the female had been done. I hung them side by side in the stairway to our bedroom. When Laura discovered them just before Thanksgiving, she was thrilled to get an early Christmas present that year.

I treasure a collage of fifteen tiny three-by-three watercolors done by my fellow Thursday Painters in Hinterland. Fourteen of them had painted a little jewel indigenous to each artist's area of interest; the fifteenth was a blank canvas to be painted by me. It was their farewell gift to us as we were leaving to make our permanent home in Winter Park. They started this tradition with me. Since then, one good friend has moved to Kansas City, the other to Durham, North Carolina. All three of us consider ourselves very fortunate to have the priceless mementoes.

A large watercolor done by Helen Logan, a Thursday Painter, is among my special paintings; I had asked her to paint it for Laura. I also love my original by Terry Leach. Of my own paintings, I would rescue only one, a very simple winter scene. When I showed it to my friends in Iowa, asking for their input, all they said was, "Sign it and frame it. It needs nothing else." I love the Tobiska oil and my roosters in the kitchen; one is small enough to grab easily, the other is rather large. We do not necessarily agree on all my selections; I would rescue two oils we commissioned Noreen Hansen to paint and a watercolor by another dear friend. Last but not least, I would save watercolors of Prague. They could be replaced with similar works if we were to return to the Golden City one of these days.

There are two small oil paintings in our bedroom; one used to hang over the fireplace in Laura's parents' home in Grosse Pointe; the other, a copy of one of Mom's paintings done by a dear friend. Both are special to us.

Laura inherited some priceless pieces of Blue Bristol from her mother. She had collected these rare pieces by visiting many an antique store throughout her life. Laura and her sisters treasure the pieces their mother left to them.

A cobalt blue biscuit jar, a gift from Mom, now resides in our office. It has always been one of my favorite things.

When I was an undergraduate at Wayne State University, I found a part-time job. After I had learned I had obtained a scholarship and a full refund of my tuition for the first year, I decided to surprise Laura with a set of beautiful dishes. My employer was going on a buying trip to Germany. I had given her an idea of what I had in mind. She custom ordered from

Hutschenreuther a service for six and many serving pieces. It was a worthwhile investment of my thousand-dollar tuition refund in the year 1966. That Christmas, Mrs. R. gave us a hand-painted china plaque by Temple Beal; she was considered one of the finest American china painters of her time.

There is the dessert service for twelve by Royal Tettau, which my mother acquired shortly after she was married; the factory rep was a regular guest at my parent's hotel in Düsseldorf. Mother acquired from him this priceless service for twenty-four. We hauled our half across the Atlantic in 1967. By then Mother had decided that Laura was a worthy recipient of some of her treasures. The dishes survived World War II and the transatlantic flight.

Lynne seldom uses her sterling silver flatware, a gift over many years from her godparents. It is service for only nine; I am the reason for the incomplete set. Laura asked for a refund at Wright Kay Jewelers on Woodward Avenue in Detroit so that I could use some of the money to buy our wedding bands. I was that broke when I proposed to marry her. No matter what jewelry I have bought her since, she would never want to part with her simple 14k Lohengrin wedding band.

Last, there are the mundane things. Obviously, we would grab our crown jewels. The computer tower would have to go because of all the valuable information stored, the most important having been copied to floppy disks. Two large boxes of negatives of possibly every photograph ever taken by yours truly have been packed. Diaries I have kept since 1978 are chock full of good information aside from my personal commentaries on events of the day and my state of mind for the past twenty-four years.

Photos and family albums that would be irreplaceable have

been added to the emergency stock piled in the garage. They are sitting next to boxes of even more mundane treasures such as tax returns for the past three years, insurance policies, and other important papers. My camera equipment would certainly be replaceable, although some of it with difficulty. My Nikon F3 is as comfortable in my hand as some of my old shoes fit to my feet. I would hate not to be able to have access to my Nikon 55mm macro lens. A collection of commemorative stamps and some rare coins were added to the pile. Perhaps the stamps could be replaced, but it might be more of a job than just taking them with us. I am saving them for one of my godchildren. Finally, I have packed up all of my personal videotapes; some would be irreplaceable since they were taken in places we may never see again. Some include footage of people who are no longer with us. Although not indefinitely preserved, we would like to keep them with us just a little longer.

Finally, there are the vital prescription drugs. What would we do without them for a few days? And I suppose we should give some thought to some clothing. So far, we have not gotten around to thinking about it.

Of course, in the back of our minds is the singular hope that we will not have to do anything to our things but enjoy them in their regular and designated places in a home that we have lovingly grown in the course of almost thirty-nine years. As the long, hot summer progresses, we look forward to Thanksgiving and singing "Bless this house ..." once again.

Getting Acquainted with Ghosts of the Past

HEKTOR'S sister-in-law, Margarethe, decided to take her youngest grandchild with her to the cemetery. It was the spring of 1994. Jessica was five and one-half years old. She was fascinated with the letters of the alphabet and began to sound out words.

Grandma Margarethe was married to Albert Birken, Hektor's older brother. Margarethe made her monthly trek to the Parkfriedhof, where the Krämers and Reuters and their respective offspring were buried. The Reuter boys were the first to find their final rest at the parklike cemetery in 1942. The two boys had been buried there within seven weeks of each other; one was twenty-two, and the other lived to be twenty-eight. By now their parents had been resting next to them for a long time.

Holding her own grandma's hand, Jessica was looking at all the beautiful flowers at the shops just outside the cemetery.

"Shall we buy a few fresh flowers to put on each of their graves?" asked Jessica.

"Yes, we will put them in the vases I keep at each of the gravesites. These tulips are colorful and will look cheery. Let's get two or three dozen, and we'll divide them among the two graves."

With their bouquet of parrot tulips in hand, they walked under the archway of the large burial center with its endlessly long hallway and many tiny cubicles where the dead were laid out. "What's that building?" asked Jessica.

"When people die, they are brought here to be publicly displayed for three days before a service is held in the chapel down the way. Afterward, they are carried to their graves," explained Grandma Margarethe.

"We just have to walk down this beautiful pathway through the rhododendrons, and we will be at the grave of your great-great-grandparents. I knew your Great-Great-Grandfather Krämer. He suffered terribly with arthritis in both hips. When Grandma Krämer died in 1950, he purposely bought this beautiful plot close to the entry; this way, he didn't have to walk very far on his visits to the grave. In later years, he was given special dispensation to be driven right up to the site."

Jessica kept looking at everything they passed, taking in the scene with her eager young eyes. They passed the fishpond, and then they were there. As usual, the grave was well kept; blue and yellow pansies, as well as cheery daffodils, were nodding to the visitors in a light breeze. Jessica stood next to her grandmother, trying to decipher the writing on the large stone. "H-a-h-n-e-n-k-a-m-m," she mouthed very slowly but audibly.

"Yes, Jessica, that is the name of Great-Granduncle Ferdinand, who was married to your Great-Grandma Helena's sister Elsa." That all sounded so complicated to Jessica.

"How come there is another name on this stone? Didn't they have enough money to buy their own?" Jessica wanted to know.

"Oh, it's not a question of money. The Krämers, your great-great-grandparents, were buried here first—Grandma Krämer in 1950 and Grandpa Krämer in 1960. Later, their second daughter, Aunt Elsa, wanted to be buried in the same spot as her parents are. When her husband, Ferdinand Hahnenkamm, died first, she put a new stone on the grave with her parents' and her husband's names engraved on it. She died just a few months ago; that's why Aunt Elsa's name has not been added yet." Margarethe didn't have the heart to tell the child that Aunt Elsa's heirs deliberately hadn't added her name on the gravestone. They considered her to be a *nothing*.

"Well, Jessica, let's walk over to the Birken's grave; it's less complicated. It's the grave of your great-grandparents, Helena and Alex Birken." As they passed the many different stones, Jessica was always trying to sound out the names of those lying there in eternal rest. Soon they stood in front of the Birken marker. Margarethe's mind took her back over the many years and the stormy relationships she had survived with her in-laws. How peaceful it was now! She focused on her happiness and the joy of being with her youngest granddaughter.

Jessica could tell that her grandmother was in deep thought and off in another time. She had no difficulty with the name Birken, since she bore the family name; however, H-e-l-e-n-a and A-l-e-x were another story. Eventually, she got her grandmother's attention.

"Yes, Jessica, that is right; they were called Helena and Alex

Birken. Your Great-Grandmother Helena, was the first of the three Krämer sisters to die; your Great-Grandfather Alex died nine years earlier."

"May I get the vase from behind the stone, Grandma?"

"Yes, you may; but be careful where you step. It looks like the caretakers have just been here. Everything looks very neat and freshly raked."

Jessica tiptoed along the side to retrieve the vase with the sharp point to make it easy to push into the soil of the grave. She had seen the water spigot just around the corner and, without much ado, decided to go ahead and fill the vase with water. Grandma Margarethe was still on another planet. When Jessica returned, she snapped out of her reverie. "Oh, there you are, Jessica; thanks for getting the water. These will look lovely with the other flowers in bloom."

After Margarethe had placed the bright tulips on the grave, she bent down to hug her grandchild. She was so thankful for the harmonious relationship she had found with her own son, Albert, Jr.; his wife, Paula; and their two beautiful girls, Jutta and Jessica. She was fulfilled and thankful for every day she could enjoy with her family. "Someday we will have another grave to visit; it will be just around the corner from here. It will be the smallest of all the graves—a single grave. Aunt Georgine has picked it out; she is the youngest of the Krämer sisters. She survived two husbands, and they are both buried in different towns. When she dies someday, she wants to be here and will be by herself."

Margarethe didn't say it aloud for the child to hear, but she thought: *They will be resting in peace in such close proximity after feuding with each other for most of their adult lives. What a shame to find peace with each other only after they're dead. Don't be morbid, just enjoy the moment,* she scolded herself as she grabbed Jessica's hand.

As they walked up the large center path of the Parkfriedhof, flanked by hundreds of gigantic rhododendrons in every imaginable color, Jessica spotted row after row of identical gravestones that appeared to be nothing but concrete poured into a mold. "What are these, Grandma? They all look the same. Can we stop for a moment?"

"Of course, Jessica, these are graves of people who died during the bomb attacks on the city in World War II." The simple graves were small. The stones were more than 50 years old, and many were covered with green moss and discolored from air pollution.

Jessica went down on her knees. She started to decipher the inscription on the first marker. "U-n-b-e-k-a-n-n-t." She thought that was a strange name. She moved on to the next stone and discovered that person's name also was "U-n-b-e-k-a-n-n-t." When the results of her serious efforts at the third, fourth, and fifth concrete markers were the same, she got up from her knees and faced her grandmother. "Isn't that strange! They all have the same name. If they came from the same family, why didn't they just put one marker on a big grave?"

"No, no, Jessica. These are all individual graves." She could tell by the child's puzzled expression that this revelation gave Jessica much to think about. "Someday, when you are older, Jessica, you will study about these things in a history class. For now, let's not dwell on the ghosts of the past. I have a great idea. Let's stop at Kikas and order the biggest dish of ice cream they offer. I'll be bad with you and have mine with whipped cream as well. Let's just not tell Grandpa where we stopped after leaving the Parkfriedhof."

"OK, Grandma—but is it all right if I order some French fries with ketchup first?"

"Yes, anything, as long as you don't get sick to your stomach." And with that pact on their lips, they passed under the archway of the great hall of the dead and headed for Grandma Margarethe's car.

When they were seated at Kikas, enjoying their ice cream with gusto, Margarethe noticed that Jessica was deep in thought. "Don't you like your ice cream, Jessica? Did we order the wrong thing?"

"No, no, Grandma. I'm still thinking about those gravestones with that strange name, 'U-n-b-e-k-a-n-n-t.' Such an odd name for a family."

"Oh no, child, it's not a family name. More likely than not, none of these people knew each other in life. Worse yet, no one knew who they were when they were buried. That is why each of the markers simply says 'U-n-k-n-o-w-n' and the year they were buried."

A Treasured Note

HEKTOR and Laura were in the final throes of departing on a lengthy trip with their visiting relatives from Germany. Suddenly, the telephone rang. Reluctantly, Hektor lifted the receiver from its cradle. As he did so, he mumbled, "I thought I had heard from the last telemarketer for the day." He was surprised when he recognized the voice of a dear friend calling from Los Angeles.

"Hi, Myrna. What a nice surprise. How are you and Osram doing? Haven't heard from you in quite a while."

"Oh, Osram just left on business for Europe. You remember my good friend, Gigi, don't you? She and I just got back from three days in Laughlin. We had such a good time. You know how I love to gamble. It just gets in my blood. Well, you won't believe what happened to me. Just before we hopped into the cab, Gigi, as usual, had to make one more potty stop. And believe it or not, here was this penny machine simply staring at me.

"So, I thought, what the heck! Gigi will be a few minutes late. I might as well not waste any time. I pulled two bucks out of my purse and stuck the money into the machine. Within a matter of seconds after I started playing, all hell broke loose.

"Lights were flashing, loud music started calling attention to the machine I was playing, and a crowd started gathering around me as the jackpot money just started gushing out at me. Well, before everything was said and done, I had turned my two bucks at the penny machine into a two-thousand dollar jackpot. Can you believe that?"

"Boy, you are one lucky lady. I don't think that could happen to me. I've never won a thing in my life, never mind two thousand dollars in exchange for a two-dollar investment. We'll be in Las Vegas sometime before we see you in LA. My family wants to visit Vegas, a place we have always avoided. Who knows, maybe I'll be lucky after all."

"Well, honey, just try the penny machines. How much can you lose?" And with that advice she said good-bye.

Hektor began thinking about that stash of rolled-up pennies sitting in some closet. As soon as he hung up from speaking with Myrna, he went on the hunt for those pennies. It didn't take him all that long to unearth the linen sack containing the rolls and rolls of Lincoln's coins. When he picked up the bag, he thought it was pretty heavy. Nevertheless, he hauled it to the garage and stuck it in one of the side pockets of the car. Who knows, he thought, they might come in handy in Vegas.

On their second day along the strip, Hektor's cousin Markus and he took turns carrying the bag of pennies to their first casino stop.

It wasn't too far from the Tropicana to the MGM except for all those steps up and down to get across the main drag. When they finally made it to the casino, looking like country bumpkins with their linen sack full of rolled-up pennies, they started searching for the penny machines. At last, they found a whole bank of them. They didn't have to wait too long before a couple of gray-haired ladies looked for greener fields among the nickel machines.

We encouraged Margo and Laura to take the vacant seats and were hoping the girls saved up some of their good luck for this adventure. Margo looked over the machine and decided she had no idea how to play the slots. "I have never played a slot machine before. Have you, Markus?" And of course, he hadn't, and neither had Hektor nor Laura. They were all looking for one-armed bandits, so often seen in old movies. Clearly, they were signs of the old Wild West and things belonging to the distant past.

"Perhaps the lady in the cashier's box will be able to tell us what to do." Hektor entrusted the three of them with the gunnysack of money and hiked over to the lady in question. "Ma'am, we have schlepped a sack full of pennies with us for thousands of miles and would like to try our luck at these penny machines. Could you help us and tell us how to use them?"

"Sorry, sir, but these machines do not accept pennies."

"I don't understand. Why do they call them penny machines if they don't accept pennies? That's ridiculous!" offered Hektor.

"Very true, sir, but slot machines accept only nickels, quarters, bills of any size, or credit cards. This is true of all slot machines anywhere in the U.S. None of them accept pennies, dimes, half dollars, or even dollar coins. Sorry, that's the way it is."

"Would you consider exchanging these for nickels or quarters or possibly even bills?"

"I wish I could, but we wouldn't have any use for the pennies. Perhaps the head cashier at the front office might exchange them for you as a courtesy. His office is two flights up. You can take the escalator over there. So sorry!"

Well, she had tried. They took her advice and schlepped the sack up the escalator, this time each of them holding one handle to lighten the burden. Of course, the answer to their request was "No!" Hektor decided they weren't dealing with the bag of pennies for the rest of their days in Vegas. The suggestion was made to try a bank for an exchange. Hektor let the girls know they would be back in a few minutes after stashing the sack of loot back into the car. No way were they lugging that heavy bag around until they discovered a bank.

So much for playing the penny slots in Vegas. After lunch, they pooled their usable change in their pockets and tried a nickel machine. Hektor sat down and acted like he knew what he was doing. Within a few seconds the machine went wild. Lights were flashing and "Macho, macho man..." was blaring from its speakers. A crowd started gathering around Hektor. What was he supposed to do? He looked over to the cashier for helpful hints. She tried to yell over the noise of the crowd and the racket made by the machine. Eventually, Laura caught on what the woman was trying to tell Hektor. She was gesticulating, pointing, and yelling to convey to Hektor to look at the screen and to touch one of the windows after another until he hit the lucky one for the jackpot. Before he had a chance to try his luck, Laura decided to touch one of the windows. Too bad; the one she hit canceled out the whole deal.

Well, their total losses were two and a half dollars. Vegas didn't get rich on them, and neither did they get rich on Vegas. Two days later they were off to California. After a short stop in Los Angeles and a lot of laughs about their adventures in that infamous city, they were headed north to San Francisco.

The last morning in San Francisco, Laura reminded Hektor of the sack of pennies. "While we were walking, I noticed several banks in the next block. Maybe after breakfast, we could take that bag and exchange those pennies for some bills. If we each hold a handle, like you and Markus did in Vegas, it won't be too bad."

Hektor agreed and thought it was a great idea to ditch the bag of copper. The first bank teller was very polite until they heaved the bag on top of his marble desk. "Do you have an account with us?" They knew their fate was sealed.

"Is there a Wells Fargo Bank nearby?" Hektor and Laura were hoping for one in the next block. Unfortunately, the closest one was three long blocks away.

"What the heck, we can handle it." So off they trudged to the Wells Fargo Bank. Having mounted fifteen steps to the imposing front entrance, they noticed a sign posted outside the door in an elegant brass stand: "Sorry, this branch is closed for renovation until Monday morning.

Please, try such and such branch office."

Of course, that particular office was another three long blocks away. When they finally arrived at the hallowed grounds of the open Wells Fargo Bank, they had to stand in a long line with their linen sack full of pennies. People were giving them strange looks as they took turns carrying the burdensome bag.

At last, the moment arrived when it was time for Hektor to haul the gunnysack of pennies into the visual field of the friendly teller. Once they had established they indeed had an account with Wells Fargo, the good young man got hold of the heavy bag and relieved them of their load. He gave the neatly rolled pennies a cursory look and accepted them at face value.

Smiling to himself, he counted the number of rolls twice and came up with the same result. There were exactly forty rolls of pennies. Looking up at Hektor with a big grin, he handed him a twenty dollar bill.

"That ought to be a lot easier to carry. You have a great stay in San Francisco." Hektor and Laura beheld the treasured note of twenty dollars merely smiling in agreement. Little did the good man know how true his words were; they were worth their weight in two thousand pennies.

The Bell

I'VE always been fascinated by bells. As a child, I loved waking up to the sound of church bells near and far, and it was often the last thing I would listen to before falling asleep at night. During the war, I lived in a house directly next to a stately church. Its bells often rang to bemoan the loss of a dear neighbor or summon the help of all to elicit people's efforts in putting out a disastrous fire in the village.

When I was in junior high, I became acquainted with and learned all 430 lines of Schiller's "Das Lied von der Glocke" [The Song of the Bell]. Many a line has long been forgotten, and others are still fresh in my mind because of their powerful images. Not only does the poem tell the tale of creating a bell, but how bells play a role in man's existence from birth to death. It is most profound in its original language.

I read Victor Hugo's *Notre-Dame de Paris* under its German title *Der Glöckner von Notre Dame* [The Bell Ringer of Notre Dame] only to be reintroduced to its famous characters Quasimodo and Esmeralda under the title "The Hunchback of Notre Dame" when reading and studying English. Quasimodo surely knew the magic of playing those famous bells. I wonder how heartbroken Victor Hugo might have been had he witnessed the destruction of Notre Dame by merciless fires in spring 2019?

Who doesn't remember the impact of the unforgettable tale of Hemingway's *For Whom the Bell Tolls*?

We were in Italy on August 6, 1978. Our hotel room in Lugano was at eye level with a church tower. Its bells began ringing in the early evening and never stopped tolling; it was almost annoying. I turned to Laura: "The Pope must have died!" The confirmation came at breakfast in the largest headline we ever saw: "Pope Paul VI Is Dead." His successor, John Paul I, was pope for only thirty-three days. His sudden death is a big question mark to this day. I wonder how long the bells rang in Italy when his death was proclaimed?

I loved the movie *The Bells of St. Mary's* with Crosby and Bergmann and proudly admired The Liberty Bell in Philadelphia.

So, what's all this interest in discussing bells? There was one in my family that was passed down from one generation to the next. When my grandparents were married in 1906, my grandfather was given a large brass bell by his older sister. Supposedly, it had been in the family for a long time. My Great-aunt Mathilde wanted Grandpa to be reminded daily from whence he came. None of them could understand why he chose to establish himself in such a distant place.

On the old farmstead, the large bell was struck to summon menfolk and children to the table when any meal was ready to be eaten.

Grandpa mounted the bell on a solid old beam in the courtyard of his first home. There, it was primarily used to scare the heck out of any and all who worked for my grandparents: maids, journeymen, apprentices, you name it. Grandpa was not a churchgoing man but insisted that anyone working for him attend on Sunday mornings. While they were off to receive blessings and/or absolutions, he went around the sausage kitchen, storage rooms, cooling houses, the store, the kitchen, and toilets with pristine white handkerchiefs in hand, making certain that all was up to his standards of cleanliness.

God forbid if he found any evidence of dirt or grease! The wrath of God would descend on those whom he knew to be responsible for a given area. At high noon, when he was certain all had returned from church, he would stand by that ominous bell and strike it with vigor. No one in the house and neighboring quarters could miss the tolling of Grandpa's summons to account for their sins.

All would line up like organ pipes and stick out their hands wanting to collect their weekly pay. Anyone who was caught by the pristine hanky did not receive a penny in pay but experienced a dressing down he or she never forgot. Only after a second and satisfactory inspection would they be paid.

My grandparents moved to their retirement villa in 1938. My mother, being the oldest of four children, became the proud recipient of the family heirloom.

In our home, it served a somewhat different purpose; yes, it alerted us mostly to the table, but never was it struck as vociferously as happened at the Krämer estate. In our relatively small kitchen, it hung on a wood-paneled back wall.

Last night, I dreamt about the bell in our kitchen. Not only could I see it, but I heard it clearly. The dream brought back all those memories stored up in that kitchen and the tiny anteroom where so many meals had been served. The bell's pleasant sound rang out and made me look for it longingly like the returning Prodigal son. How often had it summoned me to the table when Mother attempted to get everyone's attention and let us know that all was in readiness for the morning, noon, or evening repast?

When we were younger, the table was always completely set; all we had to do was to climb onto our chairs and wait to have our portions served to us. Once we were old enough to help, Mother would often ring the bell a tad more vigorously, letting us know it was time for one of us to set the table. There were no girls among the brood; so the boys had to pitch in and help with chores. Years ago, Mother had help with the household. But those days were long gone. At the height of the war, everyone learned to become self-sufficient; everyone did his or her own job to survive the war.

Until early 1943, things weren't too bad. Mother's grocery emporium flourished, and she always managed to work trades with fellow merchants. Thus, the meals she was able to serve were not too sparse by comparison to those others were able to put before their families; they had to live strictly on the rations doled out by the government. The meals weren't fancy by any stretch of the imagination; they were wholesome and nourishing, and most of the time, pretty tasty.

Mother was a good cook; that is, she had been trained in the art of cooking and baking typical German dishes and sweets. After the war was long a thing of the past, multitudes of other nationalities left their mark on the gastronomic horizon and thus influenced the conventional palates of typical Germans. Mother wasn't one of those adventuresome individuals. She stuck to the tried and true and rarely ventured into gourmet territories that smacked of Italy, France, or, God forbid, Greece, Turkey, Vietnam, or, worse yet, China.

Even in the hardest of times, she would never stoop to cooking lamb or horse meat. She would have starved and let us go to bed hungry before she would cook a meal involving either. Thus, for a goodly stretch of time, we weren't very enthusiastic about being summoned to the table by the faithful old brass bell hanging from the wall. The bill of fare for which the bell tolled in those days was a serving of "brown soup" — a.k.a. burnt flour diluted with pure H_2O and just seasoned with salt and pepper. We reached the point of wanting to simply ignore the call of the bell.

For whatever reason, the brass bell was one of the few things that never left our home on Kupferstrasse. It was a reminder of the old days before Mother chose living with empty apple crates and a mattress tossed on the bare floor. Her humble decor held up well during successive bomb attacks and eventually blended perfectly with the boarded-up windows and old blankets that substituted for the white-lacquered, heavy wooden doors that had fallen victim to earlier visitations by the RAF. Many of her treasures had been shipped to safety in the small Black Forest inn where my brother and I spent eighteen months during the war.

Returning to our hometown in the fall of 1944, we were truly exposed for the first time to the ravages of war. The center of our universe became the potbelly stove that provided us periodically with a little heat and, of course, a steady diet of the delectable brown soup. The brass bell remained at its familiar post on the back wall of the kitchen, steadily reminding us of better days of yore.

My dream ended when the dreaded alarm shook me into reality. I got up and did my dutiful two-mile constitutional; before Laura finished preparing breakfast, I searched for a copy of Schiller's "Das Lied von der Glocke" on my iPad. The powerful words of his "Song of the Bell," written in my mother tongue two hundred and twenty-one years ago, rang loudly in my head, moving me nearly to tears.

Conversations with Mariah

MY wife had stashed away our carry-on luggage. Once again, we were jilted; our generous offer of relinquishing our seats on the full plane didn't find any takers. As we arrived at our row of seats, a young girl was eagerly observing the frantic activities in preparation for take-off through the tiny window. "Mariah, you have to come over here and take the seat next to me. You can't stay by the window. The seat belongs to these people," said the man across the aisle, whom we believed to be the father.

Mariah didn't make any attempts at hiding her tears. "Why can't I stay by the window? I don't like sitting on the inside. I can't see anything from there. Micaela is sitting by the window. Why can't I?"

We looked at each other and told Mariah in one voice, "You can have the window seat if that is OK with your Daddy. You are more than welcome to stay where you are." The father had no objections. And so, the little girl stayed in the much-treasured chair by the window. My wife buckled her in, and we were all ready for take-off.

While the stewards were droning out the emergency instructions, Mariah decided to unpack her backpack. She retrieved a stuffed leopard and pulled down the tabletop in front of her seat. She wanted the spotted cat to watch with her as the plane took off. My wife asked her if the toy had a name, but Mariah informed her she had not decided yet what to call the animal. The flight attendant advised Mariah she needed to hold the leopard in her arms during takeoff.

As the 727 was lifting off at Metro airport, Mariah noticed the large cumulous clouds. The plane seemed to be headed straight for the puffy apparitions. Mariah looked at my wife with big eyes and said, “I hope we'll fly high above the clouds. Maybe I'll get to see God. I wonder what his face looks like?” She seemed thoroughly engrossed with her cloud watching, hoping to catch a glimpse of the Almighty. My wife turned to me. “Did you hear what she just asked me?” We kind of grinned at each other when I confirmed that I had overheard the child's comments.

“How old are you?” asked my wife.

“I just had my sixth birthday while we were visiting my grandma in Detroit. She took us shopping for back-to-school clothes and got us haircuts. My brother, who is ten, is looking forward to school. I'm not. For me, summer vacation wasn't long enough. My baby sister, she is two, doesn't have to go to school yet. She's lucky.”

“Where do you live?” Laura asked.

“We live in Colorado Springs. Where are we now?”

My wife looked at her watch to see how much time had

lapsed since we had taken off in Detroit. She noted that we had been in the air for ninety minutes or so.

"Why did you look at your watch when I asked you where we were?"

"I figured if I knew how long we were in the air that I could show you on the map where we are at this moment. I think we're right about here. That is halfway between Detroit and Denver." Mariah thought that was a clever way to tell where we were flying.

Then, out of the blue, she turned to my wife and said, "My Mommy is dead. She's in heaven." My wife responded immediately: "My Mom is in heaven too. We are just coming home from her funeral. Maybe your Mom and my Mom met in heaven. Wouldn't that be nice?"

"I think it would be wonderful if they could meet," replied Mariah. She then proceeded to look at the puffy clouds surrounding the plane. My wife and I pondered our conversation with the darling little girl. Before we landed in Denver, I made a final pit stop in the back of the plane. When Mariah noted that I was gone, she turned to my wife and asked, "Where did Grandpa go?" which cracked her up. I guess Mariah had us figured out all right.

The plane touched down safely slightly ahead of schedule. We made sure everything was tucked away in her backpack. We said our good-byes and wished Mariah fun in school. As the father and his three children headed for a connecting flight, we made our way quietly to the baggage claim and the bus that would take us to our car at Stapelton. "Wasn't that little girl something? She sure made that flight go by in a hurry. Don't you feel sorry for the father? I wonder if her mom died in childbirth?"

If the trip had been any longer, we might have learned the answers from Mariah or her father. As it was, we had to be thankful for Mariah's innocent and delightful conversational snippets.

Entrepreneurial Enterprises

THE Fillipusis's owned a house diagonally across the street from my parents. The one-story structure was one of the few that survived most of the bomb attacks during the war. It was heavily damaged, but a portion of it was usable. When her home had taken its worst hit, Mrs. Fillipusis moved into an apartment that stood empty in a neighboring walk-up. The homestead was boarded up by prisoners of war, who had been requisitioned by the government. The prisoners, who were engaged to assist business people in restoring their property to some kind of usefulness after each attack, were French, Belgian, and Dutch. They simply showed up at the place of business, inquiring how they might be of help to the owner. Unlike Russian prisoners, they were not guarded. They received ration cards based on the number of validating stamps they had received from the Germans whom they had helped.

As soon as Willie Fillipusis returned from the Eastern Front after the war, he salvaged what could be used of the old house. The gardens were in deplorable condition, and the remains of the family home could best be described as dilapidated. Willie turned his attention to the gardens first since he had every intention of reemerging in his former business as a successful florist. In the years before the war, he had made daily trips to Holland to secure the best blooms at the flower auction held between four thirty and six o'clock in the morning. Being there on time necessitated leaving the house before three o'clock on Monday through Friday.

The early bidders always secured the best flowers available. Whatever wasn't bought by six o'clock would be burned at the auction place. The word was that flowers not sold during the legal auction period were not fit for sale or use by anyone.

I didn't know Willie before the war but became well acquainted with his wife. Frau Fillipusis was a regular customer in my parents' enterprise that underwent several transformations. It started in 1938 as a butcher market, became a grocery store when my dad was drafted into the Army, then was a fish market after WWII, and later once again a meat market. As I watched Willie digging through the rubble of the house and working in his gardens, a buddy of mine and I took heart and approached him. There was no longer a fence to keep us out. "Hi, Herr Fillipusis. What are you doing?" we inquired of him. Not that it wasn't obvious. We did have eyes to see.

"I'm trying to fix up this house so that I can open up my florist shop once again. Don't know yet what I will have to sell. In time, my garden will produce some of the flowers. With a little bit of luck, I'll be able to buy some greens, holly, and pine cones to make wreaths and sprays for *Totensonntag* and *Allerheiligen* [Day of the Dead and All Saints] in late fall. I won't even dream about business opportunities with the upcoming Advent and Weihnachtssaison."

"Would you allow us to help when you get ready to make your first wreaths and sprays?" I asked. Peter and I always thought it would be fun to be in some kind of business and make money. At the moment, florist sounded like something fun and enterprising. I knew at a very young age that people always took flowers when they visited someone and always sent flowers if somebody had died. It sounded like a going concern. Also, flowers were prettier, less messy, and smelled a heck of a lot better than bloody meat or old fish.

Peter and I kept an eye on Willie and admired the progress he was making on his shoppe, but even more so, in his garden. Willie had decided to let us in on his little florist secrets as long as we could make ourselves useful to him as well. He handed us an old rusty bucket and a small planting shovel. "Boys, you keep an eye open when horses go by pulling the junk man's wagon. Just go up and down the streets. If you see any kind of 'horse apples,' you make sure you scoop them up with that little shovel I gave you. It will help my flowers immensely. You can do that when you are done with your homework. Then, on the weekends, I'll let you in on some of my tricks of the trade."

"Of course, we will, Herr Fillipusis. We'll be delighted to do that little favor. We'll see you Saturday morning. Where can we drop off our collections after we have gathered them? I don't think our mothers would be too happy for us to store them until we see you on the weekends."

"You see that pile of dirt and compost away from the house? That's where you can dump the horse apples." He winked at us as we walked away with our empty bucket and shovel. Neither Peter nor I had bargained for the smelly assignment. Guess we had no other choice in the matter if we wanted to pick Willie's brains, because he had given us an idea how we might make a little money of our own.

"We gathered all the horse apples we could find and were at Herr Fillipusis's florist shoppe promptly on Saturday morning. He was making a good-sized wreath for a funeral. We watched him carefully as he started out bending a firm wire into a perfect circle. That would become the base to which his greens were carefully tied. By the time he was done, it was a thing of beauty to behold. We don't know where he had gotten the greens, but they were lush and fragrant. The plain wreath was beautiful in itself. He had picked a few fresh gladiolas in his garden and affixed them on top of the wreath around a gorgeous bow he had created from ribbon that survived the war in his cellar storage room.

"Now, isn't that pretty? And isn't it too bad that the cemetery gardeners will just throw it on the heap with all the other wreaths? It's a shame. But as long as people pay me well for my creations, I can't worry about what happens to them after I make my delivery." He shrugged his shoulders and hung the wreath on the wall in his binding shop. In later years, there would be a refrigerated room holding his floral works of art before they were dispensed to his customers.

Peter and I kept our eyes and ears open and practiced what we were learning every opportunity we had. What Willie didn't realize was that he had invited the Trojan horse into his floral shop. We were intent on giving him a little competition once we knew how.

As the fall of 1946 rolled around, we were ready to try our wings. We had been working with Willie for over a year. By this time, Peter and I were going on thirteen. On our walks, we had discovered all kinds of beautiful evergreens and holly in the woods not too distant from our homes. Our mothers had saved us some flour sacks that had held the much-disliked maize flour from the United States. It tasted OK, but we never got used to the yellow color of the bread. The sacks were great. They could hold a lot and disguise the contraband we were gathering and snipping here and there. First, we collected all sorts of pinecones and tied them to thin wire. There was no harm in doing that. Snipping and trimming the evergreens on public or city property was another story. The same was true of the holly. But we were careful about where we trimmed a little here and a little there, always keeping an eye open for the forest warden. Luckily, we never got caught.

And then we went to work in mid-October in one of my parents' empty coal bunkers. Right after the war, it had been the place where the chickens roosted overnight. There still was a hint of chicken droppings. But after collecting horse apples for Willie over the past year, we were somewhat conditioned to earthy smells. And, of course, it helped that we were dreaming about all that money we were going to make.

We made mostly sprays but some wreaths as well. The sprays went faster and didn't gobble up so much of the contraband greens. Our creations were adorned with cones and holly; ribbons were not readily available and would have been too costly, cutting into our profit margin.

No one knew what we were up to, least of all the unsuspecting Willie Fillipusis. From the previous year, we knew exactly where he set up his display outside one of the largest cemeteries in town. Of course, he had a large display table and a cash register at his disposal. We also knew what he was charging for his sprays and wreaths created by the hands of a master florist.

On the Saturday before *Totensonntag* and *Allerheiligen*, Peter and I arrived early with our wares at the cemetery. We had stuffed several flour sacks with our creations and transported them on an old cart fashioned from a flatbed to which wheels from an old baby carriage had been affixed. During the final months of the war the conveyance had been used to haul fresh water from a hydrant. We used the old cart for our display; change would be made from our pockets. We had made handwritten signs displaying the price of our precious creations. We set up business kitty corner from Willie.

Peter and I decided not to be greedy; we would charge exactly half of what everyone else was garnering for their products. The signs were large enough to catch the attention of the shopping passersby. Business was brisk, to say the least. People liked the price and were only too willing to give a helping hand to the young entrepreneurs.

All went well until Willie spotted us when there was a lull at his stand and he had a chance to look around. Most of his customers were regulars who had gotten there early to have the pick from the crème de la crème. We were watching him and caught the look on his face as he spotted us. His lower jaw dropped and his eyes bulged out of their sockets. And then he let loose a tirade of not-so-mentionable German terms of endearment. He yelled them loud enough to call attention to himself, and there was no doubt about who the objects of his affection were. He was pointing at us and gesticulating in our direction as he was cussing us.

Eventually, more customers arrived at his stand and he cooled down, needing to tend to his own business. He didn't give us another look. We were all sold out by noon and took our rickety cart as we left the scene of our crime. As soon as we were a good distance from the cemetery, we sat down at the curb of the road and pulled the money from our pockets. We counted bills and coins and decided it had been a rather profitable enterprise.

Dealing with Willie and the aftermath of our entrepreneurial adventure simply had to wait. Neither Peter nor I knew right there and then how we would handle the wrath of God that surely would descend upon us before long.

We divvied up the profits fairly and hightailed it home, hiding the money from our parents and siblings. When my mother inquired where I had been all day, I simply replied that we had been selling things for the holiday at the cemetery. She assumed we had been helping Willie.

The latter showed up at our doorstep that night. He wasn't mad any longer, as he had been at the cemetery. Business had been excellent for him, and his competition had not truly done him any harm. My parents were stunned to learn what Peter and I had been up to. Before I could get a thrashing, Willie spoke up in our defense. "Yes, I was surprised and very upset at first. But to be honest with you, I admire the boys for what they did. They paid for their instruction by collecting the horse apples for me. They paid good attention to what I had to teach and learned well. I'm proud of them. More power to them for trying to make a few marks. I won't hold it against them."

I shook hands with Willie as instructed by my father, apologizing for what Peter and I had done. He accepted my apology and winked at me: "Just don't do it again next year!"

Gloriana

If you are a friend of the opera, you probably have noticed the plethora of getups many patrons of these events sport nowadays. Those who manage to dignify their attendance with a bit of decorum seem to be a distinct minority. The total lack of concern about dress is not necessarily indigenous to the venue of our latest observations; we have experienced it at the Opera House in Sydney, Australia; at the Met in New York; and in Santa Fe; as well as in Europe. Perhaps it's a sign of the times. The good news is that opera has become more accepted in wider circles rather than just among the so-called elite.

After attending a splendid performance of *La Traviata* last season in Central City, we opted for all three offerings during the current year. *La Boheme* has always been one of our favorites, and *Gloriana* sounded terribly tempting. And so we were off to the first event, experiencing a blinding rainstorm as we departed Winter Park. We wound our way over mountain passes and along Clear Creek Canyon and through the palaces of temptation in Black Hawk in spite of constant threats of impending doom from the next deluge. While not exactly decked out in black tie and a Cinderella gown, we appeared somewhat respectable for the occasion. After taking our seats, we once again admired the appearance of the old Opera House.

The crowd buzzed with anticipation of the first chords of *La Boheme*. The seat next to my wife remained unclaimed. Just seconds before polite applause greeted the conductor, its rightful ticket holder rushed down the dimly lit stairs, requiring several individuals to rise from their seats to allow the latecomer to lay claim to her prized landing place. The damsel in distress was not exactly a spring chicken, although one might have inferred so by observing her casual attire. Her obviously bleached or tinted blond hair was arranged in something resembling a French twist. She was wearing a bright yellow shorts ensemble that might have been more suitable for a stroll along the boardwalk in Atlantic City, displaying rather healthy-looking thighs and legs.

The curtain went up on the first act, with the darkness softening any visual offenses among the attendees. Glorious voices of performers were acting out the tragic story of Mimi and Rodolfo beneath the rooftops of Paris. The star of Act 2, Musetta, was clearly appreciated by the audience and especially by our neighbor in the yellow outfit. Now, it was time for the first intermission. When the bellboys announced the beginning of Act 3 in five minutes, we joined the crowd in making our way back to our seats. Perhaps our femme fatale was of the ilk that usually tends to skip out during intermission to seek happier entertainment than that often presented in the final acts of an opera.

Not so. As the lights began to dim once again, the yellow bird showed up, causing everyone to rise for her majesty's passing through the relatively narrow lane. As I glanced over my right shoulder, I could detect by the expressions on our neighbors' faces that none appreciated the commotion caused by our late entrant. Nothing changed during the second intermission. Most of us decided to give up on the lady and accorded little attention to the annoying habits of our compatriot; we decided to simply enjoy the rest of the evening and the glorious strains of Puccini's masterpiece.

As we were sipping a cappuccino in Idaho Springs, my wife couldn't help commenting, "Wasn't that lady seated next to me most annoying? I hope she isn't a regular subscriber."

"I was glad she was sitting next to you; I might have said something otherwise. Yes, she was most irritating. Her getup was bad enough, but her late entrances were something else. Well, let's see what will happen in two weeks when we see *Little Women*."

We were seated in the same row, but a couple seats to our right. Everyone seemed to be in his or her proper places. The seats to my wife's immediate left were taken, although there was still one vacant chair in our row, and several seats immediately behind us were without occupants as well. We breathed a collective sigh of relief. As the musicians were going through the final tuning of the orchestra, our infamous neighbor reappeared, this time with an entourage. As she marched down the aisle behind us, loudly counting and reciting seat numbers, she pounced on the ladies seated next to my wife, bellowing, "I have paid for this particular seat, and I have no intention of relinquishing it to anyone." She yelled for the usherette to instruct the occupants of the seats immediately to my wife's left to move their butts to their respective chairs. They arose and graciously got out of harm's way.

On this night, our annoying neighbor sported very tight and very short black velvet shorts with a white-and-red polka-dotted halter top. The ensemble was finished with black golf gloves, a giant black purse, and another huge hat.

Once she had succeeded in laying claim to her proper seat, she threw her purse on the floor in front of my wife. She then proceeded to climb over the back of her chair in a "most ladylike manner," almost striking my wife's left shoulder as she managed to finish the maneuver of hoisting her tightly packaged rump into place. When she finally plopped herself victoriously into her reclaimed space, she exclaimed with much pride to her entourage and the rest of us, "Not too bad for a seventy-three-year-old broad who has had bilateral knee surgery; haven't lost much of my agility yet."

My wife knew I was tempted to reply, "And your name must be Grace!" as her right elbow not so gently touched the left side of my ribcage. For once I decided to hold my tongue, although it was terribly tempting. Thank heavens there was only one intermission during *Little Women* for us to endure another late entrance. Now, we can't wait for the end of this opera season. We wonder what is in store for us when we attend the performance of *Gloriana* next week.

Epilogue

We had taken our seats and noted that seat #106 next to me had not been claimed yet. "Maybe tonight you will have the pleasure of having Madame Boisterous next to you." With that observation, the aforementioned made her way down the stairs. I glanced over my right shoulder and noted that she was wearing slacks and a sleeveless cotton sweater. No hat this time. Of course, she carried her giant purse and colorful plastic bags containing newspapers. As soon as she had plopped herself next to me, I couldn't help noticing the gloves again. Colorwise, they matched the drab green outfit. She started fishing for her opera glasses. Then she shuffled back and forth between the program and her carry-on newspapers. Between actions, she would take her gloves off and then put them back on. Exchanging quick glances with my wife and raising my shoulders in a questioning manner, we decided independently that the gloves had to be some kind of fetish.

The conductor made his appearance. My neighbor declined to participate in polite applause. Instead, she was flinging the opera glasses up to her eyes and gave the man a quick once-over. In some ways she reminded me of the scene in *Pretty Woman*—not in her attire, but in her unskilled motion of using the opera glasses.

As the curtains parted for the first scene of *Gloriana,* I had to tolerate running commentary intoned by my immediate neighbor. *How disgusting*, I thought. *It will be a long evening; there are two intermissions.*

After Act 1, I headed for the men's room. As usual, the line for the ladies was decidedly longer. I noticed that "Ms. Boisterous" had made her way almost to the door of the facilities, bypassing numerous ladies standing patiently in line. "You mean this is the line for the ladies' room?" I heard her complain as I kept on walking. "This is ridiculous. I will miss Act 2 if I go to the end of the line." With that she simply squeezed between two women standing closest to the portals of relief. I noticed several women shaking their heads in disbelief.

To everyone's relief, the lady, if one may call her that,

decided not to budge during the second intermission. Instead, she played her vociferous shuffle game. As we emerged from the Opera House, we looked at each other. "I hope this was the first and last season with Grace. Just to be sure, let's consider matinees next year."

Isla de los Alcatraces

TODAY we call it "Alcatraz" or sometimes "the Rock." Its discoverer, Manuel de Ayala, named it the "Isla de los Alcatraces"—the Island of Pelicans. During our most recent visit to San Francisco, we managed to garner passage on one of the ferryboat tours taking hordes of visitors to the infamous island that lies just off the shores of the City by the Bay.

It's one of San Francisco's most popular tourist attractions. We learned before our arrival that it might be difficult to get there on short notice. The best plan to succeed would be to take a city tour and combine it with an afternoon excursion to Alcatraz. And thus, we proceeded along those lines and were fortunate enough to pick up four tickets.

Of course, most visitors are of a mindset that associates an excursion to Alcatraz with its last famous inhabitants, namely Al Capone, Machine Gun Kelly, and the "Birdman of Alcatraz." People simply don't make the connection between the imagery of pelicans, birds, flight, and freedom. How ironic for those who spent years imprisoned there.

It was a perfect day for visiting Alcatraz. As the ferry pulled away from the moorings, the spires and towers of San Francisco gleamed like an alabaster city in the afternoon sun. The Golden Gate Bridge stood like a sentinel at the gate of the bay. A pleasant breeze buoyed the flight of pelicans toward their nesting place on the island, for Alcatraz became a bird sanctuary when it ceased to be a federal penitentiary in 1963.

The short trip for us on the ferryboat covered a distance that must have been insurmountable for those who had been imprisoned on the island. Few of the current visitors realize that to the best of everyone's knowledge, no one ever escaped from Alcatraz and lived. An informative talk upon arrival at the island provides the visitors with pertinent facts about the colorful inhabitants that have long since blended into the folds of history. People stand around listening with one ear while their eyes dart around looking to ascertain where to turn next.

As the birds are flying overhead, now and then bombarding those unwanted and disturbing creatures below, the visitors' minds turn toward the cell house, which is actually only a very small part in the historical scheme of the island. Before becoming a federal penitentiary, Alcatraz was a military fort, housed the first lighthouse on the Pacific Coast, became a military prison, was subject to Indian occupation, is now serviced by the National Park Service, and is viewed as a collection of historical buildings surrounded by a bird sanctuary. It is hard to believe that it has been thirty years since the first tourists arrived on the shores of Alcatraz.

I remember reading or hearing about the shark-infested waters surrounding the island. However, it is generally believed what really made the "Rock" the ultimate prison of its time were the strong ocean currents and the extremely cold temperatures of the water surrounding the prison island. Without protective diving suits developed during the space age, all attempts at escaping from Alcatraz were doomed to failure.

Upon entering the cell house, visitors are issued personal headsets, which can be tuned to six different languages of the world. The visitors are taken step by step through the cavernous structure. Looking down "Broadway" can give you the willies when perusing the tiny jail cells closed off by steel bars. Of course, one learns in detail where the most infamous houseguests languished at one time or another. Oddly enough, the location of the cell of Al Capone, perhaps Alcatraz's most famous visitor, is unknown. Apparently, he spent long stretches in a hospital isolation cell and probably had a more comfortable cot and better food in that setting.

As we walked through the gruesome halls, listening to the tales of attempted and failed escapes, prison uprisings that were cleverly engineered, and the horror stories of those condemned to lengthy stays in solitary confinement, we tried to envision what it must have been like to be imprisoned at Alcatraz.

The prisoners could look out tiny porthole-like windows and see the city of San Francisco, the Golden Gate and San Francisco–Oakland Bay bridges, and perhaps Sausalito in the distance on clear days. It's been said that on fogless and windless New Year's Eves, the prisoners could hear the revelers in San Francisco.

All the prisoners and their guards were men. The only females on the island were spouses and children of the guards. Whereas the icy and treacherous waters of the bay surrounding the tiny island essentially constituted an impenetrable wall for the incarcerated, the psychological wall of being so close to civilization and yet excluded from the joys of life had to be devastating to the human spirit. It appears that this was the intent of those who conceived of "The Rock" as a perfect place to punish those deemed unfit to live among the rest of mankind.

Emerging from the chambers of horror and total isolation into the bright sunlight of a perfect late-May afternoon, none of us said anything initially. Everyone was lost in their own thoughts as we passed one of the National Park service persons, who contemplated our demeanors and said, "Treasure your freedom."

As we translated his profound remark to our German visitors, we looked at each other and nodded in agreement. Truer words were never spoken; it was the one aspect of our visit to Alcatraz none of us would ever forget.

It's All in the Sauce

DURING our recent travels with my cousin and his wife from Germany, we heard some interesting tales relating to ordering from menus when one isn't quite certain of the language. My cousins told of an eye-opening experience they had not too long ago in Paris. They were quite certain of their wine selections. When it came to the main course, my cousin was pretty sure he had made a suitable choice for his wife and himself.

When the entrée was served, neither of them recognized anything as slightly familiar. They smiled at the garçon and each other and began to eat. It was delightfully tasteful, and they enjoyed every delectable morsel served, although they had no idea what they were consuming. Since their French linguistic skills were, to say the least, sketchy, they didn't even attempt to ascertain from the waiter what they had just eaten. On the other hand, the waiter made no effort to communicate with them in German, although he probably would have been able to converse with his patrons in either German or English. It just wasn't done, as far as he was concerned.

By the time desserts were under discussion, the bottle of

wine had done its trick, and they were laughing themselves silly. They ordered cappuccino, which works internationally, and just pointed at something on the sweets menu and took their chances. They really didn't care as long as it was something for their sweet tooth. After their first dining experience in Paris, they became more cautious in making any selections from menus they couldn't read.

While traveling with us, they relied on our interpretive skills relative to menu reading. My cousin became more adventurous after a few days. Much of his school English came back to him. Often he would read the menu out loud, letting the words echo in his auditory memory. He would then look at us and seek confirmation that his interpretation of a selected item was correct. Generally, that worked pretty well. His wife was less reliant on her English skills, which were practically nil. She knew what "hamburger" meant since that concept has been popularized thanks to the proliferation of McDonald's all over the world. The first one she ordered in Denver was a bit dry, since she had insisted that it be well done. We explained to her that she should ask for "medium," and they would be much more to her liking. Of course, in fast-food places on the road, they would always come well done regardless of how she ordered them.

When they took us out for dinner the last night they were with us, we had suggested a local German establishment. I wished I'd had my camera in readiness when Margo's eyes first met the menu. She instantly recognized all the German items presented and felt totally at home. When the waitress spoke to her in German, it was a match made in heaven. No matter how good or how bad the meal might have turned out, it would not have mattered. She was so relieved to be able to order what she wanted and to communicate readily with the wait staff without having to rely on any kind of interpreter.

And then there is yours truly. One would think that I could ascertain what a particular item was on a menu written in English. My personal disaster of ordering something at a local restaurant brought the above to mind. My wife and I were on our way to the theatre in Grand Lake and decided to grab a quick bite at a restaurant in Granby. We had stopped there once before and actually had liked what we had ordered.

We were studying the offerings and I was debating between some sort of salad with grilled chicken or salmon or a classic hamburger. As my view took in the entire menu, I saw a footnote explaining that any burger could be had on a "bean base." Having splurged the weekend before, I thought that it might be prudent to select my burger on a bean base. When the young waiter approached us for our selections, I ordered the salad Laura had chosen and my burger on a bean base.

Laura just looked at me in disbelief but didn't say anything. She thought I knew what I was ordering. When our food was placed before us, I wasn't sure what I had gotten. Laura's salad looked great. My burger was a flat little patty on a half bun floating in melted cheese.

"Why are you looking at it so critically? It is exactly what you ordered. I was shocked to hear you ask for a 'bean burger,'" she said.

"Wait a minute. I didn't order a bean burger. I ordered the burger of my choice on a bean base. I thought they were serving the burger on a bun made of beans. That was what I understood the menu to tell me. Not this thing that they have concocted."

When the waiter inquired as to our satisfaction with the

food he had just served us, I couldn't help but explain to him that I obviously had misinterpreted the menu. He offered to replace my burger with something more conventional. However, I declined and bit into the sour apple. It was OK but certainly not something I would ever order again. The shocker came when I discovered that I was paying top dollar for a soy patty. That was the ultimate insult.

As we were rushing to our car, I mumbled something about it all being in the sauce. "And can you believe this? I could even read the menu! Now I really understand what Margo felt like when she had no clue what she was ordering, always having to rely on us or Markus to make a selection. I suppose one could call it culinary Russian roulette."

Just Desserts

BEING relatively diet conscious for some time now, we haven't eaten many desserts. For some of us, it is easier to give up the sweet highlights of a good meal. Others have a much harder time and can't resist the temptation. Anticipating visitors from Germany, we knew that we would be subjected to an onslaught of unwanted calories. Therefore, we went through several weeks of calorie counting and taking off unwanted pounds, knowing each of our guests had a very sweet tooth.

As soon as our company arrived, we were exposed to regular sit-downs with cappuccino, always topped off with a healthy heap of whipped cream. As these delectable concoctions would be served, visions of the number of calories they would contain would be floating through our minds. The first thing we eliminated was the whipped topping. Those calories could be easily avoided.

Of course, it could never be just cappuccino; often it would be accompanied by some homemade dessert such as apple pie, chocolate this or that, and once in a while just a plain old fruit cup. As I kept stepping on the scales each morning, I discovered with horror that significant damage had been done to my self-imposed weight limits.

"Try watching what you eat and don't worry. We'll work on your weight after our company leaves. We'll jump on it the day they return to the Vaterland." Those were Laura's encouraging words. In the meantime, she declined having the regular calorie bombs. She is much more stoic when it comes to resisting the temptations of sweet treats.

Luckily, we went on a lengthy journey with my cousin and his wife. While we were not always successful in cutting down on the evils of sugar, it was somewhat easier to do outside our own home. Since we were usually ordering from menus, we could more readily select plain coffee instead of cappuccino. Everyone was happy and got exactly what they wanted.

Of course, the menus were a challenge at times and often subject to interpretation and translation. Rarely did we encounter a menu printed in German. While my cousin did just fine with his English, his wife was less fortunate and had to rely on her husband's word or ours. But in general, she fared just fine with cappuccino and something one of us recommended to her. She had to adjust to American portions in everything she ordered, but most of the time she was pleased with what had been chosen for her. As long as she had her regular dosage of cappuccino she was OK.

This worked while we were traveling through Utah's and Arizona's national parks as well as in Las Vegas, Carmel and Monterey, San Francisco, and Salt Lake City. The more sophisticated the environment, the more calorie-laden the dessert bombs became.

On our last leg home from our travels we stopped in Glenwood Springs for our sweet treat. We had our eye on the Hotel Colorado. It was Memorial Day, and the town was buzzing with visitors. It was a perfect day weather-wise, and lots of people were enjoying their visit to the springs. Luckily, we found a convenient parking spot. Our company was impressed with the gardens of the Hotel Colorado and envisioned an upscale Kaffeeklatsch in the offing. As we entered the hotel, we noted that the dining room was set for the evening but obviously not open for business in the afternoon. When we inquired at the front desk, the concierge informed us that none of the facilities were open for coffee and dessert until five o'clock.

We didn't want to wait around for two hours, although a certain disappointment was evident in our guests. We looked around for a somewhat suitable alternative and wound up at a Village Inn. We found a comfortable booth and made our selections. The choices were colorfully displayed in the menu and required little interpretation or translation. No cappuccino was available, but there were plenty of desserts.

As we reminisced over the adventures of the trip out West, a delightful young man served our coffee. He recognized that some of his guests were from Germany and made a fine attempt at polite chitchat in German. We sat and laughed and looked forward to lemon meringue, banana cream, and chocolate cream pie. My cousin had spotted some crepes filled with fresh strawberries and decided on his own to order his dessert. It was lighter and less calorie-laden. And then he spotted the waiter, carrying the tray. "Here comes our dessert," he was salivating.

"Are you sure that is our order?" said his wife in German. "I can see a bottle of ketchup. Why would they serve ketchup with any of our desserts?" was her follow-up. With that, our desserts, as ordered, were placed in front of us. The three of us received the pies we had ordered along with our coffee. My cousin had a large plate of crepes filled with fresh strawberries accompanied by hash brown potatoes and several strips of crisp bacon.

"That isn't what I ordered or wanted," said he. I consulted with the waiter and checked the menu again. Sure enough, there were the crepes featured with fresh strawberries, but one could barely notice the bacon and hash browns. Had I looked at the menu and the description of the item on a different page, I might have alerted him to the fact that he was ordering breakfast rather than just dessert.

All of us laughed and made the best of the situation. I inquired if I should request a doggie bag but was told not to bother. Germans are not in a habit of taking home food they didn't consume at a restaurant.

A few days later, we had our farewell meal at a local German restaurant. Everyone was pleased with the menu. It required no interpretation or translation. All were most happy with their choices, even their desserts.

In Search of Times Lost

APRIL 10, 2002, was a snowy day in the high country of Colorado. Our Air France flight departed Denver International Airport early in the afternoon. We landed safely in Cincinnati but barely made our connecting flight to Charles De Gaulle International Airport in Paris. "There is a problem with your seat assignments," announced the check-in agent. "According to your papers, you booked this flight in January. There has been a change in planes. Your seats have been already assigned to someone else. Just a moment please. I will see what I can do."

The agent operated the computer keyboard with expertise, almost playing it like an instrument, and said, "Well, here are two seats together." She proceeded to print out the boarding passes. I thought: *What wonderful seats did she manage to find us in such a hurry?* Within seconds, she handed the boarding cards to me and suggested we could get on the plane immediately. I wondered why we didn't have to wait for our seat numbers to be announced during the boarding process. We followed the agent's advice. To our astonishment, we discovered that our seats were located in business class.

The Boeing triple seven easily lifted off the runway. We were on our way. Our incredible journey across the Atlantic had begun. We basked in the lap of luxury. After we figured out all the buttons and mechanics of our chairs and the entertainment controls, we sat back and relaxed. I closed my eyes, and my mind turned back forty-eight years. This was quite different from my first Atlantic crossing on the *MS Italia* all those many years ago. Although passage with two cabin mates wasn't as bad as steerage, my first journey to the *Land of Unlimited Possibilities* wasn't exactly a trip on the Orient Express. As I looked around the cabin of the plane, I noted that there were a couple of flight attendants for every few passengers. They were passing out hot towels, pouring superb wines, and expertly presented French cheeses and other delectable hors d'oeuvres while we studied the menu announcing things to come. No questions about it; this was the way to go.

During our exceptional dinner, the captain made reference to Charles De Gaulle airport several times. I hadn't thought about the famous French general and president of France for many years. I remembered Le Grand Charles as the leader of the occupying French army who conquered the little town of Köndringen at the end of World War II. Somewhere along this journey, my feet would lead me back to the little town and the place where Aunt Klara had taken in my brother and me in 1943. It would be a nostalgic return. I wondered what changes had taken place during the passage of sixty years. In due time, I would see.

Laura and I were met by my brother Albert and his wife Margarethe at the Düsseldorf airport. The latter had risen from its ashes a second time. Founded in 1927, the airport was completely destroyed in late 1944. By 1996, it had become one of Germany's most modern airports. It was totally destroyed by fire in April 1996. Only a few months ago, it regained its former status in November 2001.

The first days of our visit were filled with a number of events. We had to get used to the new currency—the euro; the *Deutsche* mark (DM) was a thing of the past. We reconnected with family and friends. Jutta and Jessica no longer were children; they had become young ladies since we had seen them two years earlier. Else Gunders, going on ninety-four, was showing signs of aging. But she assured us, saying, "I'm staying in training, walking ninety-three steps in my stairway up and down twice a day!"

And then there were the inimitable visits to the cemetery. The Birken gravesite was in good shape; I learned that care would be provided until 2006 with the plot to remain in the family until 2016. Aunt Georgine's grave, very close by, was also in good shape. Not so the plot of the Hahnenkamms and the Krämers. Elsa Hahnenkamm's name was still missing from the grave marker.

Margarethe and Laura decided to have ladies' day at the cemetery a few days later. I went along. They cleaned the plot and planted some flowers. At the same time, I obtained the information regarding my aunt's burial date. A few days later, I made arrangements to have her name engraved on the stone of the family plot. It had always bothered me that my favorite aunt remained nameless at her final resting place.

A joint venture took us and my cousin Markus and wife Margo to Berlin. This would be my first visit to the famous capital of my homeland. I was often asked by American friends, "How come you have never been to Berlin?" I had a simple explanation, replying, "When I left Germany in 1954, Berlin was a distant and troubled place. After the wall went up, I had no desire to cross into East German territory. With my American passport showing Germany as my place of birth, I was just plain chicken. I had heard some ghastly stories about people being harassed, or worse, being kept in custody. I liked my freedom and wouldn't take any chances. We visited Dresden in 1994, five years after the wall came down."

The trip on the new and improved Autobahn took a mere four and one-half hours. After checking in at our modern hotel near Alexanderplatz, we decided to take advantage of a city tour. The weather gods did not promise too much in terms of sunshine. Armed with camera and umbrellas, we embarked on our first journey into the heart of the city.

The S- and U-Bahns, as well as streetcars and buses, provided excellent public transportation to natives and visitors alike. As the double-decker cruised along famous landmarks and streets of the city, one couldn't help but believe that Berlin constituted the largest construction site in Europe. This apparently has been true since the German people decided to make the historical city once again their capital instead of keeping the seat of government in the rather small and provincial city of Bonn by the Rhine.

Berlin is a hustling and bustling city and seems to be dominated by youth. Not that we didn't encounter mature persons. However, the presence of youth seemed to be pervasive everywhere. We got off the bus at Kurfürstendamm and took in some of the famous sites. The prices displayed in the windows of exquisite boutiques and houses of fashion moguls were downright scary. Café Kranzler is still in place, although only on the top floor; the lower two floors are now offering T-shirts. We walked up to the Kaiser Wilhelm Gedächtniskirche, the church that has been kept partially in ruins as a reminder of the devastating effects of World War II.

We got back on the bus and wound up in one of the most charming old areas of Berlin, the Nikolai District. While the Berlin Dome and the Nikolai church dominated the skyline, small specialty stores and a plethora of famous restaurants make this a must for every visitor. We had a typical Berlin dinner at a brewery/restaurant and were lucky to get a table after spending a short time sitting at the bar. Meters of beer being carried to groups of youthful patrons fascinated me. I discovered later that a meter of beer consisted of twelve large glasses. A bunch of young guys were celebrating the thirtieth birthday of one of their compatriots. After consuming several meters of beer, they were obviously not feeling any pain and entertained the entire inn. When we finally walked into our hotel room, the quiet of the neighborhood was welcoming.

As we walked to the "U" the next morning, we noted that many of the neighboring buildings were still gray and ugly, clearly showing signs of much neglect during the post-war years. We realized that our modern hotel had been built only recently in what used to be East Berlin. Obviously, it will take generations to erase the impact of more than forty years of

Communist rule. The train took us to Charlottenburg, a lovely residential neighborhood in the vicinity of the famous castle.

We toured the lovely gardens, a visit of the edifice itself to be postponed until the next visit. Our main purpose for being in Charlottenburg was to reconnect with an old friend. We had not seen Margot Bordeaux since 1979. We kept in touch with her through the years. I never forgot Margot's description of walking under the Brandenburg Gate after the wall came down. She sent us a small piece of that infamous wall.

Margot lives on the top floor of a six-story apartment building, built around the turn of the century. While her apartment had been severely damaged by firebombs, the building itself survived World War II. Climbing all those steps to her place could be a challenge. The four of us looked at each other after we climbed to the third story, took a deep breath, and went on.

"I guess one really would think twice about shopping expeditions or how often to do laundry in the basement. Of course, a health freak would view it as a convenient way of getting some excellent exercise," said I.

We all chuckled and agreed with my assessment. Margot had forewarned us in her communications that her building still did not have an elevator. When we made it to her apartment, slightly out of breath, she greeted us with a big grin. Margot looked like she had benefited from regularly ascending and descending her stairway.

After the introductions were made, we looked each other over to see what damage had been done by the passing of twenty-three years. We mutually agreed, "Not too bad!" We sat down for a drink before she presented us with a lovely dinner. Conversation flowed easily, especially after a bottle of good wine was consumed. Before long, Margot walked us to the underground that would take us to Potsdam and the Sanssouci Palace built for Frederick the Great. We were fortunate to catch the last guided tour through the palais. Perhaps the rainy weather had kept the usual crowds away from the show place.

Refreshed by cappuccino and some sinfully delectable torte, we headed back into the center of Berlin. As we emerged from the "U" at Potsdamer Platz, we were surrounded by the stupendous marvels of modernity that constitute the "New Berlin." The skyscrapers housing the Sony and Daimler corporations as well as the Deutsche Bahn have literally risen from the ashes of World War II. Nothing had been done in this area since the final devastating days of the Third Reich.

Taking in the scene at night, we decided to feast at one of the Brauhaus in the Sony Center. The food was wonderfully rich, the beer was most tasty, and the views were fabulous. We fell into bed shortly after midnight, all our senses satiated.

Our breakfast, once again a feast, gave us the strength to continue our explorations of Berlin. I simply did not want to miss any of the important sites. Unfortunately, the Brandenburg Gate was covered with an ugly shroud touting the wonders of Telecom Corporation because the gate was under reconstruction. At least we were able to walk through it; the following week the road would be closed. The crowds at the Reichstag were unbelievable. Lines were long and a three- to four-hour wait was announced. Needless to say, we didn't tour the new/old seat of the German government.

Instead, my entourage and I walked across the Pariser Platz to the Adlon Hotel. The liveried doorman stopped us in our tracks: "You can't go in there unless you are a guest of the hotel."

"We aren't guests; we are meeting someone for coffee," we said. That apparently was the right response. He let us pass. Before we entered the hallowed halls of the Adlon, I took a picture of Laura and Margo gracing the red carpet. We marveled at the foyer, its decor, and the elegant shops inside. We decided, "To heck with that snooty doorman; we'll have our coffee later at Café Kranzler."

As we walked up Kurfürstendam toward the Gedächtniskirche, the heavens opened up once again. The first of two cafés we approached were closed on Mondays; we finally settled into the Kempinski Hotel. Cappuccino and libations were pricey, but we decided to do it just to be able to say we were there. It was a fun way to end our first visit of Berlin. "Let's get the car at the hotel and beat the rush hour." And so we did.

Once on the Autobahn, the traffic lightened and the weather seemed to be improving. Not for long, however. Near Hanover, we were deluged. Pretty soon the road conditions deteriorated, and the announcements on the radio became disturbing. "Care is in order; there is a sofa in the left lane. There are children on the Autobahn! An unidentifiable object is blocking the right lane." Luckily, none of the obstacles pertained to our particular route.

The journey home took less than five hours. Laura and I invited Margo and Markus for dinner at a charming restaurant run by a Czech family. Markus had recommended the place. "I hope the road is open. I think the 'frog crossing' is over."

"What do you mean by that?" I asked.

"Well, there are certain types of frogs which are on the endangered species list. When it is their time for mating, many roads are closed simply to allow them to cross without being run over by cars." I thought I had heard everything.

Our stay with Markus and Margo ended with a delightful visit of the Sauerland, a hilly area not too far from their home. Although only a couple of hours drive from Essen, I had never been there. The little towns with their half-timbered buildings and churches spelled magic and charm. Visiting several artisans working with brass and wrought iron was one of the highlights of the journey. We stopped in the well-known ski resort of Winterberg and ended the day a most charming pizza pub in the town of Schmallenberg. Leaving the area, we noted the large maypole erected by the youth of the town while we were enjoying our pizza.

May Day (May 1) is a holiday celebrated in most European countries and is comparable to Labor Day in the United States. Following a stormy night, it turned out to be a sunny and pleasant arrival of the merry month of May. After a delightful dinner with German white asparagus, new potatoes, and tasty boiled ham, Markus and Margo took us back to the family in Werden. It had been a wonderful week of reconnecting with my favorite cousin and his spouse.

Between repacking suitcases, we managed to squeeze in a few visits with old friends. Two days later, we were again on the Autobahn, this time heading south instead of northeast. Once again, the weather gods were not their most charming. The drive was on wet and slick roads under gray skies. We were thankful that Albert had become a more sensible driver. In years past, he would have driven as fast as anyone on Germany's superhighways. While still boisterous in his behavior and constantly bitching at other drivers, at least he didn't race along the slippery roads. His new car with all the latest doodads featured a navigation system. Needless to say, it had to be put to the test on this journey. A female voice was giving directions at every turn to be taken. We decided to christen her "Susie." While Susie was fun at first, her constant admonitions would eventually grate on our nerves. It was just a bit over the top.

Having left Werden at six thirty to avoid the weekend traffic tie-ups in the Frankfurt area, we arrived safely at our destination in the Black Forest. Albert had decided to celebrate his seventieth birthday at the Ludinmühle Spa Resort, one of Germany's top twenty-five hotels.

Laura and I once had dinner at the place with family and our American friends traveling with us in 1978. At the time, it was a quaint little restaurant that had been in the family since 1702. What we encountered now was a far cry from what we saw twenty-four years earlier. Accommodations and meals can best be described as sumptuous without exaggeration; it was truly an experience par excellence. Laura and I enjoyed an outing to Freiburg with our nephew and his wife. Touring the narrow alleys and walkways leading to the old marketplace by the Münster was only slightly dampened by a steady rain. Thank goodness, we experienced all that under sunny skies in years past; the market simply is not as colorful under a gray sky.

One of the post-celebration highlights of the visit to the Black Forest was a walk back in time through the little town of Köndringen. The village of less than five hundred inhabitants has grown in the past sixty years to an enclave of over six thousand. The old church still stands proudly in the center. The storks, after an absence of many years, have returned to their nest. Now, unbeknownst to them, their privacy is invaded by a hidden camera. The activities in the nest are transmitted during all daylight hours into the old school building. Today, the school accommodates only the first four grades; the older students attend a modern new school built a few years ago. In my time, the old school made it necessary for several grades to be taught together. Such changes!

The Rebstock [Grapevine] hotel and restaurant stands empty. It is for sale. Likewise, The Loewe [Lion] is deserted. The window that used to display the menus contained a small printed notice: "Due to personal health reasons, this establishment will close December 31, 2001."

After 410 years, The Loewe, having survived the Thirty Years' War and two World Wars and other calamities, is now on the auction block and may become a parking lot for some modern structure. It gave me goose bumps. I pushed the small side door, which gave way into the old courtyard.

I looked at the others. "This is where the drinking trough for the horses used to be. Look, the old barn is almost falling down. Remember the pigsty over there? That's where the pissoir used to be. Remember taking our first bath in the large wooden bathtub in the washroom? Remember the large copper kettle to heat the water for our bath? And the still where Rudi used to make his booze? Over there, Aunt Klara kept her rabbit hutches. Look at these steps leading to the old wine cellar. That was were Aunt Klara peeked out from under the wood covers, watching the French soldiers get naked and taking a swim in the wine they had released from the gigantic barrels housed under the inn. Remember when you locked me in Rudi's barrel-making workshop? You didn't trust me when I said I had to go. Only when I started defecating against the doorjamb did you believe me and started yelling for Aunt Klara.

"I can't believe sixty years have gone by since we first laid eyes on this place. Then we were children; now you celebrate your seventieth birthday. My turn is in twenty-one months. I am reminded of Marcel Proust's *A la recherche du temps perdu* [In search of time lost]."

Most listeners didn't know what I was referring to. It didn't matter. I was simply lost in the years that had passed by. I just could not accept the fact that so much had happened in my life. In my mind's eye, I still saw the nine-year-old boy getting off the train in a strange town so many miles from my mother and home—so many years ago. I didn't see myself as the white-haired sixty-eight-year old who had returned from the New World to visit the place that kept him safe during World War II. *Where did all those years go?*

Our last stop was the cemetery. It used to be such a long way from town when the dead were carried in their heavy coffins to their final resting place. Now all the vacant lots are occupied by modern-looking houses. Driving there, it isn't any distance at all. And then we stood in front of Aunt Klara's gravesite. There was no stone befitting her station in life or her wealth. Her grave was marked by a pauper's wooden cross, already threatened by decay. The gravesite was totally neglected. The supposed caretaker was deeded an expensive piece of property on the outskirts of town where Aunt Klara's garden used to be. In exchange for the lot, the recipient was to take care of the gravesite. So much for well-laid plans.

After her burial, all everyone was interested in was the content of the will. When it was finally read, she had left everything to her favorite nephew in Switzerland. He took her money and ran, never to be heard from again. He didn't think a fancy grave marker was necessary. And thus lies the proud proprietress of The Lion in a neglected grave marked only by a pauper's wooden cross. Life does have a strange way of dealing one's cards.

A few days later, I found myself once again crossing the Atlantic. I reflected on the journey to the Vaterland and the events that had transpired. I was glad to be returning home with Laura at my side. Yes, we were indeed going home, for the New World had truly become home for me over the course of forty-eight years. Whom and what we visited were largely remembrances of a distant past.

A Memorable Christmas

THERE were only three days left in the month of November, the last November of the twentieth century. Hektor was looking out of his office window. He contemplated a splendid winter scene. Mother Nature had blessed the Fraser Valley with ample snowfall during the last twenty-four hours. Now a few soft snowflakes drifted between the gentle giants, the lodgepole pines surrounding the cozy home. They were the faithful sentinels standing guard in the forest and protecting the house from the winds of winter.

Hektor's mind traveled back in time and across the Atlantic. His thoughts took him back fifty-two years to an event that played out in 1948 at his parents' home on Kupferstrasse. Christmas of 1948 was very special to most German families living in the western part of the country. It was the first Christmas since the *Reichsmark* had been devaluated ten to one on June 6. As soon as the *Deutsche* mark (DM) came into circulation, miraculously, everything that could only be had on the black market became available in abundance.

The heart of the city became the center of attraction for

many families. Window-shopping was the thing to do during the weeks before the feast. Storefronts and windows were bursting with merchandise of the finest quality, tempting eager eyes and encouraging shoppers to fulfill their long-stifled desires for a new garment or even a piece of jewelry—anything that simply had been denied most Germans during the years of war or the deprivation of the post-war era.

Helena and Alex Birken were no different. They had taken their two sons part of the way by streetcar into town. The tracks of Streetcar 18 were partially restored; they had to walk the last ten minutes toward the Hauptbahnhof. Albert, going on seventeen, had reluctantly joined the shopping spree. Hektor, almost fifteen, could not wait to see the wonders of the mercantile world. There were so many things he wanted.

They stood in front of the Deiter's jewelry store and admired a plethora of watches in every shape, size, and price. "If I could ask for only one thing, I would love to have my own watch," said Hektor. "I'm so tired of always having to approach total strangers on the street to ask, 'What time is it?' When I start taking the train to Steele next year while I attend the School of Commerce, it would really be nice to have my own watch."

Helena Birken looked at her younger son. "Of course, a gold watch is out of the question. Which of these Kienzle watches do you like? They are an excellent make; the company has been in the watch-making business since 1883. These are made of stainless steel; they are durable and quite attractive."

"I like the square one with the light-brown leather strap. It is different."

"That's a pretty hefty price. Let me talk it over with your father when we get home tonight. There are many other things you will really need. You have to have new socks, underwear, pajamas, and some decent dress shirts for school next year. You know that we have not been able to buy anything for years. The watch is very nice, but perhaps more costly than we can afford this year."

Hektor's interest in window-shopping quickly dissipated. His mother studied Hektor's face; she could tell that her last comments had clearly put a damper on the situation. For now, she decided to leave it there. She had to think of Albert and the rest of the family, and of course, she had to be practical.

Helena Birken wasn't given to flights of extravagance. She never had been a spendthrift; she was a dyed-in-the-wool pragmatist. A year later Hektor was to discover how the other half lived. Greta Beerenbaum would not have batted an eye; she would have bought the watch on the spot. A couple hundred marks were a drop in the bucket in Greta's budget, if there was such a thing. But this was the Christmas of 1948. There would be many changes in Hektor's life in the coming year. He had no idea what lay beyond the threshold of the New Year.

Hektor had saved the pocket money he had earned by helping in the familial business. Mortar and bricks in the three store windows had been replaced by plate glass, one of the first investments to remove the last vestiges of the war years. Now fresh meats, other products, and sausages could be displayed enticingly for the eager customers. He enjoyed decorating the windows or operating one of the cash registers. These jobs entailed relatively little handling of the meats per se; he was most comfortable just dealing with the money.

He had gone into town on the second Sunday of Advent. The stores were open from one to five o'clock on three Sundays before Christmas. At Wetzel's, he had bought beautiful silk ties for his father and brother; for his mother he had selected a silk square, the dominant color being lavender, her favorite. Hektor loved the rich feel of genuine silk in his hands. He was pleased with his purchases. Needless to say, there wasn't enough money in his wallet to even think about buying presents for other relatives.

ж

The family business closed at noon on Christmas Eve. All but the last customer had been served. Helena Birken realized she needed to provide cooking instructions for a particular roast to the young woman who had rushed into the market just before closing. As always, her dismissal of each customer was punctuated by a "*Frohe Weihnachten*" as they emerged from the Birken Butchery. Store and household help had made sure that the place of business and the home were spotless. They were given their Christmas presents and sent on their merry way.

ж

Father Alex, as usual, was the first to take his bath. He had last-minute chores in the family parlor. Of course, the days of utter secrecy had long gone by. Neither Albert nor Hektor believed in the Christ Child as the bearer of "generous tidings" for many years. Nevertheless, it was Father Birken's job to make sure that all the presents were displayed most attractively at certain designated spots. Helena was always in charge of arranging the Rosenthal bowl in the center of the buffet; it was filled with home-baked cookies, marzipan, and wonderful chocolates. Hektor's spot was to the left and Albert's to the right of the centerpiece. Each had their own plate of goodies, always to be replenished from their mother's precious china bowl when she wasn't watching.

Mother Birken's entry into the dining room was the signal to fetch the elderly neighbor couple from upstairs; the traditional Christmas Eve meal of Hasenpfeffer and Spätzle was about to be served. For the first time in many years, glasses of brilliant red wine were lifted in celebration of the good times having come upon them.

The idle chitchat seemed to go on forever. Hektor was dying to see what fabulous presents his parents had selected for him. Actually, he kept envisioning the watch he had so admired a few weeks ago. *I'm sure Mom convinced Dad that it was a suitable gift for me. I told her that I really couldn't care less about any of the other stuff she was talking about. Yes, I could use some of those things. But the watch? I could be happy if I just got it and nothing else.*

Mother Birken could tell by her younger son's demeanor that he was most anxious to move into the parlor. "Shall we wait until after the presentation of the presents to have the *Schwarzwälder Kirschtorte?*" she intoned. Hektor nodded affirmatively; Albert couldn't care less about the presents. He had a pretty good idea what kind of stuff there would be for him—mostly new uniforms and sturdy, sparkling white butcher aprons. Albert was eager to get out of there; he was expected by his girlfriend Margarethe and her family, much to his parents' chagrin.

Helena Birken rose from her comfortable chair and headed for the parlor door and made an inviting gesture to the others. She sat down at the piano and played *"Ihr Kinderlein kommet"* [Oh, little children come], the old cue that all was in readiness. *At least we don't have to recite one of those damned lengthy Christmas poems like we used to when we were little,* Hektor thought. *That would keep me away from discovering what kind of a watch they bought me for another fifteen minutes.*

He caught a glimpse of the beautiful tree standing as always in the corner to the left of the parlor door. His father had hung all of the glass ornaments and electric candles, which had survived the war. The finishing touch was the perfectly draped icicles at the tip of each and every branch, giving the tree a silvery mantle that was unique; there were no carelessly tossed strands of tinsel on this tree. Hektor almost knocked over one of the chairs next to the Caucasian walnut table as he headed straight for the left side of the buffet; he knew that this was the area for displaying his Christmas presents.

He spotted immediately a cap, a woolen scarf, and mittens his mother had knitted lovingly during many nights in the past few months. There were three beautiful dress shirts, socks, some much-needed new underwear, a pair of pajamas, and several other things. *Where the hell is my watch?* he thought. *It should have been prominently displayed. Guess they decided not to buy it for me after all!* He gave all of his wonderful presents merely a fleeting glance. He looked first at his mother and then at his father and managed an insincere smile while saying, "Thank you for the lovely presents—all things I can use."

As he caught Albert's expression, his brother managed to shrug his shoulders as if to say, "I don't know what's going on."

Before he found himself a chair, he grabbed a piece of the marzipan from the large Rosenthal bowl.

"Why do you look so unhappy? Didn't the presents we selected give you any joy whatsoever?" his mother asked softly.

"We thought you would be more mature and would appreciate these items of which you truly have much need. I know what you are looking for, but it shouldn't be the only thing to make you enjoy this special Christmas. Why don't you look at your gifts more carefully? Perhaps the Christ child's messenger was a slight bit devious."

He got up and decided to take a closer look at his other gifts. First, he squeezed the socks, the scarf, and the knitted mittens. Hektor peeked inside the collars of the shirts and fingered the underwear. Finally, he took a closer look at the new pajamas. He noticed that the breast pocket was slightly bulging. Upon closer inspection, Hektor discovered the slender, black box stuck in the pocket. He popped it open with a big grin on his face. The square Kienzle watch he had liked so well during their window-shopping expedition was staring back at him. Hektor couldn't believe that his parents had decided to buy it for him after all.

He walked over to his mother and father, giving them both hugs and expressing his appreciation in a manner that had become a rarity in his young adult years; hugging them, especially his father, no longer seemed appropriate behavior. On this occasion, however, it was for him the only way to show the joy he was experiencing at this very moment in time.

He made sure the watch was wound and set at the correct time. As he put it on, he decided he would never take it off, except when he was taking his weekly bath. *With the fluorescent dial, I'll be able to tell time even in the darkness of night. What a wonderful thing; I'll never have to bother another person to learn the time of day!*

In the course of time, he purchased or was given all sorts of watches. Some would be far more valuable than the stainless steel Kienzle watch he received from his parents on Christmas Eve 1948. He lost it while skiing for the very first time in Oberstdorf in 1953. Apparently, the leather strap broke, and the treasured object disappeared in the snow. He had other watches by then, but somehow he had remained partial to the old Kienzle. True, it was just an object, but he felt like he had lost an old friend.

Returning to the present, Hektor reflected on the happenings during the Christmas holidays of fifty-two years ago. He realized that the concept of "time" and the telling of time had taken on a difference in importance. Looking back, it seemed almost impossible to believe all that he had experienced. Turning to the unknown in future time appeared almost too mysterious. He looked up from his desk, contemplating the plaque Laura had given him twenty-four years earlier. It displayed a good motto for the course of the last quarter of the twentieth century; he opted to live by its tenets for the rest of his days:

"Take time to Work—it is the price of Success.
Take time to Pray—it is the source of Power.
Take time to Play—it is the secret of Perpetual Youth.
Take time to Read—it is the foundation of Wisdom.
Take time to be Friendly—it is the road to Happiness."

The Annual Event

I don't know how you feel about garage sales. Personally, I find them rather interesting. There is such a variety of these events. They seem to take place almost any time of the year anymore. I'm not so sure what the history of garage sales is. I don't seem to recall if we had such a thing in Germany before I left in 1954.

Before the country was bombed to bits, there used to be a *Troedelmann* [junk collector] coming through the neighborhood on a weekly basis. Usually, he would be atop a rickety old cart drawn by some half-dead horse or mule. His arrival generally was heralded by some piercing tune emanating from a flute or some other undefinable instrument. People would rush out and hand over what unwanted treasures they desired to get rid of. Of course, later they would be searching through rubble to recover their treasures.

When I first came to the United States, I didn't pay much attention to those happenings. My first years in the New World were so tumultuous that I had little time to think about such mundane matters. It was only in the early 1960s, after I married for a second time, that I became aware of garage sales.

Some people called them rummage sales; a more refined term appeared to be "bazaar." Well, call them what you want—they are a great way of circulating unwanted treasures. As a matter of fact, our very first piece of furniture, I garnered at a neighborhood garage sale. I bought a Duncan Fife occasional table with removable glass top for a mere five bucks as well as a nine-by-twelve slightly worn Oriental rug for $25. Thirteen years later, I sold it for $250. The table I never could part with; just recently it was restored to the tune of $135. It continues to give us much pleasure and service—a true treasure.

I remember hearing about Mom's involvement in the Annual Antique Show sponsored by Goodwill Industries in Detroit. It's opening nights was one of *the* social events in the Motor City and a big moneymaker for the organization. The well-to-do and the not-so-well-to-do donated many of their treasures to Goodwill to be offered to generous patrons for purchase at rather handsome prices. Many of these finds were collected by Mom and handed down to her heirs.

I also remember Mom bemoaning the fact that garage and rummage sales were on an ever-rising increase in the city. People were not donating as much to Goodwill, Saint Vincent de Paul, or the Salvation Army. They were cashing in themselves in enterprising ways.

Hermione, the wife of our minister, used to brag about her ventures into the ritzy suburbs of Detroit. She made the rounds into the Grosse Pointes, and especially Birmingham and Bloomfield Hills, on trash days. "You have no idea what I have pulled out of these heaps by the curb on their regular pick-up days. These candelabra and that table came from Birmingham. To be honest with you, most of the manse is furnished in 'early curbside' from Birmingham and Bloomfield Hills. I don't go too often to Grosse Pointe. It's clear across town. By the time I get there, the very best has been picked over by the competition.

"I wouldn't dream of making any doctor's appointments early on Tuesdays or Wednesdays. I'm driving along my favorite streets before seven o'clock. That's when the pickings are best. The stuff just lends itself to our style of living and my way of entertaining. You know, I never entertain during the daytime. I love doing it at night. Everything looks great by candlelight. And of course, no one notices the dust. I just hate dusting." Hermione sure knew how to give a party.

Personally, I loved going to and doing my own garage sales. Laura was never very fond of the idea. For someone who used to hate them, she sure has learned to be involved in the annual event in Grand County. I recall our first garage sale in Detroit before we moved to Iowa. No way did Laura want to have anything to do with the sale. I wrote the ad and collected most of the stuff all through the house. The sale took place on Friday and Saturday.

I did a booming business and loved the give-and-take with some of my clients, otherwise known as bargaining or haggling. Laura couldn't stand it. Her only involvement had been the creation of shoplike tie-on aprons that held my change and moneys collected. Later, I would learn to use a fanny pack. It was safer than the open aprons.

By the end of the second day, a regular junkie pulled up to look over the dregs. "What do you want for all the rest?" I seized the opportunity immediately. "You can take it all for free, but you must take all of it."

"Got yourself a deal. Let me back up my pickup." Thirty minutes later the three-season porch was cleared of the leftover hoard. I could not have been happier with the conclusion of my very first garage sale.

Our second sale was in Hinterland, when we moved from our house to a rented flat. Laura couldn't believe the money I made on that sale and the kind of stuff that our neighbors gobbled up. I believe that the personal aspect of having a garage sale at her home was what bothered her the most. She felt like she was opening her closets for inspection by our neighbors. "Why do I want my neighbors to see and buy things that I have decided not to keep for myself? I'd much rather just give it to an organization or to our church for their rummage sale."

"Sorry, Babe, we paid good money for that, and I would like to recoup a little for my own coffers. Remember, we need to get new drapes and a few other things for the new place. It will pay for at least a few of those items." She had to agree that I was right. As long as she didn't have to confront the neighbors, she was all right with the event.

Twenty years later, she had gotten used to the idea that I knew how to turn a little profit in the garage. Not only did we sell countless of our treasures that we did not want to move to Winter Park, we actually sold our house to one of my patrons at the sale.

On the third day of the event, a lady inquired as to the purpose of the sale. "Are you moving?" she asked my sister-in-law who was helping us.

"Yes, my sister and her husband are moving to Colorado next May. Eventually, they will put this house on the market."

"Would you mind showing it to us right now? We have been wanting to buy one of these four condos for some time." Reluctantly, Elaine showed the house. She knew Laura wouldn't be happy to have strangers view her home at a time when it was not exactly in pristine order.

We had a written contract ten days later. And the rest is history. It could not have been a more painless experience, having a garage sale and selling the house to boot.

Who says garage sales are a bad idea? I don't think they are a bad idea at all. As I said earlier, they put unwanted items into circulation. Having done these sales and having been involved in the annual event in Grand County has proven to me again and again that garage sales serve a definite and good purpose. People are encouraged to donate many of their treasures that have pleased them well for many years. Now and then, it is time to part with one's hoard and share it with others. One has to give others the opportunity to get some good out of some of one's earthly possessions. Garage sales help clean out closets and garages and allow needy organizations to put much-needed cash into their coffers.

Let's not forget the downside of these sales. They take many dedicated volunteers to make them happen. There are those who do the picking up of heavy furniture, especially the dreaded sofa beds that have gone out of style or are beginning to sag just a tad. There are the countless hours of volunteers sorting through the donations, displaying them by categories and pricing them. I mean, we are talking big-time garage sales. These are regular worker bees; there is no room for queen bees. When they head home for the hives, they have earned their sustenance and rest for the night.

And finally, the first day of the sale has arrived. The cashiers are ready to fill their banks with cash and checks. The parking attendants are primed to advise the patrons where they may park and drive to retrieve their purchases. The coffee is perking, and sweet goodies are ready for sale. At eight o'clock, the race is on. Anxious buyers are swooping down on the displays in treasure heaven. Everyone is having a ball.

Sitting with my trusted cash box, I find it fascinating what people buy. The people themselves are most interesting. The best part is that it is a social event. Not only do we know most of the volunteers personally, but we know most of the customers.

"What did you find?" said I.

"I'm so glad I came just to see everybody," responded Trudi, a friend of ours.

In the end, everyone is happy. The customers have made a haul, and the fund of the Historical Association has received its annual boost from the sale. What's left on the second day is given to local charitable groups or taken to the dump, hopefully not too much to the latter. After all, we are talking big-time treasures.

Two Sides to Every Coin

I always find it interesting how certain people will look at the same situation so entirely differently. A few weeks ago, I spoke with my family in Germany. It's a weekly ritual allowing us to catch up on the events of the week. Calling has become so inexpensive, and all of us love the immediacy of the communication. It's easier, cheaper, and a lot more enjoyable than writing notes, which sometimes take forever to reach the intended receiver.

After responding to the standard question this summer, "Have you gotten any rain?" and having to decline once again, their next statement was, "I wish we could send you some of ours. We are getting much too much of it this year. I presume you have been reading and hearing about the horrendous floods that have besieged the eastern parts of Germany and most of Eastern Europe?"

"Of course! We have followed the devastating reports on television and in the newspapers." My sister-in-law talked about the horrors of destruction affecting the city of Prague. Because she had visited the Golden City recently, as had we, the impact of Mother Nature's wrath on so many cultural icons saddened us deeply. We had marveled at the splendors of one of Europe's oldest cultural centers. Best yet, we had learned that it is one of very few places that is original rather than reconstructed.

As the waters of the Moldau moved north, raising the levels of the rivers Elbe and Danube and their tributaries, the devastation moved along with it, threatening historical centers such as Passau, Salzburg, and Dresden. Passau was particularly endangered due to the confluence of three major rivers. The annual music festival in Salzburg became an instant victim to the deluge of the summer of 2002.

Perhaps the City of Dresden, restored largely in the last thirteen years since the collapse of Communist rule, was of greatest concern to us and many Europeans. *Can you imagine the Semper Opera House and the Baroque Zwinger falling victim to the vagaries of nature? The Frauenkirche is still rising from the ashes of World War II—and now this.*

We talked about the glory days of the Semper Opera, how some of Richard Wagner's great operas and eight of Richard Strauss's works premiered in the famous house. We recalled marveling at the great collections in the Zwinger and how significant the losses would be if these irreplaceable treasures were swept away by the powers of the flooding rivers. We simply could not imagine the loss of these jewels that had survived the horrors of two world wars and the reign of communism. All my sister-in-law and we were concerned about was the devastation wrought in one of Europe's most beautiful cities.

Then it was my brother's turn to address the topic of the day. There were no references to the impending disaster being visited upon priceless treasures of art and human endeavor. All he could see was the loss of billions of marks that had been invested in what used to be East Germany at the expense of taxpayers in the West. "If they had repaired and built new dams and flood walls instead of rebuilding churches, opera houses, and museums, their asses wouldn't be up the creek without a paddle. They spent my tax money foolishly. Next thing, they'll ask for billions more to rebuild some of that useless stuff a second time. The sad truth is we'll probably do it again at the cost of another increase in our income taxes."

And thus it went. We didn't make any comments and just let him rant. Through the years we have learned to appreciate him as the diamond in the rough he is. While we can buy his pragmatism to some degree, none of us subscribe to his narrow focus when it comes to objects of beauty that make life worth living. There is more to life than *Fussball* [soccer], crossword puzzles, detective stories, and the stock market. At least, so we think. We have learned to consider both sides of the coin.

What Is Important?

A couple weeks ago, we arose at daybreak for a change instead of in the middle of the night. We are so used to getting up with the birds. As I perused the scene through our sheer curtains, it looked like a promising day. I had not painted for several days due to other commitments. I felt inspired and announced to my wife that I was planning to paint all day. "What's on your agenda?" I followed up.

"I think I will wash windows today. It may be one of my last opportunities to do so before the really cold weather sets in. It has been bugging me all fall, but I simply have not had a day yet to accomplish it. You don't have to help me. I can do it all by myself."

Talk about laying a guilt trip on me. How could I sit in my studio painting while Laura was undertaking this major job? Deep in my conscience, I had known that the window washing was going to rear its ugly head one of those pretty late-fall days. I had been expecting it all along. I had hoped that the weather gods somehow would be charitable and preclude the occurrence of one of my very least favorite things to do. I knew Laura would not forget about it. *If only the weather had cooperated.*

I checked the thermometer at eight o'clock, and it was still well below freezing. Needless to say, we could not wash windows with temperatures hovering around twenty degrees. We had breakfast and then read for a while, constantly checking the rising thermometer. By eleven o'clock, the temps had reached about forty-five degrees, and Laura decided that it was time to start the undertaking. "I can't start on the east side. The sun is now too bright. I'll start on the south side in the dining room and work my way around to the master bedroom. I'll catch the east side later after lunch."

I volunteered to forget about painting and help her with the windows, as much as I hate to wash windows. "You need to hook up the outside hoses so that we can wash the screens as well. We can't leave the screens dirty. Why wash the windows?" was Laura's aside.

That's where I drew the line. "I'll make you a deal. I will vacuum the sills and the screens and wash them carefully while in place. I won't take them out and wash them outside." After pouting for ten minutes and listening to my rationales, she finally bought in to my suggestions. I guess she was pleased that I had volunteered to help with the semiannual chore. Actually, I hadn't volunteered; I was coerced or shamed into doing it.

"You make it sound like it is my job. I would like to remind you of what you say so often. 'It is our house, not mine or yours.'" Of course, my wife was right. I often say that to her. I really don't mind helping with many aspects of housework. I vacuum, I take the trash out, wash cars, usually wash the dishes, take care of the garden, and sometimes help with cooking or baking. I'm not particularly fond of dusting and positively hate window washing.

Perhaps the latter has to do with the fact that window washing in the U.S. is generally a royal pain in the butt. In Germany there is nothing to it. Most houses, even those that are a thousand years old, now have Kipp windows. Of course, the old houses have been updated as far as windows are concerned. Kipp windows can be tilted or opened by locking hinges; that is, they are easily accessible and can be washed inside and out in no time flat. Even my mother in her late seventies washed her windows at least once a week. She was like Laura; she couldn't stand dirty-looking windows. The difference was that the task was a cinch. I don't know how often in the last thirty-seven years I have heard Laura ask, "Why can't we have windows here like they have in Germany?" Ever since she first saw them in 1965, she brings up the topic whenever window washing is in the forefront.

Of course, that didn't help with the task at hand on this gorgeous late October day in 2002. I lifted out the first panel and started with vacuuming and washing screens and sills while Laura tackled washing the first window. "I'm using Elaine's new solution. She says it does just great on her windows," said Laura. I had heard about the mixture, which involved Murphy's soap and some other stuff. After she had washed the first panel, she admired her handiwork, only to discover that she wasn't too pleased with the results. "I don't like the looks of this window. It doesn't seem to get them clean at all. I'll go back to my own combination of a dash of Dawn and a good shot of ammonia!"

Down the drain went the first bucket of slightly used

window washing solution. A few minutes later, she was back with her trusted bucket filled with water, Dawn, and ammonia. She finished the second and third panels of the first window. When she checked out the results, she wasn't pleased any more than she was with the first treatment, saying, "I don't know what is wrong with these windows! I just don't understand."

I had to bite my tongue. Yes, they were not one hundred percent perfect, and what in life is? But there was a decided improvement. Finally, I said, "Why aren't we using the Ritz cloths that work so well on my glass for my paintings?"

"Well, I suppose all good things come in threes." With that she carried her bucket out to be dumped. Soon she reappeared with a bucket of clean, warm water and three of the Ritz cloths. "I'm not sure about you, but I am getting hungry. I think I'll stop now and fix us dinner."

With that, she disappeared into the kitchen. I decided to take the bull by the horns. I continued washing windows as soon as I was done with vacuuming sills and screens. I like working with the Ritz cloths and did a very nice job. By the time dinner was done, I had finished all the windows on the south and west sides. They looked pretty good to me. As I said earlier, not one hundred percent perfect but great by comparison, especially when viewed through lace curtains.

Laura didn't exactly share my views. There was a little watermark here and another drip mark there. And nothing still seemed to work just the way she had envisioned the process. I finally decided to put the whole thing into perspective. I reminded her of a very close friend who had been battling cancer for several months. Her kind husband had washed all the windows at their house. "Do you really think either of them worries about such mundane imperfections in their window-washing process? Do you believe it is of any importance to them?"

She thought about it for a few seconds and had to agree with me. As long as the windows were clean, that was all that was necessary. The rest of the job went a lot better. I decided to put on some light classical music and kept wetting and working the Ritz cloths in rhythm with the tunes of the moment. By five o'clock, every blasted window and screen in the whole house was washed. We were both glad to be done for another six months. I hoped both of us had learned what is truly important.

A Question of Longevity

MY earliest experience with the world of opera was in 1942, when I enjoyed Engelbert Humperdinck's *Hänsel and Gretel* at the city opera house in Essen, Germany. It was shortly after my eighth birthday. A year later, the opera house was completely destroyed during a bomb attack. Ironically, the opera given on that fateful evening was Richard Wagner's *Götterdämmerung* [Twilight of the Gods]. At the time, I did not realize the implications of the title glaring down from the marquis with the burned-out shell of the once-stately edifice in the background.

The love for opera must be in my genes. My father had a good voice and grew up loving classical music, particularly operatic music. My parents' hotel, Hotel Böcklin, was located on Königsallee, right across from the Apollo Theatre in Düsseldorf. My mother often related the story to me that before matinees, the theatre would play excerpts from the operatic shows performed on a given day. Internationally known, Jan Kiepura and Marta Eggerth were the stars of many performances. Supposedly, I was not two years old and listening in my crib to the recorded music. As soon as the recording of an aria would end, I would say, "Uncle more."

When World War II ended, few people were concerned with rebuilding theatres and opera houses; there were far more pressing needs. Eventually, radio stations returned to broadcasting. I loved listening to radio plays, recorded music, and, in time, to live broadcasts of whole operas. More often than not, I did this with my father; my mother was more interested in rebuilding the family business.

Two years after the end of the war, the Essen Opera began offerings in a large hall, part of a beer garden in Werden, a town established in 856 AD and located just a few miles from the inner city of Essen. It became the opera house in *diaspora* for several years. It was in this rather primitive setting that I became acquainted with many classic operas and learned to love them.

Years later, while watching the movie *Pretty Woman,* I enjoyed Edward Lewis's explanation to Vivian Ward's inquiries as they entered the War Memorial Opera House in San Francisco: "How will I understand what they are singing? How will I know if I like it?" And then his poignant and ever-so-true response: "Just watch and listen to the music; you don't have to understand a word they are singing. You will feel it, and you will either love it or hate it."

Of course, all of us who saw the movie know that she loved it. When the hard-of-hearing dowager in the adjacent booth inquires of Vivian whether she liked the performance of *La Traviata,* Vivian states, "I liked it so much, I almost peed in my pants."

Edward saves the day by translating Vivian's statement for

the lady, saying, She almost liked it better than the *Pirates of Penzance*."

From my first Saturday in the United States on May 8, 1954, I loved and appreciated the live broadcasts from the Metropolitan. Opera was not accepted and enjoyed in the U.S. in the 1950s as it is today. Yes, there was the Met, the War Memorial in San Francisco, and the Lyric Opera in Chicago. That was just about it, with very few exceptions in the hinterlands. The Met traveled during summers and brought its operatic magic to other major cities from the late 1950s into the 1980s, spreading the good word until it became prohibitively expensive to do so. Gradually, smaller opera companies sprung up in many larger and smaller cities all over the U.S. And, of course, there was Luciano Pavarotti, who enticed more individuals to become interested in opera in modern times than any other singer, including Enrico Caruso.

In our travels, we have attended many a performance in opera houses all over the world, including the famous Sydney Opera and the Teatro Colon of Buenos Aires.

Enjoying a production of an opera in a distant land or place has always been the highlight of visiting a new venue. My wife had seen Bizet's *Carmen* with the incomparable Beverly Sills while in college; that was the extent of her involvement with opera until we met. In almost fifty-six years of living with me, she has come to enjoy it almost as much as I do. While living in Detroit and attending Wayne State University in the 1960s, I managed to drag her to seven operas on successive evenings during a week-long visit by the Met. After that tour de force, she had to either love it or hate it. Lucky for me, she loved it.

When Peter Gelb took over the helm of the Metropolitan

Opera in 2006, he decided to bring opera to the masses by live broadcasting in HD to theaters all over the world, starting with six performances and a few hundred theaters during the 2006–2007 season. Anthony Minghella's revolutionary production of Puccini's *Madama Butterfly* was the showstopper of the season. The following year there were three more offerings and many more theaters. During the 2008–2009 season, twelve performances were brought to over eight hundred venues.

By popular demand, *Madama Butterfly* in the Minghella staging was once again broadcast in March 2009. Because of the three-hour difference during daylight savings time between Tucson and New York, the performance was slated to start at nine-thirty in the morning. We wanted to enjoy the opera from our favorite seats in the movie theater and arrived at about eight forty-five.

We could not believe the extent of the long line of patrons wanting to see the opera broadcast. Right in front of us stood a mother with three young girls. We were pleased to see that there was some interest in opera by younger people. Pretty soon another couple, perhaps a few years older than we, joined the line behind us. We started conversing and discovered that we had something in common.

The lady leaned forward and addressed the oldest of the girls: "I am so pleased to see you here. You will just love *Madama Butterfly*." The girl looked at her quizzically: "What's that?"

"Oh, it's the Live in HD Broadcast from the Met this morning."

"And what's that?" the girl said rather indignantly.

The lady explained to her that the broadcast originated with the Metropolitan Opera in New York and then inquired of the young lady what she and her family came to see at that hour of the day.

"We are here to see the movie about the Blue Man Group," internationally known performers who use art and music in their act."

We smiled; none of us old folks had ever heard of them. However, the lady could not let it rest there and proceeded to make her final but profound statement: "Let me tell you, my dear, people will listen to and watch Puccini's *Madama Butterfly* two hundred years from now. Do you honestly believe anyone will recall the Blue Man Group in twenty years?"

Challenging Santa

STRANGE, how our dreams allow us to travel through time. A few nights ago, I dreamed I was back in the clinic and classrooms in Hinterland, Iowa, teaching sign language and working with some of my hearing-handicapped clients. My nocturnal experience took me back thirty years to the Christmas season of 1986.

When I arrived at the University of Hinterland in 1974 as a fresh-baked assistant professor, I knew nothing about sign language since "sign" had been a four-letter word in the program where I received my degree in audiology. In other words, it was an "oral" program or one where the general consensus favored the use of hearing aids, other amplification devices, speechreading or lipreading, and anything but sign language when teaching profoundly deaf children.

Less than a year after I had started teaching and working with hearing-impaired children and adults at Hinterland, the mother of a three-year-old deaf boy consulted with me regarding her son's failure in various oral-approach programs. She scheduled her appointment with me after she had visited the

Iowa State School for the Deaf in Council Bluffs and decided that she could not leave her son in *that* or any other institution. He was simply too young for it and would be traumatized by the separation from his family. "What about sign language?" she queried.

"Sorry, I know absolutely nothing about it," had to be my response. As I beheld this caring mother with her cute and lively deaf boy, Terrance, I thought: *You may not know it now, but what stops you from learning something new?* As I vocalized my thought to the boy's mother, her eyes began to light up.

It was close to the end of the Spring semester, and I decided to have her register Terrance for the summer session. After the boy and his mom left my office, I spoke with one of our graduate students who had expressed an interest in working with a deaf client. I decided not to beat around the bush. "Gary, would you be interested in learning some basic signs and working with a three-year-old boy this summer? I'll get us some sign language books. You and I could learn and practice together during the semester break. We'll see where it takes us. What do you say?"

"Sounds like fun and a new adventure, Dr. B.," said Gary.

I checked out two copies of *The Joy of Signing* from the library, which got us started. We studied independently and then met at the clinic regularly for practice. By the end of the term break, we were ready to start working with Terrance. Right from the start, I had decided to videotape every therapy session. All of us had a ball, and Terrance seemed excited about his new way of learning to communicate.

About six weeks into the session, a clarion moment occurred. Of course, it was captured on video. Gary manipulated various objects, asking Terrance where they were. Then it was the boy's turn to hide the objects. He was imitating

Gary's question format. And then he signed, "Where is the pen pink?" Immediately he waved his hands at Gary, letting him know that he wanted to sign the question again. "Where is the pink pen?" Gary and I could not believe the progress this boy had made after a mere six weeks of teaching him language skills using sign. It was this very moment that convinced me to seriously pursue the study of sign systems and American Sign Language (ASL), ultimately allowing me to teach sign language classes and using sign language with those who could benefit from a total-communication approach. My sabbatical at the National Technical Institute for the Deaf (NTID) at Rochester Institute of Technology (RIT) in Rochester, New York, in 1981 opened up doors in my subsequent work that I had never dreamed of.

Tonja came into my life about two years later. She was the third of three cousins with whom I worked in the clinic. The first, a boy, subsequently became an orally functioning child. Karlotta, his cousin, had a more severe hearing loss but nevertheless succeeded using the oral method. I met Tonja when she was eight months old; she was profoundly deaf. For weeks, she did nothing but scream as I was holding her in my arms within a soundproof environment. Eventually, she became used to me, the room, and the clinician assigned to her. We were able to seat her in a high chair and began teaching her, using every possible means of conveying information: sign, speech, amplification, graphics, touch, and so on.

She was most receptive to visual input and learned to absorb language through her eyes. Eventually, she was mainstreamed along with hearing as well as hearing-impaired children. At age ten or eleven, she begged her parents to allow her to be transferred to the Iowa State School for the Deaf; she wanted to become fluent in ASL, live with deaf people, and become immersed in the culture of the deaf. She never did view herself as a handicapped person.

My dream brought back an unforgettable moment in my life with Tonja. Her mother had contacted me as to my willingness to play Santa Claus for all hearing-impaired children mainstreamed and served in the local school system. I had worked with many of these kids at the clinic. I agreed to do so. It sounded like fun. Tonja's mom had delivered a beautiful Santa outfit to my office—unbeknownst to Tonja, who was not quite four years old at the time.

I made my appearance at the school and enjoyed seeing many of my former charges functioning and performing at their best using either speech and/or sign language. One of the boys, Harry, hopped on Santa's lap and told me in sign what he wanted for Christmas. That moment was captured by a camerperson from the local newspaper, *The Hinterland Courier*.

Harry and I made the entire front page of next day's paper in living color. One of my colleagues cut out the page and posted it on the bulletin board across from my office. A day or so later, Tonja's mom brought me a beautiful fruit basket, a thank you from all the parents of the hearing-impaired children. At the same time, Tonja's mom wanted to retrieve the neatly boxed Santa outfit.

As we were chatting, Tonja walked behind my desk and

took me by my hand. She marched me out of my office and started to gesture toward the newspaper page on the bulletin board. She made sure she had my visual attention, starting to sign and pointing at the image in the picture.

"That isn't Santa Claus," she signed again and again, each time becoming more "expressive" in her communication efforts. Each of her pronouncements was followed by my asserting in sign that it was indeed Santa. When she wouldn't let it go, I finally signed, "What makes you think that isn't Santa Claus?"

"Because those are your hands!" was her prompt response. She had only watched them for more than three years. *What could I do but fess up?* I told her that Santa was so busy, he had enlisted me to be one of his helpers. I never was sure whether she swallowed my little white lie.

Second Chance

KAROLA picked up her glass of chardonnay and strolled out into her backyard. As she looked over to the Santa Ritas, she detected Mischief, her trusted feline companion, making her way home through the dried desert grasses. "Come here. Let me see what you have been up to. Oh my, looks like you are bringing me presents again. What have you gotten yourself into this time?" With that, Karola bent down to take a closer look at Mischief's prize. Whatever she had been carrying between her teeth, Mischief had apparently snapped up by the back of its neck. Obviously, she wanted her mistress to take a closer look at what she had so proudly conquered during her late-afternoon adventure.

"Looks to me like you are in trouble with Mrs. Hoppity, our friendly neighborhood desert cottontail. Did you sneak up on her youngins, Mischief? That wasn't very nice of you! Well, at least you were gentle with your catch. Let me take a look at the babe." She carefully picked up the wee, hairless body of the baby cottontail. Tiny squeaks and sounds emerged from the animal's body.

"This was not a good idea! Mischief, I am not very happy with you. Let's go inside and see if we can give the little girl something to eat since you robbed her of her mommy's love and care by stealing her from the nest. I don't know what I am going to do with you."

Karola's mind was racing. *This was not how I had planned to relax after a full day at the gallery.* "Darn that cat; I wish she would stick to mice and undesirable critters of the desert. What did I do with that tiny baby bottle the kids left when they were visiting from up north?" Her first guess took her to a certain cupboard in the kitchen. *I think I put it with the plastic containers. They are so handy with leftovers for the fridge.* Sure enough, here was the bottle with its tiny nipple. It was almost made for the little critter.

She washed the bottle carefully with mild detergent. Next, she rinsed it thoroughly. *I guess evaporated milk would probably work.* She filled the bottle and warmed it for fifteen seconds in the microwave. She tested it on the inside of her wrist. *Haven't done that for a few years,* she thought. *Guess it still works. It's just right—not too hot and not too cold.* "Well, little girl, let's try this."

She held the tiny body of the cottontail in her left palm. Initially, there was a lot of squirming. "I know I'm not Mom, but this is the best we can do. Here, let's give it a whirl." No way did Miss Cottontail want any part of the rubber nipple. It just wasn't like Mommy's. Karola set her charge for a moment onto a soft cloth on the kitchen table and squirted some of the warmed milk onto the tip of her right index finger. Ever so gently, she rubbed the moist finger against the tiny lips of the hare. This whole process took considerable time. Eventually, Miss Cottontail caught on. There seemed to be some attempts at sucking at Karola's finger.

"I think you've got it!" exclaimed Karola. She decided to be smart and try the bottle once again. Miss Cottontail didn't exactly hop right to the task; but with a little bit more coaxing, she began to suck. She didn't finish her bottle, but it was a beginning. Karola didn't even want to think about burping. Her little charge seemed much too tiny and fragile to be burped.

Now, what are we going to do about sleeping arrangements? Whatever I do, it better be safe from Mischief. "She might just try to play with you again. And the next time, you might not be this lucky. Her idea of fun and games lasts just so long before she decides to turn her prey into a justly earned meal ticket. You don't want that to happen to you, do you?" Karola asked Miss Cottontail.

She opened the porch door and shooed out Mischief. "Go, scat! Just don't bring home another one of Hoppity's babes. You'll be in really big trouble if you do. Do you understand me?"

When Miss Cottontail was safely in the middle of Karola's bedspread, the caretaker quickly headed for the garage, where she kept an empty birdcage. It was in pretty good shape and not too dusty. She grabbed a couple of soft rags. One of them was readily used to give the cage a lick and a promise. "This will work just fine." Karola folded the other rag into a soft padding, creating a tiny pouch in its center.

"Well, my little Cottontail, this will be your shelter until you are ready to fend for yourself." She picked up the tiny baby rabbit and gently tucked her into the soft cushioning. Thus began a real adventure for Karola and her foundling.

The tiny waif was sound asleep within seconds. Karola closed the birdcage, not making any unnecessary sounds. She placed the rabbit shelter on top of a TV table where she could keep a close eye on Miss Cottontail. *How the heck did I get myself into parenthood again at this stage of my life? Darn that cat. I really didn't bank on this for my entertainment. And what am I going to do when I have to be at the gallery in a couple of days? I suppose Miss Cottontail will be up to traveling in my car. There is a fridge and a microwave in the backroom. The music should be soothing to her little ears.* "You have the cutest little pink ears," Karola mused.

With every attempt at feeding her, Miss Cottontail caught on more readily, responding to the soft and kind-hearted voicings of Karola. She continued to hold her gently but firmly in her left hand. The warmth of Karola's skin against the hairless tiny body must have felt comforting.

By Thursday, when it was time to venture into the big, wide world at the gallery, Miss Cottontail had obviously bonded to Mother Karola. Just like a human baby, Miss Cottontail got its regular feedings and slept soundly in between. In a few days, she opened her big brown eyes and mysteriously beheld this strange creature that had become her gentle caretaker.

Karola decided to check with the Humane Society as to what needed to be done to properly raise Miss Cottontail and to prepare her for the eventual return to normal rabbit life. Answers to her many questions weren't readily forthcoming. She tried other agencies with similar responses to her strange inquiries: "Who gives a hoot about another rabbit? Goodness knows they are a nuisance and far too abundant. The way they multiply, who worries about raising one desert cottontail?!"

Perturbed, Karola turned to her trusted computer. Under NatureWorks she found "Desert Cottontail - *Sylvilagus audubonii.*"

My, aren't you sounding highfalutin. What a fancy name. I knew you were someone important. That's why I decided to take such good care of you. Miss Cottontail was getting cuter by the day, with soft little hairs beginning to cover her naked appearance. Her eyes were alert and always trained on Karola when she approached the cage.

"In a few days, your shelter will be too small for you. I'll have to find something that will allow you to stretch your growing limbs." Soon she could tell that Miss Cottontail needed something other than the evaporated milk formula she had devised. Karola learned that animals in the wild like grasses, cacti, bark, and twigs, as well as mesquite. And so, like a good mother, she made a concerted effort to provide her little offspring with a diet to its liking. From desert, woodlands, and her garden, she selected only the freshest of grasses and twigs that seemed to appeal to her charge.

When she turned six weeks old, Karola knew that she had to let go of her if she wanted the rabbit to return to her natural environment. She had done everything to make the reentry possible in terms of the creature's diet, habitat, and behavior.

And so, one fine Tuesday evening in late February, Karola took the final step. She poured herself a glass of chardonnay, picked up the picnic basket that had become Miss Cottontail's nest, and walked out into the backyard. Mischief was watching the goings-on from a Palo Verde, giving her an excellent vantage point of the periphery. "Don't you even think about it," growled Karola at her feline friend. "You just leave us alone. When I come back from this mission, you better be really nice to me if you know what's good for you!"

With that she took a healthy sip from her glass. *It's too good to spill on the ground.* She marched resolutely onward toward the open grassy area, way beyond her yard. She didn't have to worry about rattlers or any untoward critters this time of year.

In a few weeks, she could not have ventured out into the open desert at this hour. For now, she knew she was fairly safe.

Pretty soon she found a soft, grassy knoll. Karola spread the small blanket she had carried with her. She sat down and let Miss Cottontail hop out of the picnic basket. "Well, little one, it's time for me to set you free. This is what I have been raising you for. I hope I have been a good parent to you. You are a darling rabbit and a beautiful one to boot with your gorgeous brown eyes, that fluffy white tail, and those translucent, pink ears. You will have to listen to the sounds of Mother Nature and forget about my loving voice. I was there when you needed me. I could have been selfish and made you into another one of my pets. But you were born to be free and to live a free life among God's creatures in the desert. And so, I set you free."

Miss Cottontail had her eyes trained on Karola as she was speaking to her. Karola gave the rabbit a gentle push toward the surrounding grasses. Miss Cottontail decided to hop a few feet away from Karola but immediately turned to look for "Mom" and made a swift return. She proudly sat at Karola's feet and again looked up at her with those mesmerizing brown eyes. The creature didn't realize—or maybe she did—that Karola's eyes were swimming in tears. She hadn't realized that it would be this hard. She decided not to engage Miss Cottontail in any further conversation. That would make it even harder for both of them. Karola got up from the blanket and decided to walk. *Good thing I brought this glass of wine with me. I'll be ready for another when I get back to the pueblo,* she thought to herself.

She sauntered beyond her usual territory, giving Miss Cottontail gentle pushes toward the periphery. After a while, it seemed like the rabbit was catching on. Perhaps not talking to her created an aura of separation. Karola was wondering what might be going on in the little creature's brain. And then she noticed another desert cottontail. This one was clearly a male; he was slightly smaller than Miss Cottontail. Karola's foundling had spotted him immediately. The male rabbit stopped running for a moment and made eye contact with the beautiful Miss Cottontail. That did it. She hopped in his direction and was almost into his face. She gently rubbed her nose against his and he reciprocated. As the young male moved further away from Karola's vantage point, little Miss Cottontail followed him only too willingly.

Karola's eyes brimmed with tears. She lifted her glass in the direction of the two lovers. "Here's to your second chance." As she turned away and headed for the house, she took the final sip of her chardonnay.

Questioning God's Infallibility

ONE of our great joys in life is the opportunity to make new friends as we travel around the world. On our most recent voyage across the waters of the Atlantic, we were serendipitously seated with two charming couples. As we discovered, the happy foursome were lifelong friends. We were pleased when they welcomed us with open arms to join them nightly for a few hours of fellowship and conversational sharing of present and past experiences along our respective lifelines.

After the initial introductions and confessions of names, backgrounds, interests, and from where we hailed, we discovered that we had certain things in common: mutual friends, similar professional ties and interests, a love for bridge, and, of course, traveling, and the desire to discover something knew around the bend. We were off to exciting dialogues over a friendly glass of wine at the end of each day aboard ship.

Having owned up to when, where, and how long we were hitched, Serene, one of the delightful ladies, shared a most wonderful episode in her life.

"I was in my forties and had been widowed twice at that stage in my earthly existence. To tell you the truth, I had reached the conclusion that that was all there was going to be for me for the rest of my days. I had reconciled myself to that inimitable fact.

"As so often, I would chat with Mary, a close friend, over the phone. I don't remember how we stumbled once again on my state of widowhood—but we did. It certainly wasn't my idea to resurrect and revisit my marital status.

"Out of the clear blue, Mary startled me into reality by posing her fateful question: 'Have you ever considered answering an ad in the lonely heart's column in our local paper? Don't give me any funny talkback. I'm serious. You never know until you try. Who knows? Number three might be pining away just a phone call away.'

"I was flabbergasted and totally caught off guard at Mary's suggestion. After I found my voice, I confessed, 'No, I never have. And furthermore, I never will. How did you come up with that idea? Have you ever known anyone who has had a positive outcome from such a liaison?'

"'Yes, I have. Just think about the catch Harriet made by answering one of those ads. There are others who have successfully connected by taking their fate into their hands. Look at today's ads. The guy in the third ad from the top of the list sounds intriguing. He claims to be in his early fifties, charming, erudite, and is sporting a head full of beautiful hair. He's into duplicate bridge and traveling—all things you enjoy. Why not take a chance and connect with this man?'

"'I'm looking at the ad you're talking about and will think about it. I haven't got a clue how to approach the matter. I'm really not ready, willing, and able to commit myself and write to a *stranger in paradise* or otherwise. Let me sleep on this one. I'll say goodnight for now. As always, great talking with you, Mary.'

"I kept staring at that ad. *Are you out of your mind? You just told Mary you would never consider answering an advertisement in such a column. What gives with you?* Finally I grasped for a pen and stationery. Then I wondered if I should write or type my first note of inquiry? I opted for the Selectric at last; it might be easier to read and was less personal to boot. I chose to address the stranger as Mr. Erudite since that descriptor had caught my fancy. I simply stated that I was taken by his advertisement and would like to converse by phone rather than in a first face-to-face encounter. I was daring enough to include my personal telephone number but didn't give any clues other than my name, Serene.

"The phone rang at eight o'clock one evening. Hesitatingly, I lifted the receiver off its cradle as I sat down in my most comfortable favorite chair in my living room. 'Serene Eckström speaking.'

"'Hello! This is erudite Gerald Honeycott III calling,' boomed his strong bass voice over the line.

"Listening to his name and the timbre of his voice caught me off guard. For a moment, I wasn't certain how to respond. Catching my breath, I thanked him for responding to my note of interest in meeting a *Stranger in Paradise*.

"'How lovely to use that phrase! Wasn't *Kismet* a delightful musical? Sounds like an interest we have in common.'

"And thus went the evening of mutually exploring each other's backgrounds, interests, and likes and dislikes. We were thrilled not to be speaking on a party line. It would have been most annoying to other participants and to us. Later, we were wondering how unwanted eavesdroppers might have felt about and would have interpreted that four-hour-long first conversation that would ultimately represent the baseline for an enduring and happy marriage of many years.

"Halfway through that infamous first phone call, Gerald needed to fess up to a certain condition. He coughed and vigorously cleared his throat. For a split second, I wondered if I had given voice to something that might have offended him. At last Gerald spoke.

"'I suppose I should share something with you. I don't know how you would feel about living with and/or marrying a blind man; I've been blind since age eleven,' said he.

"There was a lengthy, pregnant pause. Actually, there was dead silence at both ends of the line.

"At last I got my wits about me and said, 'Goodness gracious. Even God must not be infallible. I've been praying to Him, asking Him to send me a kind man—and now—He sends me a blind man!'"

All of us around the table were totally engrossed and listening intently to Serene sharing this touching love story. A broad smile flashed across her face as she reached for Gerald's hand. "Thanks for sharing your life with me for all these wonderful years!"

What Makes Me Want to Write?

SOME of us like to be involved in sports. Others are handy and can fix anything that needs restoration around the house. Some like cleaning, cooking, baking, and entertaining. There are performers among us, be they singers, actors, musicians, or even jugglers. And there are those who enjoy watching our fine-feathered friends. All of us discover our God-given talents sooner or later.

I wasn't always allowed to explore the areas of my special interests. They were considered unsuitable, unproductive, or undesirable. Later, they would be viewed as economically unsound. What I'm trying to convey is that my inner wants and desires were suppressed for most of my life by those who knew best. Best for whom, one might ask?

Now that I'm closer to being ninety than eighty, I finally do what I always aspired to do. Well, at least some of what I hoped to achieve is now in the realm of possibility. I won't get up on a stage and make an ass of myself at this point in my earthly existence. That was a dream of a very young man whose aspirations were shattered by an autocratic patriarch. If I should have a crack at reincarnation, I might like to try my fortune at being another Luciano Pavarotti or a Vladimir Horowitz. But those are merely "ifs" that more likely than not shall remain just what they are.

Since I left the realm of practicality, that is, the world of academia where I earned my bread and butter, I have become a painter and have enjoyed success for the last twenty years. Oh, I'm not a Kandinsky, Klee, or Klimt, but I have taken a firm stab at following in their footsteps.

Lately, I've been seriously infected by the desire to commit my thoughts and inner feelings to paper, iPad, or word processor, and thank God, not to a typewriter or, even worse and unimaginable, to handwriting. I admire fellow writers who write strictly by hand, but my output would be zilch. I draw the line with a Remington Rand, but would prefer a Selectric were I denied access to word processing. I like working on my tablet but detest when it thinks itself to be smarter than I and plugs in its own choices, believing them to be of superior correctness than what I elected to write. But those are just vagaries of modern technology.

The real trick lies within the realm of those millions of synapses in our brain. I'm basically ambidextrous and consider myself somewhat gifted in both cortical hemispheres. Some have accused me of being cursed with left- and right-brainedness. Tough call. Some mornings, I can't tell right from left. It gets even worse when I watch the national news.

I suppose it's high time to address my own question. Perhaps I'm genetically predisposed to writing. My mother was addicted to reading and writing, and I learned from a very young age at the foot of the master. When nothing else was there that could be considered age-appropriate entertainment, Mother would pull out a book from her diverse library and face me: "Read this! You might learn something and appreciate your mother language. I read modern and current authors from all over the world; but when my soul is starved and my heart is bleeding, I reach for Goethe, Schiller, Eichendorff, Fontane, Rilke, Thomas Mann, Brecht, and others."

I listened, read much, and grew to love language and the doors that opened to me through clever use of that powerful instrument. Those who had succeeded in suppressing my intellectual aspirations resented my ability to give expression to my feelings in words unexpected from someone so young. One called me a smart-ass kid that ought to get his ass whipped and put into his proper place. I learned to stand my ground and went my own way. It wasn't always easy street; in time, I elected to leave my native land and discovered the New World and mastered a new language. I came to love English and the breadth of expression it allows.

Starting with the moment when I first left my parental home for the New World, I kept a daily journal recording my every adventure and giving vent to my feelings and experiences—good and bad, joyful and sad. All that writing was destroyed when an unbalanced first wife in a fit of anger burned the accounts of my first six years in the U.S. Totally disenchanted, I stopped keeping a daily journal but wrote many letters, which my mother cherished and kept. They came home to me when Mother ended her life in 1986. Between Mother's regular responses to my letters and my outpourings to her, I was often able to fill in any gaps in memory. And, starting in the summer of 1978, I resumed my regular journaling and have never missed writing a single night since.

The self-imposed discipline to put something down on paper regularly was a good foundation in preparation for a future in creative writing. Entering partial retirement in 1995, I began writing regularly. Joining a group of like-minded individuals was inspiring. Often, I would rise in the middle of darkness and chill in the house and head for the computer and write. I had dreamt about what I had written or what I wanted to write and was driven to commit those ideas to permanent storage. Yes, I felt driven to write.

I've learned the importance of committing ideas to permanency and saving the refining and restating until a later point, after which a certain distance has been gained. It's the same when I paint; depending how I feel, I may put something on canvas that takes me only two minutes and then step back and study what I just did for the next twenty. Some things simply need to percolate in order to attain their full bouquet.

Finding myself once again in the midst of fellow writers who challenge my writing with meaningful critique and counsel, the adventure of publishing has become reality. I doubt that I will ever become wealthy from the fruits of my linguistic creativity, but I have come to the realization that the process of writing is what's so rewarding. And as an old friend taught me many years ago, "It's not for the 'having.' It's for the 'doing.'"

Acknowledgments

THE author wishes to express his sincere gratitude to the staff of Wheatmark Publishing for their efforts in bringing this collection of stories to fruition. Special recognition is accorded to Wheatmark's Senior Project Manager, Lori Conser, for her dedicated and diligent work leading to the publication of the author's writings. Many thanks are due those who have encouraged the author to write, in particular the members of the Green Valley Writers' Forum and family and friends. Last but not least, the author recognizes his wife, Lynne, with heartfelt thankfulness for her endless hours of reading and providing suggestions during the writing process, critical editorial commentary, and invaluable support throughout the project.

PREVIEW OF

Lighthouse Mystery

HARALD LUTZ BRUCKNER

Chapter I

HOMER Annapolis emerged from the lighthouse, holding tightly onto the hand of his beloved wife, Sylvia. She glanced at him sideways. "You must have gotten dressed in a hurry. Look at you. The brass buttons on your uniform jacket are off by one. Here, let me straighten them out and help you make yourself presentable, not that anyone will be calling on us. Oh, my goodness. That cap of yours covers a multitude of sins as well. I believe you are dearly in need of a haircut!"

He smiled at her, inwardly liking being fussed over by his wife of many years. "I couldn't wait to get out and see what Mother Nature visited upon us during the last few days. That was quite the storm that blew in from the west. I wonder if any ships were out there that couldn't make out the powerful beam from the new lighthouse below us? I'm so glad the heavy fog is finally lifting. Can you see the rugged coastline way down there? I wish I had my glasses."

"Yes, I can. The surf is still pounding mightily against those ancient rocks. Let me fetch your glasses; then you can see for yourself. You must've been really in a hurry not to have slipped them on when you rose from your sleep sack."

Homer stood still for a moment, staring into the distance as Sylvia disappeared into the old lighthouse. He looked at his wrinkled uniform pants and mumbled, "I better slip on my oilskins before I hike down to the shore and take in the damage left by last night's storm."

Sylvia rushed to his side and gently placed his pince-nez on his masculine nose. "There, dear man, that ought to be better. What did you decide to do while I went inside?"

"I'm heading down to the shore to make a look-see. No need for you to mess up your boots and dress. It looks like you just washed and pressed this lovely frock. I'll slip on some slickers over my pants, although they look like they could stand a wash and a loving press from the hefty iron you keep on hand." He didn't wait for Sylvia's response.

He turned away from her, heading for the shed to retrieve his waterproof skins. Minutes later, Sylvia waved at Homer as he began his descent toward the sea. The wind blew his cap smack off his head, exposing a shock of snow-white hair. Picking his mariner cap off the damp ground, Homer slapped his treasured head covering back into place. Sylvia couldn't help laughing as she took in the whole scene.

Losing his cap was bad enough; he was thankful Sylvia couldn't see him sliding onto his hind end as the saturated and slippery ground gave way under his boots. *"Damn it,"* escaped his lips. He wasn't inclined to cuss, and certainly not in the presence of his dear Sylvia. He scrambled back on his feet and continued his trek toward the shoreline. Obviously, it was high tide and giant whitecaps still forced their might against the unforgiving cliffs and ate mercilessly into the white sands of the beach.

Homer thought he wasn't seeing right. He adjusted the seat of his glasses, but nothing changed. A few hundred feet from his vantage point he spotted a good-sized cutter swept onto the strand not too distant from the craggy rocks that would have spelled total destruction. *I didn't hear any distress signals or a foghorn before we retired,* Homer pondered as he tried to pick up his pace against the howling wind.

He was breathing hard as he reached the stranded vessel and began to vocalize, trying to get the attention of anyone manning the boat. Its two masts had been toppled by the power of the storm that wreaked total destruction on top deck. "Ahoy! Ahoy! Anyone there?" Homer kept yelling again and again. But all he could hear was the sound of crashing waves as they rushed ashore.

Homer wasn't sure if he could tackle climbing aboard the vessel, especially being alone. Against his better judgment, he searched for large-enough debris washed onto the beach, allowing him to create a ramp and easier access to the deck of the stranded boat.

Having overcome the initial challenge, he carefully picked his way through all the trash covering the deck. One of his feet got caught in a pile of seaweed. He was very much aware of the kelp forest near the shore. He held onto the steering wheel as he took a gander into the open door to the relatively shallow hull. Homer pushed aside a large piece of wood apparently splintered off one of the broken masts and stepped down, slowly entering the hull and casting a look around. Broken glasses and cups were scattered on the floor. There was no evidence of any human habitation.

He kicked aside some of the larger shards, as he aimed toward the bulkhead and a closed curtain on its left side.

Homer needed to know what lay beyond the heavy draped fabric dividing the hull into two chambers. As he pushed the rings suspending the weighty material to his right, he could dimly make out a body lying on the floor of the cutter. *Darn, why didn't I grab my flashlight?* He admonished himself as he carefully backed away from the scene, not wanting to touch another thing with his ungloved hands.

Homer prepared himself for the challenging hike uphill, and he knew what he needed to do. Undoubtedly, this was a case for the local police, and perhaps even forces beyond the present scene. Sylvia marveled and smiled as she watched her octogenarian lover climb up the hill from the shores of Cabrillo National Monument.

She decided to wait for him inside the lighthouse rather than see him tumble and slide on the slippery ground one more time. Sylvia was fully aware of his short temper when things no longer went the way they did when he was a much younger man. She often told him to take a good look in the mirror. He didn't like to be reminded of the fact that many years had indeed gone by.

Sylvia looked upon Homer with pride. *I've spent a lifetime with you, dear man. I cannot believe the things you continue to tackle at your age*. At that moment, her mind took her back sixty-one years.

"I met Homer in San Francisco in 1907. His parents' home on Sanchez Street had survived the earthquake. He had been lighthouse keeper at Point Arena for only two years, when the 1906 earthquake destroyed his cherished place of work.

Homer Elias was the only single man on duty. Two of the other lighthouse keepers were married and had young kids. A third couple had three adult children. Two sons were living in San Francisco; only a daughter, Jenna, was still living at the lighthouse with her parents. All who lived at the lighthouse barely escaped the collapsing tower when the quake struck.

"Homer Elias was the handsomest man that walked this earth. We fell in love at first sight and were married within weeks. I can still hear him tell me what his greatest hopes and desires were. 'Sylvia, you may not be delighted to hear this, but I've always wanted to be a lighthouse keeper. When Point Arena went down, I knew in my heart that I would return someday.'

"And so, it came to pass that the lighthouse was rebuilt to much safer standards and reopened in 1908. Homer was overjoyed to carry me as his wife across the threshold of the resurrected lighthouse. During the daytime, Homer would be busy working with the other men, but at night he was all mine.

"I had always hoped to have children of my own, a pleasure the gods unfortunately denied us. The wheel became my trusted friend, as I spent many hours spinning the wool gathered from the sheep that grazed not too far from Point Arena. Homer eventually bought me a weaving loom. How I enjoyed creating things for the children of the families who lived with us at the lighthouse. I was particularly fond of a little boy who could have been Homer's; the resemblance was uncanny.

"Joshua was born to Jenna, daughter of the oldest of the lighthouse keepers, in 1905. The boy came to his good looks from his mother, a striking blonde who was of Swedish descent. I can still see her with her thick braids, the boy always wanting to play with his mother's tresses when she held him close to her generous breasts. What I didn't realize at first was that Joshua's mother encouraged the boy to spend much time with us, especially when Homer was around.

"Sometimes Joshua would climb on Homer's lap, thrilled to be held by a man, thrilled to be fed by Homer. I would look at the two in profile, only to realize one day that Joshua had sprung from my husband's loins. I began asking the other women as to the whereabouts of Joshua's father and received nothing but vague answers. Joshua, Jenna, and the unknown father were taboo subjects no one wanted to touch.

"By the time Joshua was of school age, there was no longer any question who had blessed the boy with his handsome visage; he bore the striking hair color of his Swedish mother and his marked facial structures were those of his father.

"One may have thought I would be plagued with jealousy, but I wasn't, since Homer and I were blissfully happy in our daily togetherness. I knew that he loved me from the moment we first met. As the years went by, I realized that I would never bear Homer any children, and deep in my heart I was thankful that he had fathered a beautiful and healthy boy long before I ever came into the picture. While Jenna and I never became close friends, we treated each other with respect and civility. Once I was absolutely certain that she and Homer were Joshua's creators, I never raised any questions with either of them.

"When Homer was drafted into the Great War in 1915, he confronted me. 'I've known for many years that you discovered that Joshua is my son. Jenna and I had a single night of pleasure when I was just twenty-one years old. It was during my first year at Point Arena. I didn't know that I had fathered the boy since Jenna saw several young men at the time. When we fled Point Arena after the quake, the child was barely one year old. Yes, I saw the baby, but never knew that I was his father. It was only after you and I were married and returned to the lighthouse that I could see a certain resemblance in the three-year-old boy. I'm certain, even Jenna wasn't sure who Joshua's father was until he became a toddler and his features unquestionably resembled mine. Her parents never challenged me, being fully aware of Jenna's lust for men. Joshua is their only grandchild at this time. His grandfather told me a few years ago that he was glad to know the bloke who fathered his grandson.'

"We were lucky; Homer was considered over the hill at age thirty-two. Between his age and showing with flat feet, he was excused from having to serve in the army. He was advised that his expertise could be applied much more productively by continuing to man the Point Arena Lighthouse.

"The next three years were among the happiest in our marriage. Homer and I were in the prime of our lives and thoroughly enjoyed every opportunity of celebrating married bliss. Joshua was going on eleven when he confronted his father. 'When I look in the mirror, I see you. Are you the father I've never been told about? If you are my father, I want you to know that I've loved you from the moment I was old enough to climb onto your lap.' Homer hugged him and kissed his forehead and held the boy as tightly as he could. Joshua knew he was home at last.

"Tragedy struck our idyllic and harmonious life at the lighthouse when the Spanish influenza struck in 1918. I must have been singled out not to be touched by the devastating illness; I became Florence Nightingale of the lighthouse. Instead of sitting at the spinning wheel or weaving on my loom, I was nursing the ill. Four of the adults and five of the children on site I couldn't save, in spite of all I tried to keep them alive. Joshua lost his mother and his maternal grandparents. One of the uncles in San Francisco was taken as well.

"Homer and I talked with Joshua, now a young man going on thirteen, about his willingness to become part of our family. We legally adopted Joshua in 1920. He filled a spot in my heart that had laid barren for all those years. He was baptized and confirmed in the Lutheran faith at age fifteen. Joshua was a bright young man and excelled in school. While he loved the sea as much as his father, he didn't want to become a lighthouse keeper. Living up to his name, he became a cadet at Annapolis and we were among the proudest parents when Joshua graduated as an ensign and a commissioned officer in the US Navy in 1928. He was married to dear Loretta two years later. We became grandparents when Samuel Luke was born in 1934. Our granddaughter Mary Henrietta came into our lives two years later.

"Joshua was a lieutenant commander on the USS *Arizona* when she was struck on December 7, 1941. It was a day I shall never forget, a day that changed all our lives forever. Loretta never remarried but dedicated her life to making her children responsible citizens. Samuel followed in his father's footsteps and sails the seven seas these days, being a captain on an atomic submarine. It scares the heck out of Homer and me, but we know, he's doing what he wants to do. It's in his blood. Mary Henrietta has given us two beautiful great-grandchildren. Our lives are fulfilled. Both, well into our eighties, it seems we are still married to the sea."

About the Author

HARALD Lutz Bruckner, author of *The Blue Sapphire Amulet, Escape on the Astral Express, A Wanderer on the Earth, The Born-Again Phoenix*, and *Lighthouse Mystery*, hails from Germany but has spent his adult life in the United States. His work and educational adventures have taken him from the East Coast to the Midwest, West, and finally to the American Southwest. He's discovered that there is life after retirement from academia. Today, he enjoys painting and writing in sunny Arizona.

www.ingramcontent.com/pod-product-compliance
Lightning Source LLC
Chambersburg PA
CBHW021811110726
47902CB00006B/1734

* 9 7 8 1 0 8 7 8 5 3 5 0 5 *